Freeway 2
Englisch für FOS/BOS (Klasse 13)
Bayern

von
Jennifer Bear-Engel
Anne Herlyn
Dr. Thomas Höbel

Ernst Klett Verlag GmbH
Stuttgart • Leipzig • Dortmund

So arbeiten Sie mit Freeway Bayern

Getting started

Anhand eines thematischen Einstiegs werden das Vorwissen aktiviert und erste Themenbezüge hergestellt.

Skills

In den Topics 1 und 2 werden zentrale Skills ausführlich erklärt und angewendet.

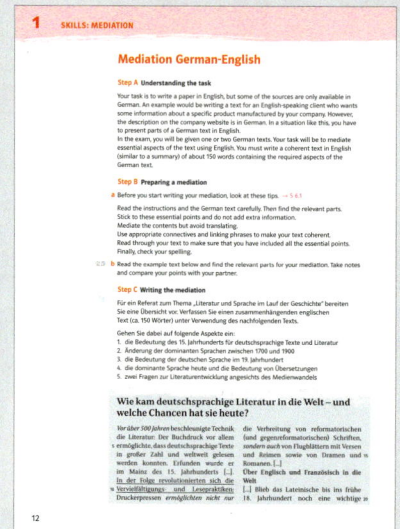

Text

Sachtexte und literarische Texte mit Vokabelannotationen und strukturiertem Aufgabenapparat werden erarbeitet.

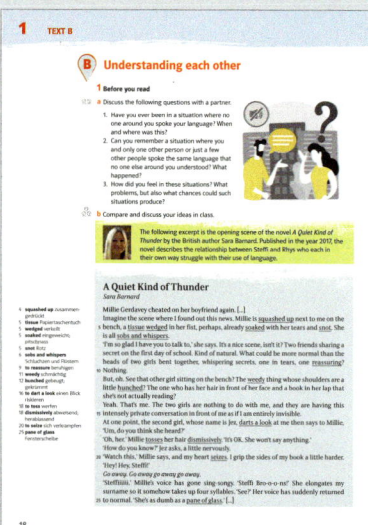

Writing

Zunächst wird anhand relevanter Aufgaben das *material-based writing* vorbereitet und schließlich in einer Schreibaufgabe mit passenden Materialien umgesetzt.

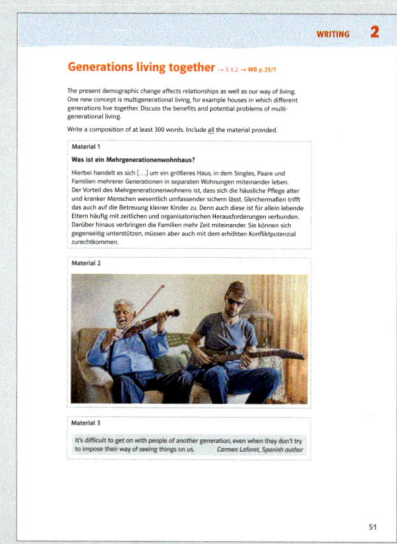

Mediation

Entsprechend einer situativen Einbettung wird der Inhalt von ein oder zwei deutschen Texten in einem kohärenten englischen Text zusammengefasst.

Discussion

Nachdem Sprechübungen die *group discussion* vorbereiten, wird im Anschluss eine Gruppendiskussion entsprechend der Abschlussprüfung durchgeführt.

Anhang

Skills files:
Alle wichtigen Kompetenzen im Überblick

Grammar files:
Kompaktgrammatik zum Nachschlagen und Lernen

Symbole

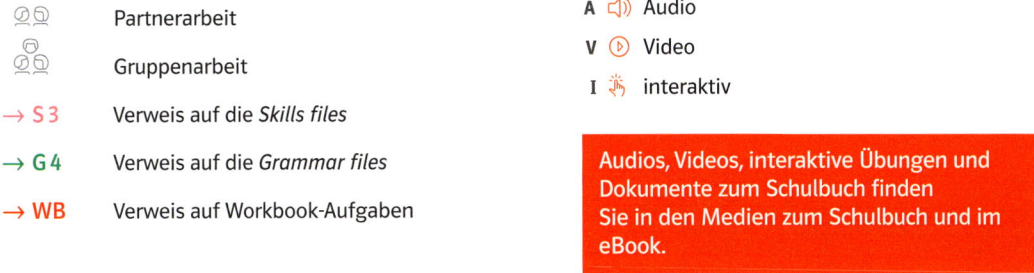

♟♟	Partnerarbeit	A 🔊	Audio
♟♟♟	Gruppenarbeit	V ▶	Video
→ S 3	Verweis auf die *Skills files*	I ✋	interaktiv
→ G 4	Verweis auf die *Grammar files*		
→ WB	Verweis auf Workbook-Aufgaben		

Audios, Videos, interaktive Übungen und Dokumente zum Schulbuch finden Sie in den Medien zum Schulbuch und im eBook.

INHALTSVERZEICHNIS

	Themen	Kompetenzschwerpunkte	
	Ihr Weg zum Abitur		8

TOPIC 1 — A common language?

	Themen	Kompetenzschwerpunkte	
Getting started	**Looking at the way English is used across the world**	Working with pictures • Working with a diagram • Listening • Looking at varieties of English	10
Skills	**Mediation German-English**	Understanding the task • Preparing a mediation • Writing the mediation • Refining your mediation skills	12
Text A	**Language and gender** For linguists, it was the decade of the pronoun (non-fictional)	Discussing the terms 'binary' and 'nonbinary' • Reading tasks • Words matter • Focus on grammar • Selecting and presenting your Word of the Year	14
Text B	**Understanding each other** A Quiet Kind of Thunder (fictional)	Talking about language barriers • Reading tasks • Words matter • Analysing a diagram and discussing sign language	18
Text C	**Global languages** The world no longer wants to learn to sing in English (non-fictional)	Talking about songs in different languages • Reading tasks • Listening • Selecting and presenting a song	23
Text D	**The power of symbols** From Z to Q: when letters become political symbols (non-fictional)	Talking about symbols • Reading tasks • Words matter • Collecting and presenting symbols	26
Writing	**Language change through social media**	Material-based writing	29
Mediation	**Bi-lingual education**		30
Discussion	**Deciding on a company language**		31

TOPIC 2 — Across generations

	Themen	Kompetenzschwerpunkte	
Getting started	**Comparing the generations**	Working with pictures and quotes • Working with a diagram • Listening • Writing a poem	32
Skills	**Working with literature**	Analysing characters, setting and plot • Analysing narrative perspective • Analysing atmosphere, suspense and language • Reading literature	34
Text A	**Young people staying at home** Two-thirds of singles in their 20s now live with their parents – here's how it affects their lives (non-fictional)	Talking about leaving home • Reading tasks • Focus on language • Creating a storyboard	36

INHALTSVERZEICHNIS

		Themen	Kompetenzschwerpunkte	
	Text B	**Generations and their view on life** One for the Money (fictional)	Making a mindmap about American families • Reading tasks • Focus on analysis • Focus on language • Continuing a story and writing a sketch	40
	Text C	**Different relationship models** PLPs: the platonic partnerships that pair up friends for life (non-fictional)	Talking about relationship models • Reading tasks • Discussing platonic partnerships	44
	Text D	**Across generations and continents** The Monk of Mokha (fictional)	Discussing the American and the Arab ways of life • Reading tasks • Talking about different cultures • Introducing a famous immigrant	47
	Writing	**Generations living together**	Material-based writing	51
	Mediation	**Generation Z in the world of work**		52
	Discussion	**Bridging the gap**		53
TOPIC 3		**Technology and us**		
	Getting started	**Talking about technology and how it affects your life**	Working with pictures • Listening • Talking about technology • Creating a mindmap	54
	Text A	**Virtual reality** Helsinki's huge VR gig hints at the potential of virtual tourism (non-fictional)	Discussing virtual reality • Reading tasks • Analysing language and communication strategies • Discussing virtual reality tourism	56
	Text B	**Robots and us** Machines like me (fictional)	Discussing living with a robot • Reading tasks • Working with texts • Continuing and performing a story	60
	Text C	**Benefits of innovative technologies** Revolutionary technologies will drive African prosperity – this is why (non-fictional)	Discussing the term 'revolutionary technology' • Reading tasks • Focus on words • Focus on analysis • Analysing a diagram and discussing SDGs in Africa	63
	Text D	**Genetic engineering** Lab-grown embryos and human-monkey hybrids: Medical marvels or ethical missteps? (non-fictional)	Discussing genetic engineering • Reading tasks • Analysing a diagram and presenting pros and cons of genetic engineering	68
	Writing	**Living with AI and androids**	Material-based writing	71
	Mediation	**In love with my car**		72
	Discussion	**A smart town for all**		73

INHALTSVERZEICHNIS

	Themen	Kompetenzschwerpunkte	
TOPIC 4	**Society now and then**		
Getting started	Talking about social change	Working with pictures • Working with a quotation • Listening • Creating a poster	74
Text A	A changing nation The Hill We Climb (fictional)	Talking about changes in the USA • Reading tasks • Analysing the poem • Talking about hip hop music • Comparing the lyrics of a poem and a rap song	76
Text B	What do we really need? How much is enough? (non-fictional)	Talking about ownership • Reading tasks • Focus on words • Focus on grammar • Discussing work-sharing and universal basic income	80
Text C	Closing the gender gap Gender diversity reforms have helped UK company boards, but they are failing in other countries – new research explains why (non-fictional)	Describing and analysing a cartoon • Reading tasks • Analysing a diagram and measures taken to close the gender gap	84
Text D	Identity in a diverse world 'Othered' in America – an old story still playing out daily (non-fictional)	Discussing the term 'other' • Reading tasks • Working with words • Listening • Analysing a cartoon and the terms 'us' and 'them'	87
Writing	Freedom vs. security?	Material-based writing	91
Mediation	Green cities		92
Discussion	Skills for the 21st century		93
TOPIC 5	**Global challenges**		
Getting started	Talking about different aspects of globalisation	Making a mindmap • Defining globalisation • Working with pictures and quotes • Listening • Creating a poster	94
Text A	Doughnut economy 'Doughnut Economic' model arrives in California (non-fictional)	Describing and analysing a diagram • Using economic terms • Reading tasks • Words matter • Talking about the global impact of food preferences	96
Text B	The USA and the world Remarks by President Biden on America's Place in the World (non-fictional)	Discussing the role of the USA in the world • Reading tasks • Analysing an inaugural address	100
Text C	Business and responsibility Empire of Pain: The Secret History of the Sackler Dynasty (non-fictional)	Defining legal terms • Reading tasks • Writing a letter to a pharma company	103

INHALTSVERZEICHNIS

	Themen	Kompetenzschwerpunkte	
Text D	**Facing climate change** What a Dutch court ruling means for Shell and Big Oil (non-fictional)	Discussing global warming and the effects of climate change • Reading tasks • Writing a speech on climate issues	106
Writing	**Global players**	Material-based writing	109
Mediation	**Terrorism and media**		110
Discussion	**A sustainable café**		111

TOPIC 6 — A global community

	Themen	Kompetenzschwerpunkte	
Getting started	**Talking about living in a 'global village'**	Making a mindmap • Defining the concept of a global village • Working with song lyrics • Listening • Creating a poster	112
Text A	**The importance of trees** The Overstory (fictional)	Talking about personal habits and the environment • Reading tasks • Writing a blog post about your favourite charity	114
Text B	**Cultural identity** Why I loved being an expat child – and what I've learned (non-fictional)	Defining the term 'cultural identity' • Reading tasks • Analysing a cartoon and ways of understanding different cultures	117
Text C	**Global water** Women helping women (non-fictional)	Presenting a non-governmental organisation • Reading tasks • Words matter • Selecting and presenting NGOs concerned with causes of poverty	120
Text D	**Economic factors of migration** Debating Brain Drain, Part 1 (non-fictional)	Researching 'push' and 'pull' factors of migration • Material-based writing • Analysing and presenting an example economic migration	124
Writing	**Different forms of citizenship**	Material-based writing	127
Mediation	**Attracting foreign workers**		128
Discussion	**Community volunteering**		129

Anhang

Skills files	130
Grammar files	168
Irregular verbs	186
Classroom phrases	188

ABITURVORBEREITUNG

Ihr Weg zum Abitur

Die Prüfung für das Bestehen des Abiturs umfasst folgende Kompetenzen:

1. Leseverstehen

In der Prüfung zum Abitur bearbeiten Sie auf Grundlage dreier Texte die folgenden Aufgaben:

- Multiple matching
- Multiple choice
- Short-answer questions
- Gapped summary
- Mediation

In *Freeway Bayern* finden Sie im Anhang des Schulbuchs die entsprechenden *Skills files* (→ S 4.1), in welchen Ihnen die wichtigsten Grundlagen für diese Aufgaben vermittelt werden. Entsprechende Aufgaben finden Sie im Schulbuch zu den Texten aller Topics (Text A, Text B, Text C und Text D).

2. Schreiben

Unter Berücksichtigung der Aufgabenstellung und dreier Materialien schreiben Sie eine *Composition* (*Material-based writing*), in welcher Sie das jeweilige Thema entsprechend diskutieren.

In *Freeway Bayern* finden Sie im Anhang des Schulbuchs die entsprechenden *Skills files* (→ S 6.2), in welchen Ihnen die wichtigsten Grundlagen für das Schreiben der *Material-based writing*-Aufgabe vermittelt wird.
Im Schulbuch finden Sie passende Aufgaben im Step *Writing* und im Step *Mediation*. Dort schreiben Sie einen kohärenten englischen Text von ca. 150 Wörtern *(Mediation)* auf der Grundlage eines längeren oder zwei kürzerer deutscher Texte.

In *Freeway Bayern* finden Sie in Topic 1 und 2 einen Step *Skills* sowie im Anhang des Schulbuchs die entsprechende *Skills files* (→ S 6.1), in welchen Ihnen die wichtigsten Grundlagen für das Schreiben der *Mediation*-Aufgabe vermittelt werden.

3. Gruppendiskussion

Der letzte Prüfungsteil umfasst die Teilnahme an einer Kommunikationsprüfung in Form einer Gruppendiskussion (*Group discussion*).

In *Freeway Bayern* finden Sie im Anhang des Schulbuchs die entsprechenden *Skills files* (→ S 2), in welchen Ihnen die wichtigsten Grundlagen für die Gruppenaufgabe vermittelt werden.
Im Schulbuch finden Sie passende Aufgaben im Step *Discussion*.

So gehen Sie vor

Ab nun heißt es üben, üben, üben – vor allem die Aufgaben, die Ihnen schwer fallen.
Lesen Sie zunächst die *Skills files* im Anhang des Schulbuchs sowie die Aufgaben im Schulbuch. Versuchen Sie dann, die Aufgaben im Schulbuch zu lösen. Wie schätzen Sie sich dabei ein?

Grammatik

„Ich kenne nur zwei Grammatikregeln: ‚klingt richtig' und ‚klingt falsch'". Falls Sie allerdings das Gefühl haben, für das Abitur das ein oder andere Thema nachschlagen zu wollen, finden Sie im Anhang des Schulbuchs alle wichtigen Grammatikphänomene in den *Grammar files*. Zudem finden Sie in den *Medien zum Schulbuch* Erklärvideos und interaktive Übungen.

Vokabular

Bei jedem Text finden Sie Annotationen zu den entsprechenden wichtigsten Vokabeln. Es ist zudem hilfreich, Listen mit thematischem Vokabular zu den verschiedenen Themen sowie nützliche Wörter und Sätze für die Schreibaufgabe und die Gruppendiskussion zu führen.

1 GETTING STARTED

A common language?

Expanding circle
Outer circle
Inner circle
e.g. USA, UK
320–380 million

e.g. India, Singapore
300–500 million

e.g. China, Russia
500–1,000 million

Braj Kachru (1932 – 2016) was an Indian linguist. He coined the term 'World English' and developed the idea of three concentric circles of the language in order to better understand how English is used in different countries.
The 'Three-Circle Model of World Englishes' was developed by him in 1985.

1 Working with pictures → WB p. 6–7/1–3

a Choose two different pictures each and describe them. Where do you think the photos were taken? Give evidence for your assumption.

b Discuss who speaks English in the countries represented in the photos. Is English used mainly by native or non-native speakers? What do you think are their main languages? Explain why English is used on the signs.

GETTING STARTED **1**

2 Working with a diagram → WB p. 8/1

a Summarise the information given in the diagram on page 10. Do you belong in any of the circles? Explain why or why not.

b Since this model was developed, English has become a common language for users around the world, and the mobility of people has greatly increased. Does the model still reflect the reality of the use of English today? Explain your answer.

A1 **3 Listening** → S 3 → WB p. 8/2

a Listen to the podcast "Across the pond". Look at the North American English words below and write down the British equivalents used in the podcast.

apartment | awesome | cookie | eggplant | movie | pants | sidewalk

b Summarise the points that Nigel and Carly make about why and how American English is influencing British English.

4 Looking at differences → S 10.3

a In small groups, collect further examples of differences between American and British English. Consider vocabulary, pronunciation, spelling and grammar. Look at the first two sections of the useful phrases below, then prepare and give a short presentation of at least three issues you have discussed about British and American English.

b There are other varieties of English. Look at the list of words and phrases and copy the table. Decide which variety of English they belong to. What are the equivalents in British or American English?

sarmie | tuque | lekker | gumshoe | arvo | to prepone | bushfire | wet market | raggamuffin | to do the needful | to small yuhself

Variety of English	Australian English	Canadian English	Singapore English	Indian English	South African English	Jamaican English
words						

c Discuss whether it is important which variety non-native language learners learn. You may use phrases from the last section of the useful phrases below.

> **USEFUL PHRASES**
>
> **Presenting information**
> As you are probably aware, …
> A good example of this is …
> What I'd like to point out is …
>
> **Structuring information**
> While in the UK they say …, in the States …
> Let's now look at / compare this to …
> On the one hand …, on the other hand …
>
> **Giving arguments**
> I'm convinced that American English …
> It's fair to say that some variants of English …
> It is important to consider that speaking a variant of English …
> Not everyone will agree that non-natives …
> We need to keep in mind that some variants …
> Another way of looking at this is …

1 SKILLS: MEDIATION

Mediation German-English

Step A Understanding the task

Your task is to write a paper in English, but some of the sources are only available in German. An example would be writing a text for an English-speaking client who wants some information about a specific product manufactured by your company. However, the description on the company website is in German. In a situation like this, you have to present parts of a German text in English.

In the exam, you will be given one or two German texts. Your task will be to mediate essential aspects of the text using English. You must write a coherent text in English (similar to a summary) of about 150 words containing the required aspects of the German text.

Step B Preparing a mediation

a Before you start writing your mediation, look at these tips. → S 6.1

Read the instructions and the German text carefully. Then find the relevant parts.
Stick to these essential points and do not add extra information.
Mediate the contents but avoid translating.
Use appropriate connectives and linking phrases to make your text coherent.
Read through your text to make sure that you have included all the essential points.
Finally, check your spelling.

b Read the example text below and find the relevant parts for your mediation. Take notes and compare your points with your partner.

Step C Writing the mediation

Für ein Referat zum Thema „Literatur und Sprache im Lauf der Geschichte" bereiten Sie eine Übersicht vor. Verfassen Sie einen zusammenhängenden englischen Text (ca. 150 Wörter) unter Verwendung des nachfolgenden Texts.

Gehen Sie dabei auf folgende Aspekte ein:
1. die Bedeutung des 15. Jahrhunderts für deutschsprachige Texte und Literatur
2. Änderung der dominanten Sprachen zwischen 1700 und 1900
3. die Bedeutung der deutschen Sprache im 19. Jahrhundert
4. die dominante Sprache heute und die Bedeutung von Übersetzungen
5. zwei Fragen zur Literaturentwicklung angesichts des Medienwandels

Wie kam deutschsprachige Literatur in die Welt – und welche Chancen hat sie heute?

Vor über 500 Jahren beschleunigte Technik die Literatur: Der Buchdruck vor allem ermöglichte, dass deutschsprachige Texte in großer Zahl und weltweit gelesen werden konnten. Erfunden wurde er im Mainz des 15. Jahrhunderts [...]. In der Folge revolutionierten sich die Vervielfältigungs- und Lesepraktiken: Druckerpressen *ermöglichten nicht nur* die Verbreitung von reformatorischen (und gegenreformatorischen) Schriften, *sondern auch* von Flugblättern mit Versen und Reimen sowie von Dramen und Romanen. [...]
Über Englisch und Französisch in die Welt
[...] Blieb das Lateinische bis ins frühe 18. Jahrhundert noch eine wichtige

SKILLS: MEDIATION 1

Übersetzungssprache für Gelehrte, wurde es zunehmend durch das publikumsfreundliche Französische und im 19. Jahrhundert durch das Englische abgelöst. *Vor allem* mit Hilfe dieser beiden Sprachen [...] wanderte deutschsprachige Literatur weiter: über das Französische des 18. Jahrhunderts nach Russland, Italien, Spanien, Portugal und im 19. Jahrhundert in die französischen Kolonien Afrikas, über das Englische nach Amerika, Indien, Japan und China. [...] Die deutsche Sprache erlangte zwar im 19. Jahrhundert durch die aktive Kulturpolitik der Weimarer Granden Wieland, Herder, Goethe und Schiller und eine avancierte Wissenschaft Bedeutung, aber diese schwand durch die zwei Weltkriege erheblich.

Übersetzen ist auch eine Form des Entstellens

Heute dominiert das Englische auf den globalen Büchermärkten. Was ins Englische übersetzt wird, hat Chancen auf internationale Literaturpreise und Übersetzungen in andere Sprachen. Diese Übersetzungen entstehen selten nur aus dem Original; *vielmehr* legen die Übersetzer häufig das Original und die englische Übersetzung nebeneinander, um Eigenes zu entwickeln.

Jedes Buch, das in einen solchen globalen Wahrnehmungsprozess hineingerät, erzählt seine eigenen Geschichten der Wahrnehmung und Ignoranz. Globale Übersetzungs- und Lesegeschichten sind oft vor allem Entstellungsgeschichten: Geschichten, die vom Buch wegführen – *nicht immer* zu dessen Schaden, *sondern auch*, um Raum für neue Aneignungen zu geben.

Ohne die zahlreichen Geschichten, Bilder, Musikstücke und Filme, die – wie die legendäre Oper Fausts Verdammnis von Hector Berlioz (1846) – aus Goethes Faust entstanden, wären die Kulturen der Welt um gemeinsame Erzählungen ärmer. Werke *wie diese* erlauben die Wahrnehmung des Selbst in einem anderen: einer anderen Geschichte oder einem anderen Text, der sich als so deutungsoffen erweist, dass er für viele Leser eine Bereicherung darstellt. [...]

Neue Medien verändern die Verbreitungswege von Literatur

Wie vor 500 Jahren finden diese globalen Literaturentwicklungen unter dem Vorzeichen eines rasanten Medienwandels statt. [...] Wird Literatur künftig vor allem Reservate für Langsamkeit, Wahrheit und den bewussten Umgang mit Medien schaffen? Oder werden die neuen Medien dazu beitragen, Literatur selbst neu zu erfinden und zu verbreiten?

Heute sind es *nicht mehr nur* die großen Verlage, die Literatur machen. Jeder kann schreiben – im Selbstverlag oder in Blogs. Will Literatur in der neuen Medienwelt überleben, könnte vor allem zählen, was in keine gängige Form passt [...]. Vielleicht wird Literatur künftig zur Kunst des Unerwarteten und Unerwartbaren?

(461 Wörter)
Deutsche Welle, 2018

Step D Refining your mediation skills

a When mediating, it is important to communicate the logical sequence within the text. Read your version carefully to check that it is coherent. Check whether X is a consequence of Y, or rather a condition / reason for Y, … Then look at the linking and qualifying phrases in *italics* in the text. Try and express these in English.

b Mediation is essentially about communicating content. It is **not** a word-by-word translation. In fact, the German texts will often use words or idiomatic expressions that are very difficult or even impossible to translate directly. It is therefore important to understand what the German text wants to say, and then find a way to render these points in English.
Look at the underlined parts of the text and mediate these into English.

 c Compare your versions in class.

TEXT A

A Language and gender

1 Before you read

a With a partner, collect ideas that you connect with the terms 'binary' and 'nonbinary.' In what different contexts are they used? In class, collect your ideas in a word web.

b Read the following quotations and choose one that you find particularly interesting. Explain it to a partner and say why you chose it. Say if you agree or disagree.

> Computers are binary, not people. All people are non-binary, for life is non-binary.
> *Abhijit Naskar, neuroscientist and author*

> A gender-equal society would be one where the word 'gender' does not exist: where everyone can be themselves.
> *Gloria Steinem, American journalist and activist*

> Sex is a matter of biology, while gender is a matter of grammar, and there is no earthly reason why sex should be involved in gender distinctions.
> *Robert Lawrence Trask, American-British linguist (1944–2004)*

> Sexuality is who you want to be with. Gender identity is who you want to be in the world.
> *Hari Nef, American actress and writer*

For linguists, it was the decade of the pronoun

The American Dialect Society held its 30th annual "Word of the Year" vote, which this year also included a vote for "Word of
5 the Decade," on January 3.
It was the year – and the decade – of the pronoun.
In a nod to shifting attitudes about gender identities that are nonbinary – meaning
10 they don't neatly fit in the category of man or woman – over 200 voters, including me, selected "(my) pronouns" as the word of the year and "they" as word of the decade.
Pronouns, along with conjunctions and
15 prepositions, are generally considered a "closed class" – a group of words whose number rarely grows and whose meanings rarely change.
So when pronouns take center stage,
20 especially a new use of "they" that expands the closed class, linguists can't help but get excited.

Pronominal importance
Word-of-the-year votes are lighthearted ways to highlight the natural evolution of 25 language. Candidates must be demonstrably new or newly popular during the year in question. Previous American Dialect Society winners have included "dumpster fire" in 2016, "fake 30 news" in 2017 and "tender-age shelter" in 2018.
Because so many words enter our collective vocabulary each year, the American Dialect Society also votes on 35 subcategories, from "Euphemism of the Year" to "Political Word of the Year." "People of means" – used by Starbucks CEO Howard Schultz in February 2019 to refer to billionaires – won the former, and 40 "quid pro quo" won the latter.
While the American Dialect Society's annual vote is the longest-running vote,

---

8 **in a nod** mit einem Augenzwinkern
8 **to shift** sich verändern
19 **to take center stage** im Mittelpunkt stehen
24 **lighthearted** unbeschwert; heiter
27 **demonstrably** nachweislich
30 **dumpster fire** Müllcontainerbrand
31 **tender-age shelter** Jugendschutzeinrichtung

other language publications, from Merriam-Webster to Oxford English Dictionary, also announce words of the year. In December, Merriam-Webster announced that its word of the year was "they."

It's rare for words as simple as pronouns – "I," "he," "they" – to get so much media and cultural attention. But that's exactly what's been happening over the past few years, which made them a tempting choice for voters.

This year's American Dialect Society Word of the Year, "(my) pronouns," highlights the trend of people presenting their preferred pronouns in email signatures and on social media accounts – for example "pronouns: she, her, hers, herself." People started doing this to help destigmatize a nonbinary person's declaration of their pronouns.

The Word of the Decade, "they," honors the way the pronoun has become a singular pronoun for many people who identify as nonbinary.

"They" has actually been used as a singular pronoun in English for centuries if the gender of someone being spoken about isn't known, or if that person's gender is unimportant to the conversation. For example, if I started telling you something funny my kid said, you might ask, "What's their name?" or "How old are they?"

Only in recent years has "they" become widely accepted as a pronoun for nonbinary individuals for whom the pronouns "he" and "she" would be both inaccurate and inappropriate. It's not the only option – some nonbinary people prefer "xe" or "ze."

A shift that didn't happen naturally

Though it can drive some pedants mad, language changes as culture changes. In English, these changes usually involve new or repurposed nouns and adjectives, like what happened with "app." Originally shorthand for a downloaded computer or smartphone application, it became a word in and of itself.

But in this case, the social push to respect nonbinary gender identity has extended so far into English that it's altering pronouns – again, a class of words that rarely changes – with a new, third-person singular gendered pronoun to accompany the longstanding pair of "he" and "she."

It helps to fill in a linguistic gender gap, just like how, in some dialects, "y'all" or "yinz" fill in the lack of a distinct, plural "you." But whereas "y'all" appeared slowly after years of unconsciously contracting "you all," the nonbinary "they" arose quickly after a conscious social movement.

This might explain why some people have adapted to the nonbinary "they" more easily than others. You probably know someone – or are someone – who has struggled with referring to an individual of nonbinary gender as "they." But what makes it so difficult? Is it discomfort with what can sound like bad grammar? Or does it have to do with our gender biases?

In a recent study, linguist Evan Bradley asked people to judge the grammar of sentences with a singular "they" as "correct English" or not. They found that singular "they" – in its centuries-old use for a person of unknown gender – was easier for people to accept. But the acceptability of nonbinary "they" depended on a person's attitudes toward gender roles.

This suggests that the difficulty with nonbinary "they" has more to do with our culture's perspective on gender than on the language itself.

779 words

Reed Blaylock, *The Conversation*, 2020

54 **tempting** verlockend
63 **to destigmatize** entstigmatisieren
65 **to honor** würdigen
81 **inappropriate** unpassend
85 **pedant** Pedant-/in
88 **to repurpose** umfunktionieren
112 **to struggle** sich abmühen
114 **discomfort** Unbehagen
116 **gender bias** geschlechtsspezifische Vorurteile

1 TEXT A

2 Multiple choice → WB p. 9/1–2

Choose the most suitable option.

1. The selection of the word of the year …
   A reaffirms gender distinctions.
   B acknowledges that attitudes about gender are changing.
   C is an attempt to change attitudes about gender.
   D is an attempt to stop changes in the attitude about gender.

2. Linguists are excited that pronouns …
   A are growing in number.
   B are a closed class of words.
   C are given increased attention.
   D do not change much.

3. New words entering the vocabulary is seen as …
   A a rare occurrence.
   B a natural process.
   C something unusual.
   D something that should be prevented.

4. 'People of means' is an expression that attempts to represent what it refers to …
   A in a more positive way.
   B realistically, as it is.
   C in a more negative way.
   D in an exaggerated way.

5. The expression '(my) pronouns' is used when people want to …
   A say they are nonbinary.
   B say they do not care what pronouns are used.
   C say they are not nonbinary.
   D show solidarity with nonbinary people.

6. Which statement about the pronoun 'they' is not correct?
   A 'They' is used for people who do not identify as either male or female.
   B 'They' has long been used to refer to nonbinary people.
   C In cases where it is irrelevant whether a person is male of female, 'they' has been used for a long time.
   D 'They' can be used as a singular pronoun when it is not known whether a person is male or female.

3 Gapped summary

Complete the summary with the most suitable words from the text (ll. 84–130). Give the line numbers of the words that you used.

The second half of the article highlights how changes in language and changes in ■ 1 are connected. While usually changes are found in nouns and ■ 2, in the case of ■ 3 'they', the speakers of the language are actually ■ 4 a pronoun, which is rarely the case. 'They' is newly used as a ■ 5 pronoun conveying information of gender, like 'he' or 'she', thus filling a ■ 6 that had existed for people of nonbinary gender. Unlike other words, which are changed gradually, the use of 'they' has changed quickly, following a ■ 7 initiative by a group of people. Different people have ■ 8 to the new use of 'they' in varying ways. Some have no problems, while others find it more difficult. This may reflect their gender ■ 9. Thus our use of language in this case is shown to be closely linked with our ■ 10 to gender.

TEXT A 1

4 Words matter → S 11

Read the definitions below and match them with the correct words in the text.
The definitions are in the same order as the words in the text.

1. not very serious
2. something that you give somebody in exchange for something else
3. happening every year
4. (of a thing or activity) making you want to have or do it
5. to change people's attitudes towards somebody / a group, so as to make them be seen less negatively
6. not fitting for a particular purpose
7. a change in something
8. an attitude towards a person, a group or an idea

5 Focus on grammar

Look at the sentences A–D from the text. Match the grammar rules 1 and 2 to the sentences.

1. We use the definite article 'the' when we believe that the listener or reader already knows what or who we are referring to or when there is information in the sentence that makes it clear what or who the article refers to.
2. With plural and uncountable nouns, no article is used when speaking generally, without specific people or things in mind.

A Pronouns, along with conjunctions and prepositions, are commonly considered a closed class (…)
B The Word of the Decade, 'they', honors the way the pronoun has become a singular pronoun for many people who identify as nonbinary.
C Though it can drive some pedants mad, language changes as culture changes.
D This suggests that the difficulty with nonbinary 'they' has more to do with our culture's perspective on gender than on the language itself.

6 A step further → S 13

a Do some online research about different organisations and their 'Word of the Year' in the recent past. Make a list of five words that you find particularly interesting.

b Compare your list with a partner. Together decide on one word that you would like to find out more about. Then collect some information on your word:

– When was it voted for?
– What does it mean?
– What was the background for it being selected at the time?

c In small groups, chose one word from your lists and prepare a five-minute presentation. Create a poster or a digital presentation and visualise your findings. Present your word to the class. → S 15 1-minute presentation

d In class, take a vote from among all the words that have been presented to select your 'Word of our Class'.

post-truth complicit fake news
strollout vax covidiot
gender-fluid cancel culture
me-too carbon footprint pandemic
protection perseverance quarantine
allyship self-isolate selfie superspreader
vaccine youthquake

1 TEXT B

B Understanding each other

1 Before you read

 a Discuss the following questions with a partner.

1. Have you ever been in a situation where no one around you spoke your language? When and where was this?
2. Can you remember a situation where you and only one other person or just a few other people spoke the same language that no one else around you understood? What happened?
3. How did you feel in these situations? What problems, but also what chances could such situations produce?

 b Compare and discuss your ideas in class.

 The following excerpt is the opening scene of the novel *A Quiet Kind of Thunder* by the British author Sara Barnard. Published in the year 2017, the novel describes the relationship between Steffi and Rhys who each in their own way struggle with their use of language.

A Quiet Kind of Thunder
Sara Barnard

Millie Gerdavey cheated on her boyfriend again. [...]
Imagine the scene where I found out this news. Millie is <u>squashed up</u> next to me on the
5 bench, a <u>tissue</u> <u>wedged</u> in her fist, perhaps, already <u>soaked</u> with her tears and <u>snot</u>. She is all <u>sobs and whispers</u>.
'I'm so glad I have you to talk to,' she says. It's a nice scene, isn't it? Two friends sharing a secret on the first day of school. Kind of natural. What could be more normal than the heads of two girls bent together, whispering secrets, one in tears, one <u>reassuring</u>?
10 Nothing.
But, oh. See that other girl sitting on the bench? The <u>weedy</u> thing whose shoulders are a little <u>hunched</u>? The one who has her hair in front of her face and a book in her lap that she's not actually reading?
Yeah. That's me. The two girls are nothing to do with me, and they are having this
15 intensely private conversation in front of me as if I am entirely invisible.
At one point, the second girl, whose name is Jez, <u>darts a look</u> at me then says to Millie, 'Um, do you think she heard?'
'Oh, her.' Millie <u>tosses</u> her hair <u>dismissively</u>. 'It's OK. She won't say anything.'
'How do you know?' Jez asks, a little nervously.
20 'Watch this,' Millie says, and my heart <u>seizes</u>. I grip the sides of my book a little harder. 'Hey! Hey, Steffi!'
Go away. Go away go away go away.
'Steffiiiiii.' Millie's voice has gone sing-songy. 'Steffi Bro-o-o-ns!' She elongates my surname so it somehow takes up four syllables. 'See?' Her voice has suddenly returned
25 to normal. 'She's as dumb as a <u>pane of glass</u>.' [...]

---

4 **squashed up** zusammengedrückt
5 **tissue** Papiertaschentuch
5 **wedged** verkeilt
5 **soaked** eingeweicht; pitschnass
5 **snot** Rotz
6 **sobs and whispers** Schluchzen und Flüstern
9 **to reassure** beruhigen
11 **weedy** schmächtig
12 **hunched** gebeugt; gekrümmt
16 **to dart a look** einen Blick riskieren
18 **to toss** werfen
18 **dismissively** abweisend; herablassend
20 **to seize** sich verkrampfen
25 **pane of glass** Fensterscheibe

I'm in the common area outside sixth form, because Mr Stafford, my new head of year, has asked to see me before the first assembly. [...]

A few minutes after Millie and Jez leave, the door to Mr Stafford's office opens and he strides through it, already beaming. I can only assume he practises the Stride & Beam in front of the mirror. [...]

I try and smile back. I start to say, 'Good morning, sir,' but the words die in my mouth halfway through 'morning' when I realize Mr Stafford isn't alone. Dammit. I was so proud of myself for mustering actual words in front of a teacher, already thinking it was a good sign for this year, the first year of sixth form, the year I'm meant to show I can do basic things like talk in front of teachers. I want to go to uni one day, and – according to my parents – I won't ever be able to do that if I can't even talk in school.

Mr Stafford is still beaming. 'Stefanie, this is Rhys.' He gestures to the boy at his side, who is smiling at me.

What fresh hell is this? Now they're parading strangers in front of me to mock my inability to speak in front of them? I can feel a familiar choking panic start somewhere in my stomach. My cheeks are starting to flame. [...]

'Oh,' he says hastily. 'Oh, it's OK. Rhys is deaf.'

My eyebrows shoot up. 'Oh!' he says again, looking mortified. 'I didn't mean . . . I meant it's OK for you to ... I didn't mean it's OK to be ... though of course there's nothing wrong with being ...' [...]

Oh dear Lord. Rhys's face breaks into a warm, if slightly amused, grin. He looks at me, then raises his hand into a wave. **Hello**.

I wave back, automatically. **Hello**. I let my hands fall into the familiar patterns. **My name is Steffi**.

Nice to meet you. Rhys taps two fingers to his right ear. **Deaf?**

I shake my head, touching the tip of my finger first to my own ear and then to my mouth. Hearing. I hesitate, trying to figure out how to explain myself. I could fingerspell 'selective mute', but he probably doesn't know what that means, and it's not really even accurate any more. **I can't** – I begin, meaning to say that I can't talk, but that's not accurate either, because I can talk, physically speaking. Oh God, both Rhys and Mr Stafford are staring at me. I can feel my face flaming. I finally sign, a bit lamely, **I don't talk.** Which is the worst response ever.

But Rhys smiles, raising his eyebrows a little as if in appraisal, then nods, and I'm so relieved I smile back.

'Wonderful,' Mr Stafford says, looking like he wants to pass out with relief. 'Wonderful. Steffi, Rhys is starting at Windham sixth form today. I thought it would be a good idea to introduce the two of you. Rhys will have a communication support worker helping him out, of course, but I thought it would be nice for him to meet a fellow student who knows sign language. So he can feel more at home.' [...]

'I suppose I'll have to learn some sign language too, won't I, Mr Gold?' Mr Stafford turns his head to Rhys only as he says the final bit of this sentence, clearly oblivious to the fact that Rhys will have completely missed all that came before it.

But still Rhys nods cheerfully, and I feel a sudden fondness for him. He must be all right if he lets Mr Stafford act like such a well-meaning buffoon without making things awkward for him. I wish I could be more like that, but I make things awkward for everyone. People just don't know what to do with someone who doesn't speak.

[...] I just carry on smiling nervously and wait for Mr Stafford to fill the inevitable silence. He does, bless him. 'Well, on to assembly, then, the two of you. Steffi, what's the sign for assembly?'

---

26 **common area** Gemeinschaftsraum; gemeinsamer Bereich
29 **to stride through** durchschreiten
29 **to beam** strahlen
33 **to muster** zusammenbringen; *hier:* artikulieren
37 **to gesture to** deuten auf
39 **to parade** paradieren; vorführen
39 **to mock** verhöhnen; verspotten
40 **choking** erstickend; würgend
43 **mortified** gekränkt; beschämt
52 **to fingerspell** das Fingeralphabet benutzen (*Methode zum Buchstabieren von Wörtern mit Handbewegungen*)
53 **mute** stumm
58 **appraisal** Würdigung
60 **to pass out** in Ohnmacht fallen
66 **oblivious to** nicht bewusst; nicht wahrnehmend
69 **buffoon** derbe(r) Komiker-/in
72 **inevitable** unvermeidlich; unausweichlich

1 TEXT B

75 **obediently** gehorsam
75 **spark of mischief** Funke von Unfug; Anflug von Schalk
76 **deadpan** unbeweglich; ausdruckslos

75 I'm about to <u>obediently</u> make the sign when a <u>spark of mischief</u> lights from nowhere in my mind. I turn to Rhys, keep my expression completely <u>deadpan</u>, then sign **Welcome to the hellmouth.** Rhys's whole face lights up into a surprised grin. Oh yeah, strange new boy. The silent girl is FUNNY. Who knew? (1020 words)

2 Multiple matching → WB p. 10/1–2

Match all the pieces of information (A–I) with the correct character (1–4).

1 Millie   2 Jez   3 Mr Stafford   4 Rhys

A … is a good friend of Millie's.
B … is a teacher of Stefanie and Rhys.
C … feels insecure about Stefanie's problems.
D … treats Stefanie in a condescending way.
E … is worried Stefanie might reveal a secret.
F … is a new pupil at Stefanie's school.
G … tells her friend a secret.
H … reacts to Stefanie's communication in a friendly and accepting way.
I … tries to help Rhys integrate.

3 Multiple choice

Choose the most suitable option.

1. Millie talks about cheating on her boyfriend …
   A to Stefanie, not caring about Jez.
   B to Jez and does not want Stefanie to hear.
   C to Jez, not knowing that Stefanie is listening.
   D to Jez, not caring that Stefanie is listening.

2. What is Stefanie's problem?
   A She cannot hear.
   B She cannot talk at all.
   C She cannot talk in certain situations.
   D She cannot do sign language.

3. Stefanie is trying to talk to her teachers because …
   A she wants to study.
   B she would otherwise get bad grades.
   C she would otherwise not pass her A-levels.
   D people make fun of her.

4. What does Stefanie refer to when using the phrase 'fresh hell'?
   A a threatening gesture Mr Stafford made
   B a new and bad situation
   C a life-threatening incident
   D a very hot and uncomfortable place

TEXT B 1

5. What is not true about Rys?
   A He has someone in class to help him.
   B He cannot hear.
   C He uses sign language to communicate with Stefanie.
   D He cannot communicate with his teachers at all.

6. Stefanie has positive feelings towards Rhys because he …
   A is friendly to her.
   B makes her laugh.
   C does not make Mr Stafford feel uncomfortable.
   D knows sign language.

7. What is not a paraphrase for "I … keep my expression completely deadpan" in line 76?
   A My expression remains matter-of-fact.
   B I make a poker-face.
   C My face doesn't show any emotions.
   D I express my emotions clearly.

8. When Mr Stafford asks Stefanie to sign 'assembly,' she …
   A secretly makes a joke.
   B does as she is told.
   C tells Rhys that she likes him.
   D tells Rhys she does not like Mr Stafford.

4 Words matter

a Match the following words and phrases from the text with the correct definition.

1. to whisper
2. to grip
3. to elongate
4. dumb
5. starting to flame
6. pattern
7. to hesitate
8. relief
9. support
10. fellow student
11. cheerfully
12. to make things awkward

A temporarily unable or unwilling to speak
B to cause problems when handling a situation
C to hold on to something very tightly
D a feeling of happiness that something not very nice has ended
E a person who is going to the same school or university as you
F practical and emotional help
G to talk in a very low voice
H in a way that shows that you are happy
I to make something longer
J a regular way in which something happens
K to become red in the face
L to make a pause before you say or do something

b Choose five words from **a** and write sentences about the main characters in the story extract.

5 Mediation

Beantworten Sie folgende Fragen auf Deutsch. Sie beziehen sich auf den Text ab Zeile 31.

1. Wie reagiert Stefanie, als sie merkt, dass Mr Stafford nicht allein in seinem Büro ist?
2. Warum hat Stefanie Schwierigkeiten, Rys Frage, ob sie taub ist, zu beantworten?
3. Warum will Mr Stafford, dass Rys und Stefanie sich kennenlernen?
4. Was veranlasst Stefanie, Mr Stafford als einen „well meaning buffoon" (Zeile 63) zu charakterisieren?

6 A step further

a How do others react to people whose hearing is impaired? Collect examples from the text and add ideas of your own.

b Compare your findings in class.

c Should sign language be made a mandatory subject at school in order to help people whose hearing is impaired? Discuss in class. Consider the infographic when formulating your arguments.

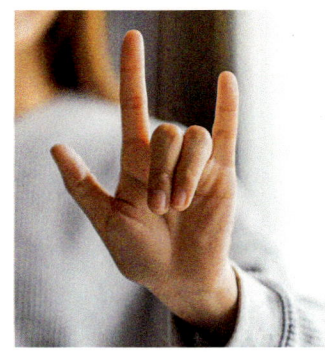

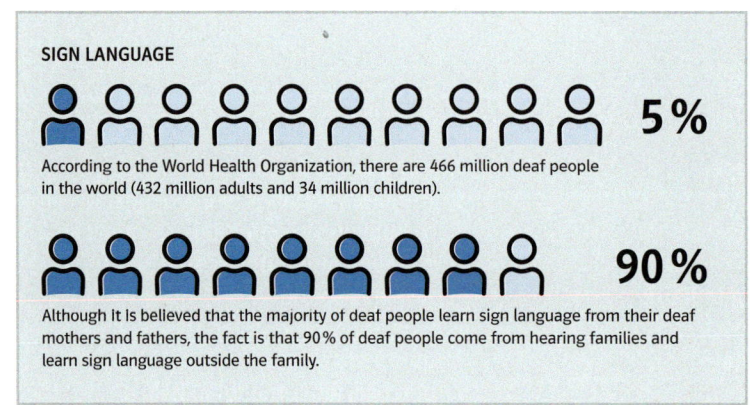

SIGN LANGUAGE

5%
According to the World Health Organization, there are 466 million deaf people in the world (432 million adults and 34 million children).

90%
Although it is believed that the majority of deaf people learn sign language from their deaf mothers and fathers, the fact is that 90% of deaf people come from hearing families and learn sign language outside the family.

TEXT C

C Global languages

1 Before you read → S 15 Think-pair-share

a Think about the songs you like listening to. Try to estimate the percentage of these songs that are in English, German and other languages.

b Compare your favourite songs with a partner. Discuss whether and if so, why you prefer to listen to music in English or in another language.

c Exchange and compare your ideas in class.

The world no longer wants to learn to sing in English
Pop fans in the Anglosphere are growing more tolerant of different languages

The US and UK music charts tend to provide slim pickings for English speakers
5 curious to hear other languages. Linguistically adventurous 1980s pop fans might have gleaned a few words of German from Austrian singer Falco's tribute to Mozart, "Rock Me Amadeus"
10 ("*Er war Superstar / Er war populär*"). And Los Del Río's "Macarena" is why much of the anglophone world can enunciate "*Dale a tu cuerpo alegría Macarena*" with something approaching fluency. Whether
15 the meaning is grasped ("Take joy in your body, Macarena") is another matter.

Hits such as these are rare beacons of cosmopolitanism amid a landscape of linguistic monotony. In the Anglosphere,
20 English has come to be treated as pop music's lingua franca. But there are signs that the mother tongue of "Sussudio" and "Ob-La-Di, Ob-La-Da" may not be ruling the airwaves for much longer. A new
25 report into the state of the global music industry in 2018 reveals the consolidation of new power centres. For the fourth year in a row, Latin America was the continent with the highest rate of revenue increase,
30 at almost 17 per cent. Asia is now the second biggest regional market after North America. Like a sleeper hit single inexorably climbing the charts, China has risen to number seven in the top
35 10 countries.

Although most of the world's most successful acts come from the Anglosphere, non-English speakers are muscling in. South Korean boy band BTS
40 were the second most successful act globally last year, after Canadian rapper Drake. Chinese singer Tia Ray was number seven in the global singles chart. She is a former talent show contestant influenced
45 by Mariah Carey who has named herself after Ray Charles — western pop with Chinese characteristics, as Deng Xiaoping might have said.

The ebb and flow of musical cultures is
50 complex. As well as exporting their songs around the globe, Anglosphere acts have been open to sounds from other places. But the language barrier has impeded traffic the other way. Even the US, with its
55 large population of Spanish speakers, has had a strikingly monoglot chart history. When BTS's "Fake Love" entered the Billboard top 10 last year, it was only the 17th primarily non-English language
60 song to do so.

The industry report paints an optimistic picture of music streaming services as a force for good. Contrary to fears that streaming would cement English's
65 supremacy, local repertoire is in fact flourishing. Simultaneously, the anglophone public appears to be growing more tolerant of different languages. The

4 **slim pickings** mageres Angebot
12 **anglophone** englischsprachig
12 **to enunciate** artikulieren
15 **to grasp** begreifen; verstehen
17 **beacon** Leitstern; Leitfeuer
18 **amid** mitten unter
24 **airwaves** *(nur Pl)* Äther *(fig)*; Radiowellen
26 **consolidation** Festigung
29 **revenue** Verkaufseinnahmen; Ertrag
33 **inexorably** unaufhaltsam
39 **to muscle in** sich hineindrängen
44 **contestant** Kandidat/-in; Bewerber/-in
53 **to impede sb** jdn behindern
56 **monoglot** einsprachig
64 **to cement** festigen
65 **supremacy** Vorherrschaft; Überlegenheit
66 **to flourish** großen Erfolg haben; gedeihen

1 TEXT C

69 **trickle** kleine Menge; Rinnsal (*fig*)
76 **Panglossian** übertrieben optimistischer Mensch
80 **diabolical** teuflisch; Teufels-
82 **reformulation** Neufassung; Neuformulierung
84 **exceptional** außergewöhnlich; besonders
96 **to predominate** vorherrschen
97 **to spell** *hier*: bedeuten
98 **emergence** Verbreitung; Aufkommen

trickle of non-English songs in the US and UK charts is picking up volume. In 2017, Luis Fonsi and Daddy Yankee's "Despacito" became the most streamed track ever worldwide. K-pop has been credited with boosting Korean learning in US universities.

To music tech Panglossians, we are entering a future for pop in which The New Seekers' "I'd Like to Teach the World to Sing (in Perfect Harmony)" has somehow achieved a diabolical mating with the Duolingo language-learning app. What this really means is a reformulation of anglophone supremacy in pop music. English is no longer the exceptional language. Instead, it is becoming *primus inter pares*, the leader of the pack. K-pop songs mix English words and Korean: the results have been termed "Konglish". "Despacito" required a remix with Canadian singer Justin Bieber to become a global smash hit. The new single from Mexico's Sofia Reyes sums up the direction of travel. A collaboration with the UK's Rita Ora and Brazil's Anitta, "R.I.P." mixes English, Spanish and Portuguese lyrics. With English predominating, it does not spell RIP to Anglosphere dominance, but rather symbolises the emergence of an anglophone-led multipolar world. English is dead, long live English. (628 words)

Ludovic Hunter-Tilney,
The Financial Times, 2019

2 Short-answer questions → WB p.11/1–2

Copy the table and take notes. Then complete the table with the information from the text. Leave the spaces with – – – empty.

song title	interpreter	language	other information
Rock me Amadeus		German	
Macarena	Los del Rio	– – –	
Sussudio	– – –		– – –
Ob La Di, Ob La Da	– – –		– – –
I'd Like to Teach the World to Sing (in Perfect Harmony)			
RIP			

3 Mediation

Beantworten Sie folgende Fragen auf Deutsch.

1. Warum sind Hits in anderen Sprachen weltweit immer noch eine Seltenheit?
2. Wie hat sich der Markt in Südostasien und China in den letzten Jahren entwickelt?
3. Welchen Einfluss haben Streamingportale auf den Musikmarkt?
4. Welche Rolle spielt die Sprache Englisch inzwischen in der Popmusik?

TEXT C 1

4 Gapped summary

Complete the summary of the final part of the text with the most suitable words from the corresponding section (ll. 61–100). Give the line numbers of the words that you used.

> The final part of the text deals with the effect that streaming services have on the ■ 1 of English in the world of pop music. Because English-speaking listeners have become increasingly ■ 2 of other languages, a song like 'Despacito' became the song that has been ■ 3 most frequently in the whole world, and has caused the ■ 4 of Korean at US universities to rise. No longer seeing English as the ■ 5 language of pop music, musicians have begun to ■ 6 English with other languages. This kind of ■ 7 has created results that achieve ■ 8 success. Because of English still ■ 9 in these mixed songs, the music world is not experiencing the end of English dominance in pop music, but rather the ■ 10 of an English-led multilanguage music world.

5 Listening

A2 a **L**isten to the podcast "English as a global language". Put the topics into the order in which they are mentioned in the podcast. There is one topic that is not mentioned.

- A Where English is spoken
- B Differences between British and American English
- C Why English is a global language
- D Other languages in culture and advertising
- E The role of English in culture

b Listen again and answer the following questions.

1. What role does English play in different areas of culture?
2. Why has English become a lingua franca?
3. In what areas are other languages prominent? List the examples.

6 A step further

a In small groups, choose one of the songs that are mentioned in the text and in 2. Do some research and complete the table that you copied. Find further information on the songs and the singers.

b Prepare a three-minute presentation of your song in which you offer the information you have collected. Consider the following aspects.

– Which language or languages were chosen for the song? What effect does the choice of language have on the listener?
– What is your personal opinion on the song in general, and on the language(s) in the song. → S15 1-minute presentation

25

TEXT D

D The power of symbols

1 Before you read

a Look at these political symbols. What do they stand for? Take notes.

b Compare your notes with a partner. Then list further symbols that you know and present your results in class.

From Z to Q: when letters become political symbols

1 Painted on the side of <u>tanks</u> and <u>emblazoned</u> on the shirt of Russian gymnast Ivan Kuliak, the letter Z has come
5 to represent support for Russia's invasion of Ukraine. It has even been <u>incorporated into</u> the spelling of place names such as КуZбасс in south central Russia.

2 In some countries, the Czech Republic
10 for instance, there are even discussions about whether displaying the letter should be a criminal offence. Its rise comes shortly after another lesser-used letter from the Latin alphabet – Q –
15 became a part of far-right politics in the US (and abroad) through the <u>conspiracy theory</u> QAnon.

3 The use of symbols is a fundamental part of any political conflict — part of the
20 propaganda strategy that tries to shape the public narrative. But what is most interesting is how these effective symbols <u>emerge</u>, and that some of them <u>resonate</u> so powerfully that they end up banned as
25 a form of hate speech.

4 The war for public opinion that runs alongside the actual war in Ukraine has given rise to a host of symbols representing support for one side or the other. Twitter
30 is full of people adding the Ukrainian flag emoji to their name. The <u>defiant</u> words of the Ukrainian defenders of Snake Island – "Russian warship, go fuck yourself!" – have become a powerful <u>underdog</u> slogan, and
35 even the basis for an official Ukrainian postage stamp. On the other side, the most notable symbol has been the simple Z. There have been many theories about why this letter has become a pro-war symbol, and what its origins might be. Is it
40 because it represents the Russian word for west (zapad), the direction in which Putin's tanks are rolling? Or is it shorthand for Za pobedu — "for victory"? There is
45 also the <u>oddity</u> that the Cyrillic alphabet doesn't have a sign resembling Z. The zed sound is written as 3.

5 The circumstances of a symbol's origin are only a small part of its story. It's the
50 way symbols come to resonate in society, and how people <u>impose</u> meanings on them, which transforms <u>arbitrary</u> signs into powerful instruments of propaganda.

6 Political symbols can take pretty much
55 any form you can imagine. In 2013, penguins became the symbol of anti-government protesters in Istanbul. When violent clashes between police and protesters first broke out, all the national
60 TV channels chose not to cover them. CNN Türk instead ran a documentary about penguins – which protesters then adopted as an emblem for their struggle, and to <u>mock</u> the broadcaster.
65

7 The use of letters of the alphabet as political symbols is a little unusual for the simple reason that individual letters <u>aren't meant to have</u> any <u>intrinsic</u> meaning of their own. They're supposed merely to
70 represent sounds which, when combined, produce words which only then have a meaning.

8 When the Nato phonetic alphabet (Alfa, Bravo, Charlie and so on) was being
75 developed, one of the criteria for words

---

2 **tank** Panzer
3 **to be emblazoned on** an etwas prangen
6 **incorporate into sth** einfügen; eingliedern in etwas
16 **conspiracy theory** Verschwörungstheorie
23 **to emerge** entstehen; auftauchen
23 **to resonate** mitschwingen; mitklingen
31 **defiant** aufsässig, herausfordernd
34 **underdog** Außenseiter-/in
46 **oddity** Kuriosität
52 **to impose on** aufzwängen; aufdrängen
53 **arbitrary** willkürlich
65 **to mock** verhöhnen; verspotten
69 **to be meant to have** haben sollen
69 **intrinsic** intrinsisch; immanent

used to represent letters was that they should "be free from any association with objectionable meanings". They should be politically and culturally neutral, in the same way the letters themselves are.

The neutrality of alphabetic letters was also behind the World Health Organization's decision to use Greek letters to designate new COVID variants. Prior to this, the variants had been named according to their place of origin, but this risked stigmatising locations or countries by having them forever associated with the virus. Even then, certain letters had to be omitted in case they accidentally led to unwanted associations. The Greek letter Xi, for example, was skipped as it resembles the surname of the president of China, Xi Jinping.

9 What this shows is that language is always potentially political, precisely because it's at the heart of how humans interact – and human interaction itself is always, at some level, political. Words and symbols have a denotative meaning – their literal "dictionary definition" – but they also carry traces of the history of their use, which colours the connotations they have for people. It's not surprising that the two recent instances of alphabetic letters as political symbols have adopted the two least used of all the letters. Z has traditionally been seen as superfluous in English –- so much so that Shakespeare made it the basis of an insult in King Lear: "Thou whoreson zed! Thou unnecessary letter!" And Q has associations with words such as query and question. So neither was a completely blank canvas before their use was co-opted.

10 Ultimately, however, it's the way that signs are actually used that transforms them into symbols. It's a matter of who they're used by, for what purpose. Once this usage begins to spread through society and is adopted by supporters, highlighted and debated by the media – and, in some cases, banned – its meaning quickly gets embedded in the culture. Eventually, it becomes part of the everyday vocabulary we use to make sense of the world. (825 words)

Philip Seargeant, *The Conversation*, 2022

79 **objectionable** anstößig
85 **to designate** benennen; bezeichnen
86 **prior to** früher; vor
88 **to stigmatise** stigmatisieren; abstempeln
91 **to omit** auslassen
91 **accidentally** versehentlich; zufällig
93 **to skip** auslassen, überspringen
101 **denotative** bedeutend; bezeichnend
104 **connotation** Konnotation; Assoziation
109 **superfluous** überflüssig
114 **query** Anfrage
115 **blank canvas** leere Leinwand
116 **to co-opt** nutzen
125 **embedded** eingebettet

2 Multiple matching → WB p.12/1–2

Match the following subheadings (A–L) with the correct paragraphs from the text (1–10). There are two more subheadings than you need.

A From sign to symbol
B Letters as objective signs
C Literal and associated meanings
D Pictures as symbols
E The development of symbols
F The power of symbols in conflicts
G The symbolic value of names
H The symbolic value of the letter Z
I The Ukraine war and its symbols
J The unusual origin of a political symbol
K Two recent political symbols
L What letters are

3 Short-answer questions

Answer the following questions. You may use words from the text.

1. How are symbols used in political conflicts?
2. Why is it unusual that Z became a symbol during the Russian war against Ukraine?
3. How do letters grow into symbols?
4. Why are Greek letters used for the variants of Covid 19 and not the country of origin?
5. What terms does the author use to describe the main meaning of a word and the ideas that people associate with words?

TEXT D

4 Words matter

Find the matching words and phrases in the text for the following definitions.
The number in brackets tells you the corresponding paragraph. Give the line numbers.

1. an illegal act that you can get punished for (two words) (2)
2. information used to promote a political cause or point of view (3)
3. expressing hate towards a group of people, often encouraging violence (two words) (3)
4. clearly showing an attitude of opposition (4)
5. an image representing something (a country, an idea etc.) (6)
6. to disapprove of somebody, giving them a bad image (8)

5 Multiple choice

Choose the most suitable option.

1. In the Czech Republic …
   A showing the letter Z publicly is outlawed.
   B there are thoughts of making the public display of the letter Z unlawful.
   C the letter Z has been introduced into certain place names.
   D the letter Z does not exist.

2. Which of these statements is not true?
   A The reason why the letter Z has become the symbol of support for the Russian invasion of Ukraine is unclear.
   B Z could have several different meanings in this context.
   C Z represents the number 3 in the Cyrillic alphabet.
   D The Cyrillic alphabet does not have a letter that looks like Z.

3. Penguins became the symbol of protests in Istanbul because …
   A the protesters needed an indirect symbol of their struggle.
   B a documentary about penguins was cancelled because of the protests.
   C broadcasters wanted to make fun of the protesters by showing a documentary on penguins.
   D a Turkish TV channel showed a documentary on penguins instead of covering the protests.

4. The symbolic letters discussed in the text are …
   A not used frequently in English.
   B very common letters in the English language.
   C not connected with any associations of their own.
   D deemed central to the English alphabet.

5. The media play a role in signs developing into symbols because …
   A the symbols originate in the media.
   C the media ignore the symbols.
   B the media discuss the symbols.
   D the media change the symbols.

6 A step further → S 15 Think-pair-share

a Symbols surround us. Photograph or download some of them.

b Make notes on what the symbols mean, and discuss in how far they help us communicate.

 c Create a poster in which you present a selection of the symbols you have found and their meanings. → S 15 Gallery walk

Language change through social media → S 6.2 → S 10.2 → WB p.13/1

It is a well-known fact that social media has developed its own language and has had an impact on the language we use in general. Critics fear that language is being corrupted by social media, while others find little reason to worry about these changes. Discuss the following issue:

'Should we worry about, or should we greet the developments in language that have been caused by social media?'

Write a composition of at least 300 words. Include all the material provided.

Material 1

Material 2

Generational language gap?

In a recent study of 2,000 parents, conducted by Samsung, 86% of participants said that they felt teens and young people spoke an entirely different language on social media. According to the study there is now a 'seismic generational gap' regarding how modern informal language is being used. The study was carried out by Professor John Sutherland at University College London, who is the UK's leading expert on the English language. He claims that the rise of the emoji could be the next phase in language and communications.

Material 3

Sprachen sind bei weitem das wichtigste Vehikel kultureller Entfaltung und zugleich das wichtigste Element nationaler – übrigens auch persönlicher – Identität. *Helmut Schmidt, deutscher Politiker (1918–2015)*

MEDIATION

Bi-lingual education → S 6.1

In Deutschland wird diskutiert, welches der beste Zeitpunkt zum Erlernen einer Fremdsprache ist. Ist es sinnvoll, bereits in der Kita oder im Kindergarten anzufangen?

Als Vorbereitung für einen internationalen Workshop zum Thema planen Sie, den anderen Teilnehmenden die Inhalte des folgenden Artikels auf Englisch zur Verfügung zu stellen. Verfassen Sie einen englischen Text (ca. 150 Wörter), in dem Sie auf die folgenden Aspekte eingehen:

1. Vorteile der Mehrsprachigkeit und einer (frühen) mehrsprachigen Erziehung
2. Gründe für diese Vorteile
3. Skepsis gegenüber frühem Fremdsprachenlernen und Gegenargumente
4. Wichtige Maßnahme für die Umsetzung in Kitas.

Massive Vorteile durch zweisprachige Erziehung
Christoph David Piorkowski

Kinder sollten bereits in der Kita zweisprachig aufwachsen können. Denn: Schon in der Grundschule ist es für das Hirn etwa 100-Mal so schwer, eine Fremdsprache zu lernen. Zu dieser Einschätzung kommen namhafte Bildungswissenschaftler und Neurobiologen, die auf Initiative des früheren VW-Vorstandsvorsitzenden Carl Hahn am Montag in Berlin ihre Forschung präsentierten.

„Menschen, die mehrere Sprachen lernen, können sich zwischen verschiedenen Kulturen souverän bewegen und beherrschen meist auch ihre eigene Sprache besser", sagte der Heidelberger Bildungswissenschaftler und Koordinator der internationalen Pisa-Studien, Andreas Schleicher. Außerdem bewirke eine zweisprachige Erziehung, dass man sich langfristig besser konzentrieren könne, neue Aufgaben leichter bewältige und ein geringeres Risiko für Alzheimer habe, ergänzte Martin Korte, Lernforscher und Neurobiologe an der TU Braunschweig.

In Deutschland jedoch werde die Chance, Kinder über frühe bilinguale Erziehung für den internationalen Bildungswettbewerb fit zu machen, leichtsinnig verspielt, so die Forscher. Demnach hätten es die späteren Erwachsenen deutlich schwerer, sich auf den globalen Arbeitsmärkten gegen selbstverständlich mehrsprachig aufwachsende Briten und Chinesen zu behaupten. Ein wirtschaftlicher Schaden in Milliarden-Höhe sei die Folge dieses ungenutzten Bildungspotentials.

Mehr kognitive Flexibilität
Anders als in vielen anderen OECD-Ländern herrsche hierzulande mehrheitlich die Auffassung vor, dass Kinder in der Kita lieber spielen sollten, kritisiert Rüdiger School von der Saxony International School (SIS) Carl Hahn. Der Gegensatz von Lernen und Spielen aber sei künstlich. „Das Lernen von Fremdsprachen macht Kindern großen Spaß." Außerdem seien Kinder, die in bilingualen Kindergärten aufwüchsen, in der Grundschule nicht bloß in Englisch oder Deutsch den Kindern aus herkömmlichen Kitas voraus – sondern zum Beispiel auch in Mathematik.

Was aber bedingt deren Vorteile? „Zweisprachige Kinder verfügen über deutlich mehr kognitive Flexibilität", erklärt der Neurologe Manfred Korte. Der Stirnlappen werde durch den Wechsel zwischen verschiedenen Sprachsystemen bestens trainiert, was die Selbstreflexion und die Fähigkeit stärke, aus eingespurten Denkwegen auszuscheren.

So müssen sich zweisprachig aufwachsende Kinder besser konzentrieren lernen, weil sie die gehörten Laute zunächst dem jeweiligen Sprachcode zuordnen müssen.

„Nach dem zehnten Lebensjahr wird eine zweite Sprache nicht mehr von den biologisch dafür vorgesehenen linkshemisphärischen Hirnarealen verarbeitet, sondern über Gedächtnisareale in der rechten Hirnhälfte", sagt Korte. Dies mache den Spracherwerb mühsamer, bewirke, dass man weniger „wendig" sei und außerdem einen Akzent habe. „Nach dem zehnten Lebensjahr hört man eine Sprache nicht mehr so gut, es fällt uns dann schwerer etwas nachzusprechen".

Gerechtere Bildung durch Zweisprachigkeit

Auch mit dem Mythos, dass frühkindliche bilinguale Erziehung die Bildungsschere weiter auseinandergehen lasse, räumen die Wissenschaftler auf. [...]

„Der sozioökonomische Status aller Kinder verbessert sich, wenn sie zweisprachig aufwachsen", sagt Korte. Um soziale Gerechtigkeit zu verbessern, müsse man auch frühkindliche Zweisprachigkeit fördern. So zeigen Studien, dass die spätere Leistungsfähigkeit von Menschen oft in der Kindergartenzeit festgelegt wird. Kitas können die Abhängigkeit des schulischen Erfolges vom Elternhaus verringern.

Wichtiger als den Betreuungsschlüssel zu erhöhen, sei es dabei, in die Ausbildung des Personals zu investieren, meint Andreas Schleicher. [...]

(468 Wörter)
Tagespiegel, 2021

Deciding on a company language

You are working in the German branch of an international company. Most of the employees are German, but there is an increasing number of international colleagues, not all of them with a good command of the German language. The suggestion has been made to introduce English as the official company language. However, not all the German colleagues are comfortable with this.

A staff meeting is called with the aim of coming up with guidelines for language use at the branch. The participants are asked to agree on one of these four suggestions.

1. English should be the official company language and is to be used at all times. German employees are to be offered free English classes.
2. English and German should be official company languages. In the presence of someone who doesn't speak German, English should be spoken. Minutes of meetings and other important documents should be provided in English and German.
3. German should be the official company language and employees who don't speak German should be expected to learn enough German to cope with everyday communication. Minutes of meetings and other important documents are to be provided in English and German.
4. German should be the official company language to be used at all times. Those employees who don't speak German are to be offered free German classes.

a Choose one of the suggestions and say why you think this suggestion is the best.

b Discuss the suggestions and try to convince the other participants of your solution.

c Try to come to a conclusion and formulate a suggestion to be presented to the management.

2 GETTING STARTED

Across generations

> The young, no doubt, make mistakes; but the old, when they try to think for them, make even greater mistakes.
> *Bertrand Russell, Welsh philosopher (1872–1970)*

> There is a certain power when old and young come together – we can do more together than we can on our own.
> *Shane Claiborne, American sociologist and author*

> The old say, 'I remember when.' The young say, 'What's the news?'
> *Gelett Burgess, American artist, art critic, author and humourist (1866–1951)*

> Sooner or later the young always betrayed the old.
> *Pearl S. Buck, American author (1892–1973)*

1 Working with pictures → WB p.16–17/1–2; 18/1

a Look at the pictures. What do you see? What is their message? What have they got to do with the topic 'Across generations'? → S 10.1

b With a partner, look at the quotes and talk about their message. Decide which quote fits the topic theme best and which one is the least fitting. Give reasons for your choice.

c In small groups look at the list of adjectives below. Relate them to the pictures or quotes. In which way would you associate them with different generations?

active | boring | conservative | dynamic | experienced | flexible | hedonistic | liberal | mature | modern | old-fashioned | outspoken | open-minded | progressive | reactionary | spoiled | wise

GETTING STARTED 2

2 Comparing the generations

a Look at the diagram: A stands for your generation, B for your parents' and C for your grandparents' generation. AB represents what you and your parents have in common, AC depicts what you have in common with your grandparents and so on. Copy the diagram.

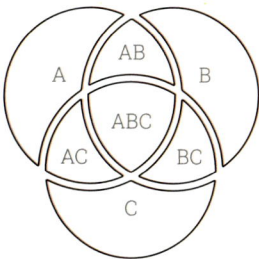

 b Get into small groups. What are the values, ideals, idols, goals, worries, hopes, dreams etc. of your generation? Make a list.

c Ask your parents and grandparents about their values, ideals etc. Make two more lists.

d Put the information from **b** and **c** into the correct sections of your diagram from **a**. Then present your results in class. → S 15 Gallery walk

e Discuss the following questions on the basis of the information gained from your completed diagram.

1. Where do you see the biggest differences between the different generations?
2. Where do you see the potential for conflict? Why?
3. Where can the generations learn from each other? What can they learn?
4. How does your diagram relate to the pictures and quotes on page 32?

3 Listening → S 3

a In 1970, Cat Stevens wrote the song 'Father and Son.' Find the song online and listen to it. What is the song about? Write down 3–5 keywords.

b Listen again and take notes on each verse. Who is speaking? Which points do father and son mention? What is the position of each one at the end of the song?

c Discuss the views and arguments of both father and son. Do you know of similar situations and conversations? What was the outcome of these conversations?

d 'Father and Son' is quite old. Find a modern song about the differences between generations. Prepare a fact sheet with the following information and present it to the class. → S 15 1-minute presentation

title | singer | year of release | genre | main message

4 Writing a poem → S 5

a Look at the poem on the right. Each line begins with a letter of the word 'friend'. Choose one of the following expressions and write a similar poem.

family | parents | grandparents | growing up | generation gap

Fear I don't know, as you
Remain at my side
In every situation,
Exciting or sad, good or bad, you
Never, ever will
Desert me.

b Exchange your poem with a partner. Is it appropriate for the expression? → S 15 Tip-top

33

2 SKILLS: LITERATURE

Working with literature

Step A Analysing characters, setting and plot → S 8.2 → S 8.5

a When reading a fictional text, the reader is like a literary detective looking for information about different aspects of the story:

- Where and when do these things occur? (the **setting** – time and place)
- Who is involved? (the **character**s and their relationships)
- What happens? (the action/events and the development of the **plot**)

Look back at text A in Topic 1 *(A Quiet Kind of Thunder)* on page 18 and analyse setting, characters and plot.

b Characterisation can be explicit or direct when the reader is told what a character is like by the narrator, another character or by the character themselves, but it can also be implicit or indirect. The reader must infer what characters are like from what they do, say or think. In addition, what people wear, their physical appearance or the gestures they make, all convey information about a character. By which means is Rhys characterised in *A Quiet Kind of Thunder*?

c What makes the reader interested in a story?

In some texts narrative passages create tension or suspense by means of an exciting plot, or by introducing an element of surprise. In others there are slower, more descriptive passages giving details or creating a particular atmosphere.
Look at text B in Topic 3 *(Machines like me)* on page 60 and analyse what attracts the reader.

Step B Analysing narrative perspective → S 8.3

When authors write a fictional text, they have to choose a narrator to tell the story. This can be done through the eyes of characters in the story or from the perspective of an observer. Narrative prose can have an unlimited or a limited narrative perspective.

> The author writes, the narrator speaks and a character takes part in the story.

- A first-person narrator is limited. The narrator tells the story from their perspective, either as the protagonist or simply as an observer.
- A third-person narrator can be limited. They may know everything about one character or be an observer. Third-person narrators can be subjective; however if they don't report on a character's thoughts or feelings, they can be objective or impersonal.
- A third-person narrator can also be unlimited. This is an omniscient or 'all-knowing' narrator who may know everything about several characters' thoughts and feelings and may even comment on a character's behaviour.

Analyse and compare the narrative perspectives of *One for the Money* (p. 40) and *The Monk of Mokha* (p. 47).

SKILLS: LITERATURE 2

Step C Analysing atmosphere, suspense and language → S 8.4

a Atmosphere is the mood the author creates by describing feelings, setting etc. Suspense is created when the author raises questions or holds back information, making the reader want to read on to find out what will happen. Without suspense, the reader loses interest. Think about books that you have read which caught your attention and made you want to go on reading. Discuss your book with a partner.

b Authors create certain effects through language choices, such as sentence structure and length, register, and stylistic devices (e.g. alliteration, metaphor, simile). Authors also use dialect or local words to depict the particular time, place or culture. Direct speech makes readers feel they are experiencing the situation live. The reader's emotions may be influenced by the description of feelings or actions. Look at this excerpt from *A Quiet Kind of Thunder* again and analyse the stylistic devices the author uses.

> Mr Stafford is still beaming. 'Stefanie, this is Rhys.' He gestures to the boy at his side, who is smiling at me.
> What fresh hell is this? Now they're parading strangers in front of me to mock my inability to speak in front of them? I can feel a familiar choking panic start somewhere in my stomach. My cheeks are starting to flame.
> […]
> 'Oh,' he says hastily. 'Oh, it's OK. Rhys is deaf.'
> My eyebrows shoot up. 'Oh!' he says again, looking mortified. 'I didn't mean … I meant it's OK for you to … I didn't mean it's OK to be … though of course there's nothing wrong with being …'

> To understand literature better and to get deeper into it, think of those aspects above when reading the literary texts in this book or any other kind of literature.

Step D Read yourself

a While analysing literature is important, it is far more important that you actually read and discover great stories and ideas. Do some research and make a list of six important classical writers from the English speaking world. Compare your list with a partner's. Talk about what you know about the authors.

b There are many more interesting great writers. Do some research and match the authors (A–L) with the genres (1–6) There are two authors for each genre.

1 contemporay
2 crime and mystery
3 humour and comedy
4 travelling and culture
5 romance
6 SciFi

A Isaac Asimov
B Bill Bryson
C Lindsey Davis
D Janet Evanovich
E Dashiell Hammett
F Patricia Highsmith
G Ian McEwan
H Jan Morris
I Zadie Smith
J Nicolas Sparks
K Nora Roberts
L P. G. Woodhouse

c Which genre interests you most? Do some research on a novel you have read or would like to read. Compile a fact sheet with the following information and present it in class.
→ S 6.6 → S 15 1-minute presentation

title | author | publication date | genre | summary of plot

35

2 TEXT A

 **A Young people staying at home**

1 Before you read

a Do a survey with some older people. At what age did they move away from home? What was the reason for moving out? Collect your results in class. → S15 Round robin

b Now look at the title of the following text. Does the headline correspond with your results from **a**? Talk about it in class.

Two-thirds of singles in their 20s now live with their parents – here's how it affects their lives

1 Gone are the days when living at home in your 20s was seen as an embarrassing sign of arrested development. Today, 63% of single adults between the ages of 20 and 29 live with their parents, as do just over half of 25- to 29-year-olds. This inevitably raises issues about how families share costs, and what sort of living standards both older and younger generations can maintain in this arrangement.

At the Centre for Research in Social Policy at Loughborough University, we […] found that, for young adults with modest means, high housing costs and difficulty saving money are the main motivation for living with parents. As well as saving on rent, a combined household can share the cost of council tax and water bills, save on heating and potentially save money by bulk buying food and other goods. Our research identified potential savings of about £7,000 a year, as a result of a single person living together with their parents, rather than separately.

Arguably, living this way also makes efficient use of the UK's limited housing stock, by keeping family homes fully occupied. Yet our research – based on focus groups of young adults and parents who live in such situations – identified some thorny dilemmas within these living arrangements, particularly where they are not a temporary transition, but may last for years. […]

2 The parents we spoke with saw sharing the family home as a way of helping their sons and daughters to get established. Some hoped it would assist them to save for a deposit on a house, or take other steps towards independence. But many parents couldn't help observing cases where their children leveraged this help to spend far more than they expected, for example by buying the latest technological gadgets, or eating out frequently. As a result, parents wondered whether they were wrongly subsidising such a lifestyle, when their grown-up children should be taking more financial responsibility.

Young adults living with their parents maintained that some such expenditures were justified; for example, they thought if you live in your parents' home, you will eat out more often than if you had your own place, where you are more likely to socialise by asking a friend around for a meal.

Difficulties are bound to arise when related adults live together, and to some extent pool their economic resources, while still living largely separate lives. This creates economic relationships full of ambiguities, as parents desire to do the best for their sons and daughters, without having the same control over how their children live as they did when they were dependent. At the same time, young adults have to negotiate living as independent adults, within their parents' "domain". […]

3 These tensions emerged most clearly in discussions about how much young people living with their parents should

---

5 **arrested development** angehaltene Entwicklung; aufgehaltene Entwicklung
8 **inevitably** unvermeidlich; unausweichlich
9 **to raise issues** Probleme aufwerfen
12 **to maintain** erhalten; bewahren
15 **modest means** bescheidene Mittel
20 **council tax** Gemeindesteuer
21 **bulk buying** Großeinkauf
28 **limited housing stock** begrenzter Wohnbestand
33 **thorny** dornig; kompliziert
41 **deposit** Kaution; Anzahlung
44 **to leverage** zum Vorteil nutzen
49 **to subsidise** subventionieren; bezuschussen
54 **expenditure** Ausgabe
61 **be bound to arise** vorprogrammiert sein
66 **ambiguities** Unklarheiten

TEXT A 2

contribute to household costs. Both the young adults and parents taking part in our study agreed that, while parents would pay most household bills, they should receive some contribution from the young adult in the form of a regular "board" payment.

But there was little agreement on how to establish a fair price for this payment. [...] All of our participants felt that it would depend on the financial situations of both the young adult and their parents.

Some parents argued strongly that trying to create a formula for this contribution missed the point that a family relationship is not a commercial relationship, as with a landlord: it is guided by emotions, not just rational principles.

4 [...] We found that the additional cost to parents of having a son or daughter at home – such as buying more communal groceries or spending more on heating – could be fairly modest, compared with the savings made, costing a minimum of about £100 a month.

This means that with only a relatively small contribution, a young adult can ensure that their parents are not out of pocket, while still retaining large savings from living at home. [...]

5 Yet these calculations make some important assumptions about the parents' situation. One is that the parents themselves are well off enough to provide a decent home, [...]. The calculations also assume that, because parents had a bedroom available when their son or daughter was growing up, they would still have it when they reach adulthood.

Keeping a spare bedroom can imply serious additional costs for less well-off families. They might have to maintain high rates of private rent or be unable to downsize to ease the transition to retirement. [...]

[...], it's crucial to remember that not all parents own their home and have plenty of spare space, as well as the financial resources to support their adult children.

6 What's more, if it becomes more common for people to live at home with parents even into their 30s, this will begin to affect parents' retirement plans. The transition from work to retirement is typically managed with the help of a reduction in housing costs, [...].

If the parents are still sharing a home with their children when making these decisions, they may need to become more disciplined to negotiate a fair contribution towards the costs of keeping a room available for their sons and daughters to live in. Yet our research shows just how hard that is for parents, who will never see a son or daughter as a paying lodger, but always as part of the family. (905 words)

Donald Hirsch, *The Conversation*, 2019

---

77 **to contribute** beitragen; beisteuern
80 **household bills** Haushaltsausgaben
83 **board payment** Kostgeld
93 **landlord; /-lady** Vermieter/-in
97 **communal** gemeinschaftlich
105 **to retain** behalten; bewahren
116 **spare** übrig; frei
116 **to imply** bedeuten
120 **to downsize** (sich) verkleinern
122 **crucial** entscheidend; wesentlich
142 **lodger** Mieter/-in; Untermieter/-in

2 Multiple matching → WB p.19/1–2

Match the correct heading (A–H) with the paragraphs from the text (1–6). There are two more headlines than you need.

A Saving despite paying
B No money to move out
C A necessary long-term perspective
D Reckless spending
E Paying their way
F Negotiating difficulties
G Difficult dynamics
H It might not be that simple

3 Mediation

Beantworten Sie folgende Fragen auf Deutsch. Sie beziehen sich auf die Abschnitte 1, 3 und 6.

1. Wie wurde es früher betrachtet, wenn Kinder lange nicht ausgezogen sind?
2. Worin sind sich alle einig, wenn es um Höhe der Kostenbeteiligung geht?
3. Wozu fordert der letzte Absatz die Eltern auf? Was ist dabei die Schwierigkeit?

TEXT A

4 Multiple choice

Choose the most suitable option.

1. According to the paragraphs 1 and 2, …
   A almost two thirds of all adults in their 20s live at home.
   B the average single person living together with their parents has £7,000 a year of savings.
   C for a lot of young adults, making ends meet is the reason not to move out.
   D it is clear that families share costs for heating and bulk food buying.

2. The phrase "some thorny dilemmas" (l. 33) refers to the fact that …
   A these living arrangements are mostly not a temporary transition.
   B the parental assistance does not always produce the intended result.
   C young people find it hard to save for a deposit on a house on their way to independence.
   D young adults have problems taking more financial responsibility.

3. What is not mentioned in section 2?
   A Young adults would go out less if they had their own place.
   B Sharing the same house but living independent lives can lead to difficulties.
   C As they want the best for their children, parents want to maintain control over them.
   D It is not that easy for young people to live independently in their parents' home.

4. According to the text, what is true?
   A There is disagreement as to whether parents should receive regular board payment from their children.
   B There are guidelines on how to establish a fair price for the contribution to household cost.
   C As parents are not commercial landlords, children should pay what they feel is right.
   D If the children's contribution is to cover the additional costs, it should be at least £100 a month.

5. The phrase "these calculations make some important assumptions" (l.107) means that …
   A not all parents are in the financial position to have their adult children living with them.
   B many parents want to downsize to ease the transition to retirement.
   C adult children living at home have a negative impact on the retirement plan of the parents.
   D retirement necessitates a reduction in housing costs.

6. On the whole, the text …
   A is strongly in favour of young people moving out as soon as possible.
   B would recommend that parents let their kids stay at home if financially possible.
   C tries to present a balanced view taking into account various aspects of the issue.
   D suggests that kids should only continue to live at home if they contribute to the cost.

5 Focus on language

a Look at the text on pages 36–37 again. Which arguments does it present? What is the main point of each argument and how is this supported with facts, examples etc.?

b How does the author connect ideas and thoughts? Make a list of the useful phrases.

c In small groups, find further statistics on the topic. Collect data and use it to write one argument in a style similar to this text.

6 A step further

For many young people going to university is the first step to moving out of the family home.

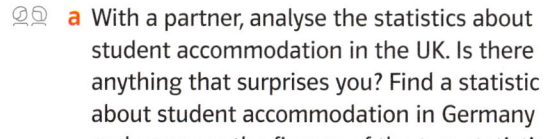

a With a partner, analyse the statistics about student accommodation in the UK. Is there anything that surprises you? Find a statistic about student accommodation in Germany and compare the figures of the two statistics. Are there significant differences? → S 10.3

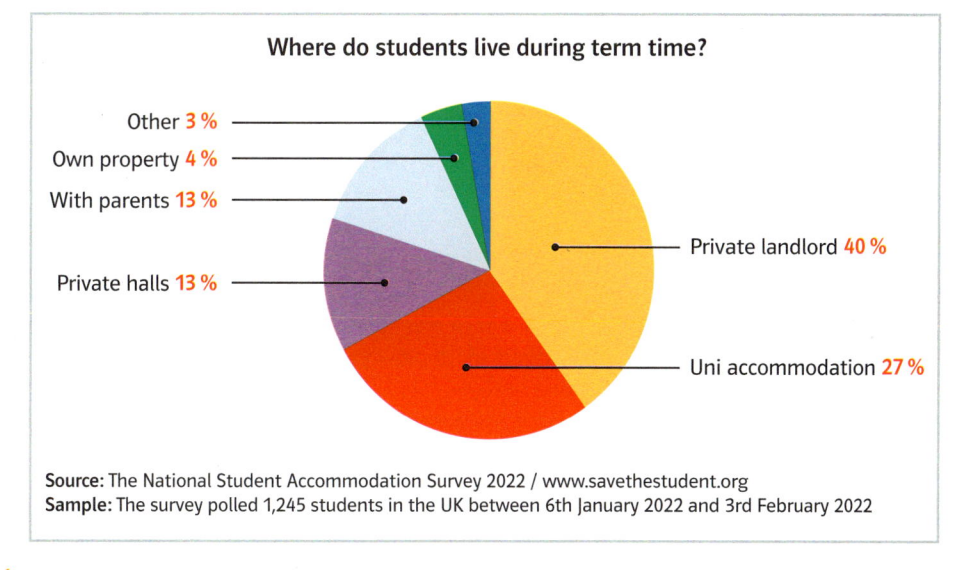

Where do students live during term time?

- Other **3 %**
- Own property **4 %**
- With parents **13 %**
- Private halls **13 %**
- Private landlord **40 %**
- Uni accommodation **27 %**

Source: The National Student Accommodation Survey 2022 / www.savethestudent.org
Sample: The survey polled 1,245 students in the UK between 6th January 2022 and 3rd February 2022

b In small groups, go to the websites of British universities (for example Birmingham, Cambridge, Cardiff, Guildford, Liverpool or Oxford) and do some research on student accommodation.

Find out about:
– What kind of accommodation is available for students in the city?
– Does the university provide accommodation? If so, is it on campus or off campus?
– How much does it cost to live in student accommodation?
– How do you apply for a place?
– What are the requirements you have to fulfill to be eligible for student accommodation?

c Present you results in class. → S 15 1-minute presentation

d Use the information from your research and the text on pages 36–37 to prepare a storyboard for a video about a young adult living at home or a young person moving out to study. → S 12

GOOD TO KNOW

A **storyboard** helps to visually organise a story. It consists of a sequence of illustrations or pictures to show what is going on in a scene and how the story evolves. Think of it as sort of a comic book.

2 TEXT B

B Generations and their view on life

1 Before you read

a Which American series do you watch? What do the typical families in these series look like? Reflect on whether there are any clichées. → S15 Round robin

b In small groups, make a mind map about your idea of the typical American family.

c Present your mind maps in class. Discuss what seem to be core values and ideals of American families.

One for the Money is the first volume of the Stephanie Plum series by Janet Evanovich. The novels are a mixture of crime, comedy, romance and action. Stephanie Plum is a young woman from Trenton, New Jersey, who works as a bounty hunter. In this extract she is not trying to bring criminals to court but she is on a more dangerous mission – dinner with her family. Her family live in the Italian neighbourhood of Trenton called Chambersburg.

One for the Money

I turned off Hamilton onto Roosevelt. Two blocks to my parents' house, and I could feel familial obligation sucking at me, pulling me into the heart of the burg. This was a community of extended families. There was safety here, along with love, and stability,
5 and the comfort of ritual. The clock on the dash told me I was seven minutes late, and the urge to scream told me I was home.

I parked at the curb and looked at the narrow two-story duplex […]. It was a small, tidy house crammed with kitchen smells and too much furniture, comfortable with its lot in life. […]

10 My mother was at the open screen door. "Stephanie," she called. "What are you doing sitting out there in your car? You're late for dinner. You know how your father hates to eat late. The potatoes are getting cold. The pot roast will be dry."

Food is important in the burg. The moon revolves around the earth, the earth revolves around the sun, and the burg revolves around pot roast. For as long as I can remember,
15 my parents' lives have been controlled by five-pound pieces of rolled rump, done to perfection at six o'clock.

Grandma Mazur stood two feet back from my mother. "I gotta get me a pair of those," she said, eyeballing my shorts. "I've still got pretty good legs, you know." She raised her skirt and looked down at her knees. "What do you think? You think I'd look good in them biker
20 things?"

Grandma Mazur had knees like doorknobs. She'd been a beauty in her time, but the years had turned her slack-skinned and spindle-boned. Still, if she wanted to wear biker shorts, I thought she should go for it. The way I saw it, that was one of the many advantages to living in New Jersey—even old ladies were allowed to look outlandish.

---

3 **familial obligation** familiäre Verpflichtung
3 **burg** *(ugs.)* Burg; Festung
4 **extended family** Großfamilie
5 **dash** *hier:* Armaturenbrett
6 **urge** Verlangen
7 **curb** Bordstein; Straßenrand
8 **two-story** zweistöckig
8 **duplex** Doppelhaus; Zweifamilienhaus
12 **pot roast** Schmorbraten; Schmorfleisch
15 **rump** Rumpsteak
18 **to eyeball** beäugen; begutachten
21 **doorknob** Türgriff; Türknauf
22 **slack-skinned** schlaff; faltig
22 **spindle-boned** spindeldürr
24 **outlandish** seltsam; sonderbar

TEXT B

25 My father gave a grunt of disgust from the kitchen, where he was carving up the meat. "Biker's shorts," he muttered, slapping his palm against his forehead. "Unh!"
Two years ago, when Grandpa Mazur's fat-clogged arteries sent him to the big pork roast in the sky, Grandma Mazur had moved in with my parents and had never moved out. My father accepted this with a combination of Old World stoicism and tactless mutterings.
30 [...]
"You should wear a dress," my mother said to me, bringing green beans and creamed pearl onions to the table. "Thirty years old and you're still dressing in those teeny-bopper outfits. How will you ever catch a nice man like that?"
"I don't want a man. I had one, and I didn't like it."
35 "That's because your husband was a horse's behind," Grandma Mazur said.
I agreed. My ex-husband had been a horse's behind. Especially when I'd caught him flagrante delicto on the dining room table with Joyce Barnhardt.
I hear Loretta Buzick's boy is separated from his wife," my mother said. "You remember him? Ronald Buzick?"
40 I knew where she was heading, and I didn't want to go there. "I'm not going out with Ronald Buzick," I told her. "Don't even think about it." [...]
My mother plunged on. "All right, then how about Bernie Kuntz? I saw Bernie Kuntz in the dry cleaner's, and he made a point about asking for you. I think he's interested. I could invite him over for coffee and cake."
45 With the way my luck was running, probably my mother had already invited Bernie, and at this very moment he was circling the block, popping Tic Tacs. "I don't want to talk about Bernie," I said. "There's something I need to tell you. I have some bad news...."
I'd been dreading this and had put it off for as long as possible.
My mother clapped a hand to her mouth. "You found a lump in your breast!"
50 [...] "My breast is fine. The problem is with my job."
"What about your job?"
"I don't have one. I got laid off."
"Laid off!" she said on a sharp inhale. "How could that happen? It was such a good job. You loved that job." [...]
55 "I've been out of work for six months."
"Six months! And I didn't know! Your own mother didn't know you were out on the streets?"
"I'm not out on the streets. I've been doing temporary jobs. Filing and stuff." And steadily sliding downhill. I was registered with every search firm in the greater Trenton area, and
60 I religiously read the want ads. I wasn't being all that choosy, drawing the line at telephone soliciting and kennel attendant, but my future didn't look great. [...]
My father forked another slab of pot roast onto his plate. He'd worked for the post office for thirty years and had opted for early retirement. Now he drove a cab part-time.
"I saw your cousin Vinnie yesterday," he said. "He's looking for someone to do filing. You
65 should give him a call."
Just the career move I'd been hoping for—filing for Vinnie. Of all my relatives, Vinnie was my least favorite. Vinnie was a worm [...]. "What does he pay?" I asked.
My father shrugged. "Gotta be minimum wage."
Wonderful. The perfect position for someone already in the depths of despair. Rotten
70 boss, rotten job, rotten pay. The possibilities for feeling sorry for myself would be endless.
"And the best part is that it's close," my mother said. "You can come home every day for lunch."
I nodded numbly, thinking I'd sooner stick a needle in my eye.   (918 words)

---

27 **fat-clogged** verstopft (von Fetten)
29 **stoicism** Gleichmut; stoische Gelassenheit
29 **muttering** Gemurmel
37 **flagrante delicto** in flagranti; auf frischer Tat
40 **to head** (in eine Richtung) steuern
42 **to plunge on** sich vorwärts stürzen
46 **to pop** einwerfen
48 **to dread** fürchten
49 **lump** Knoten
52 **to get laid-off** entlassen werden
58 **filing** Ablage; Archivieren
61 **telephone soliciting** Telefonwerbung
61 **kennel attendant** Hundehüter/-in
63 **to opt for** wählen
63 **retirement** Ruhestand
69 **in the depths of despair** völlig verzweifelt
74 **numbly** wie betäubt

TEXT B

2 Short-answer questions → WB p. 20/1–2

Answer the following questions. You may use words from the text.

1. What are the advantages of the area where Stephanie's parents live?
2. Which reaction shows that Stephanie has ambivalent feelings about the burg?
3. Which phrases underline the almost religious importance of meal times in the Plum family?
4. What is a sign for Stephanie that she lives in a liberal state?
5. What are Stephanie's father's survival tactics?

3 Gapped summary

Complete the summary with the most suitable words from the text. Give the line numbers of the words that you used.

Stephanie is on her way to her parents' place in the burg, a ■ 1 with a rather traditional background. For Stephanie, her parents' house, a ■ ■ 2, is a place that evokes ambivalent feelings. While the family offers her a safe haven, it is also a place where she is perhaps too ■ 3 with the way things are. But at least, Grandma Mazur, who has been living with Stephanie's parents for ■ ■ 4, is there as a guarantee to liven things up. While Stephanie's mum wants her daughter to give up ■ ■ 5, Grandma Mazur is keen on trying out ■ 6, despite the fact that she is no longer the ■ 7, which she has apparently once been.
That evening the dinner conversation does not go quite according to plan because instead of talking about a potential ■ 8 for her, Stephanie, she reveals that she has got problems as she has been ■ ■ 9. The job situation is so problematic that Stephanie might even consider asking her cousin Vinnie for a job even though this is not the ■ ■ 10 of her dreams.

4 Multiple matching

Who could have said this? Match the sentences and questions (A–J) with the people (1–7). Who would they have said it to? You can use each person several times.

1 Stephanie Plum   3 Stephanie's father   5 Vinnie   7 Joyce Barhardt
2 Stephanie's mother   4 Grandma Mazur   6 Bernie Kuntz

A It's not my fault that I am more attractive than you.
B Why didn't she die instead of him?
C It wasn't your fault. Luckily, you didn't have a gun then.
D Don't be so impatient. She can't be much longer.
E Get out before I impale you with something far less pleasant.
F Trying to look respectable might help in many ways.
G I am desperate. So even though I hate doing this, here I am.
H Too much admin. I hope someone replies to my ad.
I Health is the least of my worries.
J What is Stephanie up to these days?

TEXT B 2

5 Focus on analysis

a With a partner, make a table about aspects of Stephanie Plum's family. Who would you consider to be conservative and traditional, who seems to be unconventional and modern? Give reasons for your choice.

b Compare your results from **a** with the images of family you found when you did exercise **1**.

c Discuss how the values presented in the text on pages 40–41 and in the films and series compare with your values and the values of your parents. You can use your diagram from page 33.

d Would you rather like to live like Stephanie's family or like Stephanie? Why? Talk to a partner.

6 Focus on language → S 8.2

a Read the points on analysing novels on pages 34–35, then look again at the text on pages 40–41. Which elements of the plot turn the normal dinner scene into comedy? Think about what seems to be traditional and what less so.

b How does Janet Evanovich tell the story? How does she use language to achieve this comical effect? Make a list of some stylistic devices. Give the line numbers.

7 A step further → S 6.7

a In small groups, choose one of the following scenarios to continue the story.
  – Scenario 1: Stephanie, her parents and Grandma Mazur are at the shopping mall. Grandma Mazur goes clothes shopping.
  – Scenario 2: Stephanie has her job interview with Vinnie. On the way out she bumps into Bernie Kuntz.
  – Scenario 3: Stephanie and Grandma Mazur are at the shopping mall where their paths cross with Stephanie's ex and Joyce Barnhardt.

b Write a continuation of the story as a sketch using stylistic devices from exercise **5**. Then act it out in your group.

c Perform your sketch in class. Give each other feedback. → S 15 Tip-top

2 TEXT C

C Different relationship models

1 Before you read

a Which types of relationships and family models do know? Collect your ideas in class. → S 15 Round robin

b In small groups, talk about these models and which ones you consider more traditional and which more modern. Then talk about the pros and cons of each model.

c With a partner, discuss which model(s) you would prefer for yourself. Why? Which is not an option for you?

PLPs: The platonic partnerships that pair up friends for life

Deena Lilygren, a mother in her 40s, has been living with her best friend Maggie Brown for years in Kentucky, US. During the time they've been co-habiting, Brown met her future husband. He moved in with the pair of best friends, proposed to Brown, they got married and eventually, all three of them bought a house together. When he moved in with them – and again when he proposed – Brown told him she and Deena "were a package deal", says Lilygren. "She wanted to be sure he didn't have the expectation that so many people seem to have – that marriage is the time when you let go of your friends."

Brown and Lilygren have a relationship that goes beyond most friendships. Lilygren considers them "platonic life partners", meaning they are each other's primary partners – the way people often relate to spouses or romantic partners, only romance and sex don't factor into their relationship.

Barely uttered in the past, the phrase 'platonic life partners' has been popularised lately by two women in their 20s from Singapore, April Lee and Renee Wong. The pair discuss their platonic life partnership (PLP) on TikTok, where Lee has more than 51,000 followers. […] As Lee put it in a piece about their partnership for Refinery29, they were not just best friends but "supportive financial partners", helped each other reach their life goals more effectively and wanted to be together not just temporarily as roommates, but for the long haul. […]

For some who are currently in PLPs, like Lilygren, the phrase is an important way to not just define their living situations, but also stress the value of non-romantic partnerships. "As a culture, we really devalue friendship when compared to relationships like marriage – we're expected to have transient, secondary friendships that become marginalised when one friend gets married," says Lilygren, "and there really isn't a word for a friend who is a partner in life." 'PLP' fills that void. […]

From colonial times up until about 1850, people entered […] marriages for "pragmatic" reasons, says Eli Finkel, professor at Northwestern University, Illinois, US […]. "The distinct functions of marriage during this era revolved around basic survival – literally things like food, clothing and shelter," he says. For women – who were kept out of the workforce and unable to make a living independently – having a husband was key to getting by. This changed for many in places like the US and Britain by the late 1800s, however. There, middle class women could attend college, paving the way for them to enter the workforce, explains US-based LGBTQ

---

1 **platonic** platonisch; nicht körperlich
6 **to co-habitate** zusammenleben
12 **to propose (to so)** (jdm.) einen Heiratsantrag machen
23 **spouse** (Ehe)partner/-in
24 **to factor** eine Rolle spielen
35 **supportive** unterstützend; stützend
39 **for the long haul** auf Dauer; langfristig
45 **to devalue** entwerten; abwerten
47 **transient** vorübergehend; flüchtig
48 **marginalised** an den Rand/ ins Abseits gedrängt
52 **void** Lücke; Leerraum
63 **be key to** der Schlüssel zu etwas sein
67 **to pave the way for sb** jdm. den Weg ebnen/ bahnen

TEXT C 2

historian Lillian Faderman. Women no longer had to rely on husbands for income, and some chose to live with other women instead. [...]

From the mid-1800s up through the 1960s, Finkel says marriage had left the "pragmatic era" and landed in the "love-based era", meaning people formed lifelong partnerships for love and intimacy, rather than survival. Industrialisation brought young people to cities, making them, "for the first time ever... geographically and economically independent of their families", says Finkel. With this freedom came an emphasis on "emotional fulfilment" in lifetime matches.

The 1960s, he adds, brought another shift in what people largely looked for in life partners in the Western world. "Love and intimacy remain necessary, but they're no longer sufficient," he says. Marriages [...] and life partnerships have evolved to a point at which many expect their significant other to be their everything, fulfilling multiple roles including sexual partner, cohabitator, co-parent, emotional support system and financial partner, among other things. That can be a lot to ask of one person, and "many relationships are buckling under the strain", adds Finkel. PLPs offer an alternative way to engage in long-term relationships. A platonic partner isn't expected to fulfil sexual and romantic needs, and those with a PLP don't see their romantic partners as their primary emotional support system. Some merge finances with their PLP, as many might expect from a married couple, and others don't, or do partially. [...]

Overall, entering a PLP has a lot in common with entering a marriage. Some even do get married, in part for the legal rights that come with the arrangement (like ensuring their partners will be considered their 'next of kin'), or to show their commitment to each other to family members and friends who may not otherwise understand. The practical discussions about how to share a life still apply, along with added negotiations about how to incorporate each member's romantic partners into the relationship and/or living arrangement.

People who aren't familiar with PLPs often struggle with the idea two people can share such deep intimacy and not have a sexual relationship. It took Florida-based Jay and Krystle, who talked about their PLP to The Cut, going viral on TikTok about their relationship for their family and friends to finally grasp that they were totally platonic, in spite of their marriage. For Lilygren, writing about her relationship with Brown is what ultimately helped explain the trio's arrangement to Brown and her husband's families.

"They started taking us more seriously as a family unit, which is beautiful," says Lilygren. But the article also received some backlash. "There were a lot of negative comments online because people cannot imagine that our situation isn't sexual, which is too bad." [...]

[...] as more young people talk publicly about their decisions to enter PLPs, they're spreading the word that it's an option for lifelong partnership. [...]

(908 words)
Jessica Klein, *BBC*, 2022

93 **significant other** bessere Hälfte
99 **to buckle** einknicken; zusammenbrechen
115 **commitment** Verpflichtung; Verbindung
119 **negotiation** *hier:* Aushandeln; Verhandeln
120 **to incorporate** berücksichtigen; integrieren
128 **to go viral** viral werden; sich wie ein Virus im Internet verbreiten
130 **to grasp** verstehen
140 **backlash** Gegenreaktion; Gegenbewegung

2 Short-answer questions → WB p. 21/1–2

Answer the following questions. You may use words from the text.

1. Which business idiom is used to describe two people as very close?
2. Where has the phrase PLP been made known?
3. What does having a phrase like PLP underline?
4. What was the central focus of marriage until about 170 years ago?
5. What is the negative result of the shift the 1960s brought about?
6. According to Lilygren, what is still unthinkable for many?

2 TEXT C

3 Multiple matching

Match the possible statements (A–J) with the most suitable people (1–8). You can use each person only once. There are two more statements than you need.

1. Deena Lilygren
2. Lilygren's child
3. Maggie Brown
4. Brown's husband
5. April Lee
6. Eli Finkel
7. Lillian Faderman
8. Jay and Krystle

A No, I am not a bigamist even though there are two women in our house.
B Tying the knot was for a long time more a question of necessity than emotion.
C I wanted to tell the world that this was far more and deeper than just flat sharing for a while.
D I made that clear from the start. Either both or none.
E What's in a name? But without one it is at times difficult to explain a situation to others.
F It would help marriages if they were less love-based and a bit more pragmatic.
G Only after financial independence became possible, did women have such a choice.
H Writing about it has been like a liberating coming out.
I It was only online that we could make them understand that we have a wedding ring but no sex.
J If I can live with it, why can't others let them be? People have such dirty minds.

4 Mediation

Beantworten Sie folgende Fragen auf Deutsch. Sie beziehen sich auf den Text ab Zeile 40.

1. Welches Problem sieht Lilygren mit Blick auf das Verständnis von Ehe und Freundschaft?
2. Erklären Sie aus dem Textzusammenhang, was mit dem Satz „marriage had left the 'pragmatic era' and landed in the 'love-based era'" (Zeile 74–76) gemeint ist.
3. Was meint der Text mit der Aussage, dass PLPs eine Alternative seien?
4. Eine PLP ist keine Ehe. Warum heiraten diese Menschen trotzdem ihre Partnerin oder ihren Partner?
5. Welche Faktoren gibt es in einer PLP, die neben denen, die auch in einer Ehe vorkommen, geklärt werden müssen?

5 A step further

a Imagine you had the chance to interview the different people portrayed in the text. In order to understand the idea of PLPs better which questions would you ask? Whom would you ask them? In small groups, write down these questions.

b Exchange your questions with another group. Look at the text again and speculate what the answers might be. Then present your answers in class.

c Considering your answers from b, discuss what the advantages and disadvantages of a PLP are.

TEXT D 2

D Across generations and continents

1 Before you read

a Look at the illustration. What do you think belongs to the typical American way of life? In small groups, collect your ideas in a list.

b What do you know about the Arab world and in particular about Yemen? Where does your knowledge come from? Write down your ideas.

c Look at your notes from tasks a and b and discuss in your group what challenges a Yemeni person might experience in America.

Dave Eggers is an American writer, editor and publisher. In his novel *The Monk of Mokha* Eggers tells the true story of Mokhtar Alkanshali, a young Yemeni American man raised in San Francisco, who dreams of resurrecting the ancient art of Yemeni coffee but finds himself trapped in Yemen in the midst of civil war. The following excerpt is about Mokhtar when he was still a teenager and far from trouble.

The Monk of Mokha

Mokhtar's parents […] sent him to Yemen. They thought he needed a change of location, **1**, some fresh air. Mokhtar went from his family's one-bedroom apartment in the Tenderloin to his grandfather's Hamood's six-story home in Ibb. There, Mokhtar had his
5 own bedroom. […] The house had dozens of rooms, a balcony overlooking a lush valley in the center of the city. It was a castle, really, built by Hamood from nothing.
Hamood was more than a patriarch; in the Alkanshali family his influence was impossible to escape. And though he was in his late sixties, he still travelled a hundred miles a day, from Sana'a to Ibb, or out from Ibb to the villages, **2**. He was no longer a tall
10 man – age had shrunk him, thinned him – but his mind was quick; he was witty and tough. Though largely retired, he was still an éminence grise in Ibb. When he walked into a wedding hall, everyone stood. Some kissed his hand, others kissed his head – **3**.
He was born in the 1940s in Al-Dakhla, a small village inside of Ibb, the fifth of eight children. From a young age he was his father's favorite. When he was still young, only
15 nine or ten, his father was embroiled in a land dispute with another tribesman **4**. The dispute landed him in prison, and there, his health quickly deteriorated. Knowing his end was near, he summoned only one of his children, Hamood, to his cell and this act of favoritism soured Hamood's relations with his siblings, especially his older brothers. After their father's death, these brothers ostracized him and would not grant him any of
20 their father's land.
At thirteen, Hamood decided to set out on his own. Without shoes and carrying only a knapsack, he left Ibb and walked to Saudi Arabia. He told this story to Mokhtar often. […] In Saudi Arabia, a land awash in oil money and far wealthier than Yemen could ever be, Hamood sold water in the side of the road. He cleaned restaurants. He did any odd job he
25 could, and he saved money to send home to his widowed mother. […]
In his late teens, Hamood went back to Yemen and married a young woman named Zafaran, **5**. They traveled to Sheffield, England, where Hamood had heard there was

5 **lush** üppig; üppig bewachsen
10 **to shrink** schrumpfen (lassen)
10 **witty** witzig; geistreich
11 **éminence grise** (aus dem Französischen) graue Eminenz
15 **to be embroiled in** verwickelt/verstrickt sein in
15 **dispute** Streitigkeit; Konflikt
15 **tribesman** Stammesangehöriger
16 **to deteriorate** sich verschlechtern; nachlassen
17 **to summon** bestellen; einbestellen
18 **siblings** *pl* Geschwister
19 **to ostracize** verbannen; ächten
22 **knapsack** Rucksack
23 **awash** überschwemmt

47

TEXT D

28	**steel mill** Stahlwerk; Stahlhütte
29	**assembly line** Fließband; Montageband
33	**undaunted** unerschrocken; unverdrossen
38	**bewildering** verwirrend
41	**custom touch** individuelle Note
43	**array** Reihe; Sammlung
53	**to grind down** abschleifen; unterdrücken
54	**sarong** Sarong (Wickeltuch)
54	**to assimilate** sich anpassen; integrieren
61	**to carry oneself** sich benehmen
62	**to concoct** sich ausdenken; aushecken
62	**far-flung** entlegen; weit verstreut
64	**courtyard** Hof; Innenhof
65	**caravan** Karawane
65	**flatbed truck** Tieflader; Flachbett-LKW
70	**ephemeral** vergänglich; kurzlebig
73	**to cut corners** Abstriche machen
76	**mold** Ausprägung; Tradition

good-paying work in the steel mills. Eventually he left for Detroit, where Yemenis were finding work building cars. Hamood worked the assembly line at Chrysler, installing air
30 bags, until, **6**, he followed Yemeni friends to New York.

With his savings, he bought a corner store in Harlem and made it profitable. He bought another in Queens, and though he had to contend with gangs and the Mafia, he was undaunted. The market in Queens did well, too, and soon Hamood was loaning money to his sons and […] all of whom opened their own grocery stores and liquor stores in New
35 York and California, all of which paid dividends to Hamood and allowed him to retire in his fifties.

He bought five acres in Ibb, and gave the builders a sketch he'd drafted himself. It was a bewildering drawing, even by the wildly eccentric architectural standards of Yemen. […] He began building the house in 1991 and never finished. When Mokhtar arrived and
40 throughout the year he spent in Yemen, there were always workers in the house. At any time there were five craftsmen adding custom touches, all according to Hamood's specifications […]. Walls were covered with his collections of daggers, swords, cowboy hats, holsters and guns. He had a Beretta, an array of Colt .45s, a collection of pistols he'd seen in Bond films and John Wayne movies. Hamood had seen every film John Wayne
45 had ever made, and collected holsters, hats, wore cowboy boots – anything Wayne had worn, he wanted.

When Mokhtar got to Ibb, **7**, he had no interest in John Wayne and no interest in Yemen. He missed the action in San Francisco. Hamood sent him to a local school, private and rigorous, and made him walk to it, **8**. Mokhtar spoke some Arabic, but no one in the
50 school spoke English. He was one of the only Americans there. He didn't wear his clothes correctly. He didn't know the proper response to standard greetings. He didn't know the right Yemeni way to walk, act, smile, not smile. To fit in, he decided he would become super-Yemeni. He worked on his Arabic, ground down his accent, dressed like Yemeni kids, with a sarong and sandals and the right kind of jacket. He tried to assimilate and
55 master local customs, **9**. […]

But soon Zafaran and Hamood began to trust him with tasks small and significant. "Go to the bank and cash this check," Hamood would say, and would hand him a check for three million riyals – about fifteen thousand dollars. Mokhtar would return, navigating the streets of Ibb carrying an enormous bag of money like a cartoon bank robber.
60 Hamood had business all over Ibb, and all over Yemen. He brought Mokhtar on his rounds, teaching him how a businessman carried himself, how a leader walked and talked. The tasks Hamood concocted for him were far-flung and grand. One time he gave Mokhtar a bundle of cash and instructed him to go to Taiz, **10**, and come back with six tons of a certain kind of stone he needed for the courtyard of the house. Mokhtar
65 returned that evening leading a caravan of three full flatbed trucks.

When Mokhtar made a mistake, Hamood was angry only if Mokhtar made an excuse. "Own the error and correct it," he said. Hamood had a thousand proverbs and maxims. His favorite was Keep the money in your hand, never in your heart. He used that a lot. "What does it mean?" Mokhtar asked.
70 "It means that money is ephemeral, **11**," Hamood said. "It's a tool. Don't let it get into your heart or your soul."

Mokhtar spent a year with Hamood and Zafaran and returned to the United States changed. Not entirely reformed – there was still significant corner-cutting in high school – but he'd studied classical Arabic, awakened to his Yemeni heritage, and though
75 Hamood hoped Mokhtar might become an imam or attorney, Mokhtar began instead to see himself in Hamood's mold, as a man of enterprise. A man who liked to move.

(1071 words)

TEXT D 2

2 Multiple matching → WB p. 22/1–3

Match the missing phrases (A–N) from the text with the gaps (1–11). There are three phrases more than you need.

A who had the favor of the ruling powers
B moving from person to person
C yet destined for something more
D a few years later
E but he never forgot it
F but the embarrassment was unending
G attending weddings and funerals and mediating tribal disputes
H just after eighth grade
I who were natives of Ibb or Aden
J two hours away
K an immersion in his ancestry
L forty-five minutes each way
M a sign of the utmost respect
N who had grown up in a neighboring Ibb village

3 Gapped summary

Complete the summary with the most suitable words from the text. Give the line number of the words that you used.

> At high school Mokhtar constantly ran into trouble. There was simply too much ■ 1. Mokhtar lacked a sense of direction. That is why his parents sent him to Yemen to live with his grandfather Hamood for a ■ 2. For Mokhtar it was quite an experience and a big change from a small ■ 3 in San Francisco to the huge castle-like house of his grandfather. For Mokhtar, living with the ■ 4 of the Alkanshali family was a full immersion into Yemeni ■ 5 and culture. It was probably a stroke of good luck that Mokhtar's grandfather was a self-made man who had worked his way up from rags to riches while working in Saudi-Arabia, ■ 6 and the USA before finally settling down in the city of ■ 7. In a sense, for Mokhtar, Hamood bridged the cultural gap between the USA and Yemen. Eventually, Mokhtar improved his ■ 8 and dressed and behaved like Yemeni. Hamood also taught Mokhtar how to carry himself as a businessman and a ■ 9. All this made a ■ 10 contribution to Mokhtar's education and formation.

4 Multiple choice

Choose the most suitable option.

1. Which is wrong?
   A It was not Mokhtar's idea to spend some time in Yemen.
   B Hamood lived in a village near Ibb.
   C Although he was mainly retired, Hamood was still very active, moving around a lot.
   D Mokhtar had to share a room at home.

2. Which is true about Hamood?
   A His father never owned property.
   B He was born in a town.
   C Together with his siblings, he was at his father's deathbed.
   D He didn't spend his teenage years in Yemen.

3. What is not mentioned about Hamood?
   A He has been to Europe.
   B He already knew some people in New York when he went there.
   C Zafaran and Hamood have more than one child.
   D He lived in Harlem for some time.

2 TEXT D

4. Coming to Ibb, Mokhtar …
   A was keen on becoming like his grandfather.
   B considered Ibb less interesting than San Francisco.
   C spoke mainly English with the people around him.
   D at once tried to assimilate and master local customs.

5. Hamood …
   A was angry when Mokhtar made mistakes.
   B found it hard to trust Mokhtar with more than small tasks.
   C took Mokhtar to many places in Yemen.
   D made sure Mokhtar always kept money in his hands.

5 Mediation

Beantworten Sie folgende Fragen auf Deutsch: Sie beziehen sich auf die Zeilen 14–20 und 66–76.

1. Wie war das Verhältnis von Hamood zu seinem Vater? Wie beeinflusste dies sein Verhältnis zu seinen Geschwistern und welche Folge hat das für ihn?
2. Was erwartet Hamood von Mokhtar anstelle von Perfektion?
3. Wie formuliert Hamood seine Einstellung zu Geld und was meint er damit?
4. Erklären Sie aus dem Textzusammenhang, was im letzten Absatz mit der Aussage „Mokhtar […] returned to the United States changed […], awakened to his Yemeni heritage" gemeint ist, bzw. auf welche Veränderungen bei Mokhtar angespielt wird.
5. Was ist Mokhtars Selbstverständnis nach seiner Zeit im Jemen?

6 Talking about different cultures

a With a partner, look at the text on pages 47–48 again. Which parts and aspects would you consider traditionally Yemeni, which ones typically American? Take notes. Also name the character these aspects are connected with in the text.

b In small groups, discuss the following aspects:
   1. What is the main theme of the text?
   2. Which developments and changes do the main characters go through?
   3. Which culture is the text predominantly about?

7 A step further

a *The Monk of Mokha* tells the story of Mokhtar Alkanshali, who is a real person. Do some research on how the book continues and about Mokhtar's career. Would you like to read the book? Give reasons.

b In small groups, research online about a famous immigrant to the USA. Make a timeline about their life and important stages. What success and challenges did this person experience?

Example: Arnold Schwarzenegger

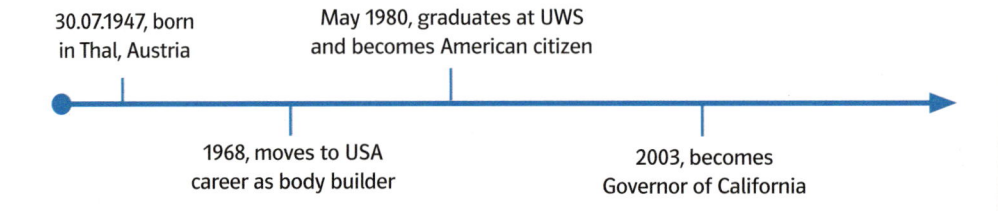

- 30.07.1947, born in Thal, Austria
- 1968, moves to USA career as body builder
- May 1980, graduates at UWS and becomes American citizen
- 2003, becomes Governor of California

Generations living together → S 6.2 → WB p.23/1

The present demographic change affects relationships as well as our way of living. One new concept is multigenerational living, for example houses in which different generations live together. Discuss the benefits and potential problems of multigenerational living.

Write a composition of at least 300 words. Include all the material provided.

Material 1

Was ist ein Mehrgenerationenwohnhaus?

Hierbei handelt es sich […] um ein größeres Haus, in dem Singles, Paare und Familien mehrerer Generationen in separaten Wohnungen miteinander leben. Der Vorteil des Mehrgenerationenwohnens ist, dass sich die häusliche Pflege alter und kranker Menschen wesentlich umfassender sichern lässt. Gleichermaßen trifft das auch auf die Betreuung kleiner Kinder zu. Denn auch diese ist für allein lebende Eltern häufig mit zeitlichen und organisatorischen Herausforderungen verbunden. Darüber hinaus verbringen die Familien mehr Zeit miteinander. Sie können sich gegenseitig unterstützen, müssen aber auch mit dem erhöhten Konfliktpotenzial zurechtkommen.

Material 2

Material 3

It's difficult to get on with people of another generation, even when they don't try to impose their way of seeing things on us.   *Carmen Laforet, Spanish author*

2 MEDIATION

Generation Z in the world of work → S 6.1

Sie sollen ein Referat zur Zukunft der Arbeitswelt halten, das speziell auf die Sicht junger Menschen eingeht. Zur Vorbereitung verfassen Sie einen zusammenhängenden englischen Text (ca. 150 Wörter) unter Verwendung des nachfolgenden Textes.

Gehen Sie dabei auf die folgenden Aspekte ein:
1. Worum ging es in der Umfrage und wer wurde befragt?
2. Worauf legt die Generation Z neben dem Gehalt am meisten Wert? (3 Aspekte)
3. Was ist der Hauptwunsch bei der Gestaltung der Arbeitszeit? Welches Problem ist damit verbunden?
4. Was ist für die Generation Z neben Karriere sehr wichtig und was eher weniger?
5. Welche Unternehmensformen werden präferiert? Warum?

Generation Z wünscht sich Arbeitgeber mit Werten

[...] Was wünschen sich also die Menschen, die nach 1995 geboren sind und gerade ins Berufsleben einsteigen, von ihrem Arbeitsplatz? Hierzu hat Zenjob, eine Online-Plattformen für Nebenjobs, für die Studie „Future of Work" im Mai 2021 rund 1.200 Vertreterinnen und Vertreter der Gen Z und 500 Millennials in Deutschland befragt. [...]

Der Großteil der Generation Z legt Wert auf eine Unternehmenskultur, in der ehrlich und offen kommuniziert wird. [...] Auf Position zwei befindet sich das Gehalt, das somit auch für junge Beschäftigte eine große Bedeutung hat. Dennoch sind es vor allem die „inneren Werte" eines Unternehmens, die für die heute Unter-25-Jährigen in ihrem Job wichtig sind. Das betrifft zum einen die Offenheit für neue Ideen und Konzepte, die die jungen Beschäftigten bei ihrem Arbeitgeber einbringen wollen, und zum anderen die Themen Nachhaltigkeit und soziales Engagement. Weiter unten ranken Ansprüche an die Unternehmensstruktur wie Diversität, flache Hierarchien und Firmenfeiern. [...]

Bei der Frage, ob sie sich die Arbeitszeit frei einteilen möchten, sind sich die jungen Menschen uneins: Die Hälfte aller Befragten gab an, dass sie sich feste Arbeitszeiten wünscht, die andere Hälfte äußerte dagegen das Bedürfnis nach Flexibilität im Arbeitsalltag. [...] Wichtig ist den Vertretern der Generation Z vor allem Autonomie: 83 Prozent gaben an, sich ihre Zeit selbst einteilen zu wollen, um nach dem eigenen Rhythmus arbeiten zu können. Gleichzeitig stellt diese Eigenorganisation die jungen Arbeitskräfte aber auch vor einige Herausforderungen. Jeder Zweite erklärte, dass das in der Praxis noch nicht immer gelingt. Die andere Hälfte der Befragten sprach sich zudem dafür aus, dass Mentoring und belastbare Rahmenstrukturen von Unternehmen ihnen bei der Selbstorganisation helfen würden. [...]

Klar ist: Die Karriere ist zwar ein wichtiger Teil des Lebens der Generation Z, aber nicht das oberstes Arbeitsziel. Das sagen rund zwei Drittel der Befragten. [...] An den obersten beiden Stellen der Bedürfnispyramide stehen die Vereinbarkeit des Jobs mit dem Privatleben (69 Prozent) sowie die Flexibilität (55 Prozent). Dahinter folgen die persönliche Identifikation mit dem Unternehmen (55 Prozent) und vielfältige Aufgaben (53 Prozent). Die Sicherheit des Arbeitsplatzes ist für 45 Prozent der Generation Z besonders wichtig, dagegen gab nur rund ein Viertel der Befragten an, es sei für sie elementar, dass ein Unternehmen besonders digital und fortschrittlich aufgestellt ist. [...]

Was die Unternehmensform angeht, so haben die Teilnehmenden unterschiedliche Präferenzen. Sowohl bei der Generation Z (32 Prozent) als auch bei den Millennials (37 Prozent) liegt jedoch der Mittelstand klar vorn. Die Kombination aus Sicherheit und eher familiärer Umgebung scheint für die junge Generation besonders attraktiv zu sein. Für jeweils circa ein Viertel ist das Arbeiten in Startups und die Selbstständigkeit die ideale Arbeitsform. Etwas abgeschlagen liegen bei beiden teilnehmenden Gruppen die Großkonzerne: Nur rund ein Fünftel würde sich dafür entscheiden. […]

(449 Wörter)
Online Redaktion, *Haufe*, 2021

Bridging the gap

There is a difference between how the older generation and today's youth see themselves and each other. This generation gap often leads to misconceptions the different age groups have of the other and to misunderstandings between young people and their grandparents.

Your school is planning a project to help bridge this gap. In preparation for this project, you meet to discuss what the biggest differences between the generations are and how you could start a dialogue between the generations to further mutual understanding.

In addition to these ideas also think about what would be an appropriate forum and format (exhibition, website, public debate …) for such a conversation between young people and the generation of their grandparents.

During the discussion, you can talk about the following questions:

- How has the world changed for youth since the days when your grandparents were young and today?
- Which developments would you consider negative and which ones positive?
- What were and are the key issues and topics for your grandparents?
- What are the key issues and topics in your generation?
- What characterises each generation?
- What do the generations have in common?
- What would be a good forum for a dialogue between generations?

a Present one or two of your ideas (about one minute).

b Discuss and explain your ideas and views.

c Sum up your ideas and different positions. Try to come to a conclusion.

3 GETTING STARTED

Technology and us

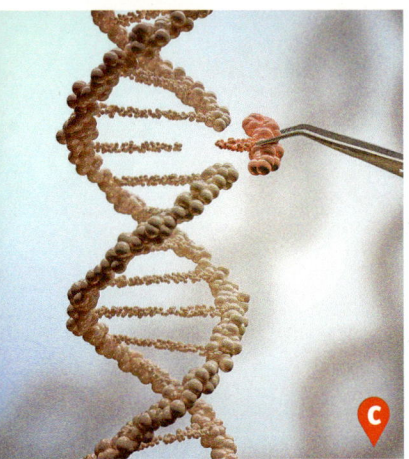

1 Working with pictures → S 10.1 → WB p. 26–27/1–2; 28/1–2

Look at the five pictures relating to science and describe them. Say which aspect each one depicts and what effects these might have on society.
Use the words below to help you and compare your results with a partner.

control panel | smart home | Internet of Things | genetic engineering | 3D-printer | augmented reality | genetically modified organisms | DNA | artificial intelligence | ethical issues | VR glasses

USEFUL PHRASES

Discussing a topic
On the one hand … On the other hand … | One of the advantages/disadvantages of … is … | In my opinion, … has more risks/benefits because … | In my mind, it is clear that … | Due to technological/scientific progress … | Another important aspect is (that) … | The main reason/result is that … | All in all, we can say (that) …

GETTING STARTED **3**

2 Talking about technology

a What do you think are the most important technological inventions? Present your ideas to your partner and then in class. → S 15 Think-pair-share

b Look at the useful phrases on page 54. In small groups, discuss which technological developments make your lives easier. Agree on a list of at least five inventions or innovations you cannot imagine living without. Give reasons for your choice. Share your ideas in class. → S 15 Gallery walk

3 Listening → S 3

a Listen to the first part of the podcast 'Benefits and risks of technological developments' and answer the following questions.

1. What is the title of Michael Southwater's book?
2. According to Carrie Spencer, what does technology offer us?
3. What does a smart factory use data for? Give two examples.
4. Which positive examples of facial recognition technology does Carrie mention?
5. What are the positive and negative aspects of drones mentioned? Name two each.

b Listen to the second part and choose the most suitable answer.

1. Carrie agrees that technology has always been used for …
   A making money.
   B doing unpleasant things and breaking the law.
   C communicating with people all over the world.

2. In Michael's opinion, …
   A driverless cars do not help the environment.
   B there will be no driverless cars on the road.
   C technology can help solve more important issues than driving cars.

3. According to Michael, augmented reality has been used positively for …
   A selling furniture and teaching.
   B improving the world as we know it.
   C exploring different historical periods.

4. When talking about genetic engineering, Carrie argues that …
   A the public should be informed about the potential health risks involved.
   B society should try to live in a more sustainable way before turning to science.
   C technology must be used immediately to modify crops and fight global hunger.

4 Creating a mind map

a Look again at the pictures on page 54. Which aspects of today's increasingly interconnected society do they represent? In small groups, make a mind map of these issues.

b Add the aspects and arguments mentioned in the podcast in task **3** to your mind map.

c Find other images or aspects that reflect your view on this issue. Add them to your mind map and present it in class. → S 15 Gallery walk

3 TEXT A

A Virtual reality

1 Before you read

a In small groups, read the following quotes and make sure you understand their meaning. Discuss the ideas presented in the quotes. With which do you agree? Where do you disagree?

> Virtual reality is a technology that could actually allow you to connect on a real human level, soul-to-soul, regardless of where you are in the world.
> Chris Milk, American innovator, artist and entrepreneur

> Crucial to science education is hands-on involvement: showing, not just telling; real experiments and field trips and not just 'virtual reality'.
> Martin Rees, British astrophysicist

> I like live audiences, with real people – virtual reality is no substitute.
> Hillary Clinton, American politician

b What role does virtual reality play in your daily life? Present specific examples to the class. Can you relate them to the quotes above? → S15 Round robin

Helsinki's huge VR gig hints at the potential of virtual tourism

[...] According to Finland's National Police Board, this year's Vappu Eve (the festive
5 night before May Day, when the country traditionally enjoys public fun and frolics) was "exceptionally peaceful". Citizens largely respected calls to stay at home. And yet ... I found myself at a gig in
10 Helsinki's Senate Square with almost 150,000 other people. I was dressed as a giant pineapple called Temperamenttinen Satuilija (Temperamental Fabulist!), and was tossing champagne at Finnish rap
15 duo JVG as they performed live on a stage, in front of the city's neoclassical cathedral. Just another day in lockdown.
Though it happened in real time, the event was held in the virtual world. While
20 Temperamenttinen – my avatar – was bopping in the Nordic twilight, I was at home, at my computer, cat on knee, finger on mouse, sending gestures and fizz-bottle emojis to the duo, who could see the feedback as they performed. I can't say 25 it had the buzz of being at a "proper" concert. And JVG weren't my personal jam. But, technically, it was impressive. Without the requirement of a VR headset, I was watching humans, performing in 30 real time, in front of an interactive audience, within a world of meticulously rendered make believe.

Virtual Helsinki – launched in late 2018 – is the physical capital's digital twin. It was 35 built using 3D modelling from open data (supplied by the city), as well as drawings and images. It allows users to experience key landmarks as they choose, and it claims to be one of the world's most 40 realistic VR experiences.
The platform is part of the city's bid to become the virtual capital of the world. "We are embedding digital innovation into all of the city's activities. Simply, 45 digitalisation builds better cities – it

---

6 **frolics** Späße
13 **fabulist** Geschichtenerzähler/-in
14 **to toss** werfen
21 **to bop** tanzen; wippen; hüpfen
28 **personal jam** *hier:* persönlicher Geschmack
32 **meticulous** sorgfältig; akribisch
42 **bid** Bewerbung
44 **to embed** einbinden

means personalised services and more choice," says Laura Aalto, CEO of Helsinki Marketing. Helsinki is a good test-bed for VR: big enough to enable the development and trial of significant innovations, small enough for it to be feasible. The Covid-19 lockdown has spurred such a trial. [...]

The live show was watched on 460,000 computers. With a conservative estimate of 1.5 viewers per computer, that is almost 700,000 people – Finland's biggest online event. Of those, 149,403 attended by creating avatars, though the camera largely focused on the band and, with only 500 avatars visible at a time, you'd have been lucky to pick yourself out on screen – even dressed as a pineapple.

The gig was a success, but what does it – and virtual tourism more widely – mean for the future of travel? Helsinki is seeking to be a pioneer of sustainable tourism, and allowing people to visit without racking up carbon emissions certainly aids that.

"The travel industry needs to reinvent itself and I hope this encourages other destinations to experience with digital platforms," says Mikko Rusama, chief digital officer at City of Helsinki. "Some are suspicious and think no technology can replace a real visit – which in a way is true. But VR can bring about new experiences that are impossible in real cities."

Virtual Helsinki plans to develop its content – art exhibitions, shopping experiences, "re-lived" historical events – and to make it all multi-user. "Multiplayer functions enable visitors to become social in virtual cities," says Rusama. "That will have a big impact on people's interest to explore places virtually."

But, when we're permitted to move again, will the city have made actually visiting it feel unnecessary? "No, the idea is to offer visitors an alternative way of experiencing the city in addition to travelling here," says Aalto.

"Customer behaviour is likely to change radically post-corona [virus]. We won't stop travelling but the reasons will be different. We need a stronger "why"; visits will be more in line with what we stand for. The winners in the future tourism industry are those that can understand and meet the values of visitors."

[...] [D]estinations across the world are brainstorming ways to create virtual content to keep visitors interested [...]. There are 360-degree tours: we can scan the mountains of Switzerland, the skyscrapers of Dubai or the Great Barrier Reef; and 3D modelling allows us to take tours of Egypt's ancient wonders that offer such clarity we can see chisel marks on the walls. Also, festivals and events have moved online [...].

And we can expect more, believes Dr Timothy Jung, founder and director of the Creative AR & VR Hub at Manchester Metropolitan University. "The role of VR will increase," he says. "The tourism industry may need to consider hybrid experiences – a combination of real and virtual – in the future. And, after this forced isolation, people will be more open for virtual experience as an alternative way of socialising and enjoying life. It might be accepted as the new normal within tourism." (800 words)

Sarah Baxter, *The Guardian* website, 2020

---

52 **feasible** machbar
53 **to spur** anspornen
55 **estimate** Schätzung
58 **to attend** teilnehmen (an)
62 **to pick oneself out** *hier:* sich erkennen
66 **to seek** sich bemühen
69 **to rack up** steigern; aufblähen
73 **destination** Reiseziel
85 **to enable** ermöglichen
87 **impact** Auswirkung
99 **in line with** im Einklang mit
111 **chisel marks** Meißelspuren
122 **forced** erzwungen

2 Multiple choice → WB p. 29/1–3

Choose the most suitable option.

1. The phrase 'And yet' (l. 9) underlines the fact that …
   A this Vappu Eve was less fun and frolics but exceptionally peaceful.
   B the author was dressed as a giant pineapple.
   C there was a rap concert in front of Helsinki's cathedral.
   D there was a concert with thousands of people despite lockdown.

3 TEXT A

2. Which is wrong according to lines 18–33?
   A The Vappu Eve gig was held in the real and virtual world.
   B There was some interaction between the audience and the performers.
   C A VR headset was not required to join the virtual event.
   D The author was more impressed by the technology than the music.

3. Virtual Helsinki …
   A was invented in 2018.
   B uses data mainly supplied by the city.
   C has earned Helsinki the title 'virtual capital of the world'.
   D enables people to visit the city's key landmarks virtually.

4. Which is true for lines 42–53?
   A Helsinki offers activities to embed digital innovation everywhere.
   B Cities can be improved through digitalisation.
   C There are more personalised services and more choice in Helsinki.
   D Helsinki is big enough for VR to be feasible.

5. What is not explicitly mentioned about the Vappu Eve's gig?
   A The live show was probably watched by 700,000 adults.
   B There were thousands of avatars.
   C They mostly showed the band.
   D Even in a crazy outfit it would have been difficult to spot this person on screen.

6. Virtual tourism …
   A is a pioneer project for sustainable tourism.
   B enables low-emission sightseeing.
   C shows that the travel industry will have to change dramatically.
   D is intended to replace a real visit.

3 Short-answer questions

Answer the following questions. You may use words from the text (lines 42–126).

1. What is the goal of Finland's capital?
2. What should ideally follow from Helsinki's virtual tourism?
3. What is the potential strength of virtual tourism for the 'travellers'?
4. What are Helsinki's plans for the future?
5. Which phrase describes virtual tourism as a complementary concept to conventional tourism?
6. What is key for tourism to be successful in the years ahead?
7. What might be a promising model for future tourism?

4 Multiple matching

Match the people (A–F) with the statements they might have said (1–10).
You have to use some people twice.

A Finland's National Police Board   C JVG   E Mikko Rusama
B Sarah Baxter (author)   D Laura Aalto   F Timothy Jung

1. This is not about replacing visits but about the need for innovation and extending possibilities.
2. Not a replacement for the real thing, but the way it was done: "Wow!"
3. It is not just one thing among others, it is integral to everything we do.

4. So little to do despite it being such a big event. Why can't it always be like that?
5. We need technological developments, but also people to become more open to VR.
6. It is about offering an experience on top of coming here.
7. Still, spotting friends there is just as difficult as at a real gig.
8. This is going to grow and become more the norm than it is now.
9. It can't replace the real experience, but better this than no reaction at all.
10. Becoming a part of history, socialising virtually – all this can make VR more attractive.

5 Analysing language and communication strategies

a Summarise the central topic of the text on pages 56–57 in one sentence.

b With a partner analyse the structure of the text, including answers to the following questions.

1. What are the different paragraphs about?
2. Which paragraphs deal with the actual topic of the text?
3. What is the function and point of the other paragraphs?

c What is the author's attidude towards VR and virtual tourism? In small groups, analyse which vocabulary she uses and how she uses language to emphasise and underline her point of view. Present your findings in class.

6 A step further

a In small groups, do some online research about VR tourism in your region. Which kind of VR tourism is there?

b In your group, think about (further) possibilites for VR in your region/town. Come up with some ideas of what should be represented in VR and what it could look like. How could your town/region advertise VR tourism?

c Discuss which ideas and which advertising concepts seem attractive/convincing/important? Copy the table and complete it. Give reasons for your choice. Find ways to optimise your ideas from **b**. Present your results in class. → S 15 1-minute presentation

idea	attractive	convincing	important	remarks

3 TEXT B

B Robots and us

1 Before you read

a Pepper is a social humanoid robot able to recognise faces and basic human emotions. Pepper was designed for human interaction and can engage with people through conversation and his touch screen. Can you imagine living with a robot like Pepper? Say why or why not.

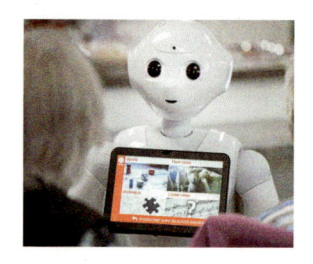

b Share your findings with a partner and make a list of pros and cons.

> Ian McEwan is an English novelist and screenwriter. His novel *Machines like me* takes place in an alternative year 1982 when "the first truly viable manufactured human with plausible intelligence and looks" is produced – 12 Adams and 13 Eves.
> After the Eves were sold out immediately, the first-person narrator, Charlie, has purchased one of the Adams. Miranda, his neighbour, helps Charlie to get the robot started.

Machines like me
by Ian McEwan

It was religious yearning granted hope, **1**. Our ambitions ran high and low – for a creation myth made real, for a monstrous act of self-love. As soon as it was feasible, we had no choice but to follow our desires and hang the consequences. In loftiest terms, we aimed to escape our mortality, confront or even replace the Godhead with a perfect self. More practically, we intended to devise an improved, more modern version of ourselves and exult in the joy of invention, the thrill of mastery. In the autumn of the twentieth century, it came about at last, the first step towards the fulfilment of an ancient dream, the beginning of the long lesson we would teach ourselves that however complicated we were, however faulty and difficult to describe in even our simplest actions and modes of being, we could be imitated and bettered. And I was there as a young man, an early and eager adopter in that chilly dawn. […]

I was among the optimists, blessed by unexpected funds following my mother's death and the sale of the family home, which turned out to be on a valuable development site. The first truly viable manufactured human with plausible intelligence and looks, believable motion and shifts of expression went on sale […]. Adam cost £86,000. I brought him home in a hired van to my unpleasant flat in north Clapham. […]

Adam was not a sex toy. […] He was advertised as a companion, an intellectual sparring partner, friend and factotum who could wash dishes, make beds **2**. Every moment of his existence, **3**, he recorded and could retrieve. He couldn't drive as yet and was not allowed to swim or shower or go out in the rain without an umbrella, or operate a chainsaw unsupervised. As for range, **4**, he could run seventeen kilometres in two hours without a charge or, its energy equivalent, converse non-stop for twelve days. He had a working life of twenty years. He was compactly built, **5**, dark-skinned, with thick black hair swept back […]. Miranda said he resembled 'a docker from the Bosphorus'. Before us sat the ultimate plaything, **6**, the triumph of humanism – or its angel of death. Exciting beyond measure, **7**. Sixteen hours was a long time to be waiting and watching.

---

3 **yearning** Sehnsucht; Verlangen
5 **to hang the consequences** die Konsequenzen tragen
5 **lofty** hoch; erhaben
8 **to exult** frohlocken; triumphieren
14 **to be blessed** gesegnet sein
15 **development site** Entwicklungsstandort (von Bauland)
16 **viable** brauchbar; funktionsfähig
20 **factotum** Faktotum; Mädchen für alles
21 **retrieve** abrufen; zurückholen
24 **charge** *hier:* Aufladung
24 **converse** sich unterhalten
26 **swept back** nach hinten gekämmt

TEXT B 3

30 I thought that for the sum I'd handed over after lunch, Adam should have been charged up and ready to go. It was a wintry late afternoon. I made toast and we drank more coffee. Miranda, a doctoral scholar of social history, said she wished the teenage Mary Shelley was here beside us, observing closely, not a monster like Frankenstein's, but this handsome dark-skinned young man coming to life. I said that what both creatures
35 shared was a hunger for the animating force of electricity. [...]
I couldn't think of myself as Adam's 'user'. I'd assumed there was nothing to learn about him that he could not teach me himself. But the manual in my hands had fallen open at Chapter Fourteen. Here, the English was plain: preferences; personality parameters. [...] Glancing at the next page I saw that I was supposed to select various settings on a scale
40 of one to ten.
I'd been expecting a friend. I was ready to treat Adam as a guest in my home, 8 . I'd thought he would arrive optimally adjusted. Factory settings – a contemporary synonym for fate. My friends, family and acquaintance, all had appeared in my life with fixed settings, with unalterable histories of genes and environment. I wanted my expensive
45 new friend to do the same. Why leave it to me? But of course, I knew the answer. Not many of us are optimally adjusted. Gentle Jesus? Humble Darwin? One every 1,800 years. Even if it knew the best, the least harmful, parameters of personality, which it couldn't, a worldwide corporation with a precious reputation couldn't risk a mishap. Caveat emptor.
50 God had once delivered a fully formed companion for the benefit of the original Adam. I had to devise one for myself. [...]
The user's handbook merely granted an illusion of influence and control, the kind of illusion parents have in relation to their children's personalities. It was a way of binding me to my purchase 9 . 'Take your time,' the manual advised. 'Choose carefully. Allow
55 yourself several weeks, if necessary.' [...]
Before lunch I'd sent Miranda an email inviting her to dinner that night. Now she'd accepted. She liked my cooking. During the meal I would make a proposal. I would fill in roughly half the choices for Adam's personality, then give her the link and the password and let her choose the rest. I wouldn't interfere, I wouldn't even want to know what
60 decisions she had made. She might be influenced by a version of herself: delightful. She might conjure the man of her dreams: instructive. Adam would come into our lives like a real person, with the layered intricacies of his personality revealed only through time, through events, through his dealings with whomever he met. In a sense he would be like our child. What we were separately would be merged in him. Miranda would be drawn
65 into the adventure. We would be partners, and Adam would be our joint concern, 10 . We would be a family. There was nothing underhand in my plan. I was sure to see more of her. We'd have fun.

(892 words)

37 **manual** Anleitung; Handbuch
42 **adjusted** angepasst
44 **unalterable** unveränderbar; unveränderlich
48 **precious** wertvoll
48 **mishap** Panne; Missgeschick
49 **caveat emptor** ausschluss der Gewährleistung
51 **to devise** entwickeln
57 **proposal** Vorschlag; Angebot
59 **to interfere** eingreifen; einmischen
61 **to conjure** herbeizaubern
62 **layered** vielschichtig
62 **intricacy** Komplexität
64 **to merge** zusammenführen
66 **underhand** heimtückisch; hinterlistig

2 Multiple matching → WB p. 30/1–3

Match the phrases (A–M) with the gaps (1–10) from the text. There are three phrases more than you need.

- **A** square-shouldered
- **B** and 'think'
- **C** but frustrating too
- **D** the skin was warm and soft to touch
- **E** thanks to breakthroughs in electrical storage
- **F** emotionally overwhelming
- **G** the dream of ages
- **H** and providing legal protection for the manufacturer
- **I** our creation
- **J** it was the holy grail of science
- **K** everything he heard and saw
- **L** technology meets human-like precision
- **M** as an unknown I would come to know

3 TEXT B

3 Gapped summary

Fill the gaps in the summary with the most suitable words from the text sections ll. 3–20 and l. 41 to the end. Give the line numbers of the words you used.

> Even before Mary Shelley wrote Frankenstein, it had been like a ■■ 1, a dream of mankind, to create an artificial human that would be an ■ 2 edition of us. Thus, when they finally become available, Charlie, who sees himself as a keen ■ 3 of technological progress, does not hesitate and buys Adam. While the manufacturer advertises Adam as a ■ 4 capable of doing all kinds of household chores, Charlie had expected Adam to be more like a ■ 5. Ultimately Charlie dreams of Adam, Miranda and himself becoming a ■ 6. To achieve this, Charlie has a ■ 7 for Miranda. Each of them is to choose independently about half of the different settings for Adam's ■ 8. Yet, whether they can indeed influence and control Adam or whether it is just an ■ 9 of power remains to be seen.

4 Mediation

Beantworten Sie folgenden Fragen auf Deutsch.

1. Um welches ideologische Ziel geht es bei der Erschaffung von Maschinen wie Adam?
2. Woher hat Charlie das Geld für Adam?
3. Warum wünscht sich Miranda, dass Mary Shelley Adam sehen könnte?
4. Wie denkt Charlie über die Auswahl, die Miranda für Adam treffen könnte?

5 Working with texts

a How are Adam and other artificial humans in the text referred to and described? With a partner, make a list of the words and phrases used. Which phrases are more negative and which are more positive?

b Look at your list again. In small groups, discuss the following questions:

1. Which aspects of Adam are already present in today's technology?
2. What is the potential and danger of such technology?
3. Where is there the need to be careful, where can we be optimistic?
4. Does Adam have rights? If no, why not? If so, which rights should he have?

6 A step further

a How will Charlie and Miranda program Adam? If you were Charlie or Miranda, how would you have programmed Adam? Take notes.

b In small groups, discuss how the story of Charlie, Miranda and Adam might continue.

c Come up with some ideas how you would film it, which genre it could be and which actors should be in it. What kind of music would you use? Give reasons for your choice.

d Present your ideas in class. Discuss which idea is the most creative / most convincing.
→ S 15 Tip-top

C Benefits of innovative technologies

1 Before you read

a Think of a definition for the term 'revolutionary technology' and discuss it with a partner.

b List examples of what you think were revolutionary technologies in the past.

c Look at the pictures and consider how revolutionary technologies might be used to increase prosperity in African countries.

> **GOOD TO KNOW**
>
> **evolution**
> = a slow and gradual change or development
> **revolution**
> = a sudden, dramatic and complete change

Revolutionary technologies will drive African prosperity – this is why

1 Right now, we're at a tipping point in Africa's development. We're hurtling
5 headlong into the Fourth Industrial Revolution (4IR), which has the potential to turbocharge the socio-economic development of the entire African continent. We've got the youngest
10 continent in the world, with 60 % of Africa's 1.25 billion people under the age of 25. If we make the right decisions in the next few years, we could pave a bold new path of African prosperity.

15 **2** In Africa, 4IR's potential is limitless. Its technologies, like artificial intelligence (AI) and the internet of things (IoT), offer a new vision for economic growth, innovation, development and human
20 well-being. It can solve a host of business and societal challenges, from providing better healthcare and basic services to creating more efficient governments, and helping businesses become intelligent
25 enterprises that drive growth and prosperity.

3 Our governments and institutions have a massive opportunity to start using AI and digital platforms to do life-
30 changing things: Like delivering safe drinking water to our people, improving the quality and reach of education, and even giving people the ability to identify themselves, to be able to access
35 government grants, open bank accounts and vote in elections.

We know Africa suffers from a massive infrastructure deficit. But the beauty of 4IR's technologies is that you don't need big legacy systems and programmes in
40 place to start rolling them out. We're already seeing numerous case studies and examples of how developing countries can move quickly to new digital approaches that can transform public
45 service delivery in critical areas like farming, healthcare and education.

4 Take agriculture as an example. Today, small-scale agriculture accounts for about 80 % of food production and nearly 70 % of
50 all jobs in Africa. Imagine what can be achieved if we use data to help small-scale farmers to improve their production: better use of land and water, less food

3 **tipping point** Umkehrpunkt
4 **to hurtle** rasen; sich schnell bewegen
5 **headlong** kopfüber
13 **to pave a path** den Weg bereiten
13 **bold** kühn; mutig
15 **limitless** unbegrenzt
20 **host** *hier:* Vielzahl
25 **to drive** voranbringen
32 **reach** Reichweite
35 **grant** Zuschuss; Stipendium
38 **deficit** Defizit
40 **legacy system** veraltetes System
41 **to roll out** starten; auf den Markt bringen
52 **small-scale** in kleinem Maßstab

TEXT C

57 **revenue** Ertrag; Einnahmen
58 **surplus** überschüssig
59 **subsistence** Lebensunterhalt
82 **fraud** Betrug
82 **leakage** Leck; undichte Stelle
87 **to empower sb** jdn befähigen; bevollmächtigen
89 **loan** Darlehen; Kredit
100 **coding knowledge** Programmierkenntnisse

being imported, improved food security – and the ability for farmers to start generating revenues for themselves by selling surplus produce, and breaking free from subsistence.

5 We can use technologies like AI to improve access to healthcare across the continent for the most vulnerable and needy communities. It can even help make diagnoses in rural areas, where there are precious few doctors. And we're already seeing technology changing the face of education in countries like India, where they've launched a national teacher platform that builds capacity by allowing teachers to provide richer content, while giving administrators access to data about student study patterns. Digital platforms are not only transforming teaching, but changing the way we think about learning.

6 Another relatively quick win for Africa would be to roll out digital identification systems, as India has done with its Aadhaar system, which can play a major role in driving financial inclusion and reducing corruption through reduced fraud and leakages in social benefits payment systems. Once people have digital identities, they can do anything from getting a SIM card to arranging a bank account or pension.

7 If you empower people with their personal information and data, they can use this data to get better loans, get better skills and ultimately earn better salaries. On a continent like ours, developing a high-performing digital ecosystem will provide a unique chance to stimulate the economy and create jobs.

8 But the real promise of 4IR is to unlock a new future for Africa's estimated 700 million young people. We're going to have to move quickly, though. Today, fewer than 1% of African children leave school with basic coding knowledge. We – big business, governments, NGOs and civil society – must do more to give our youthful workforce the skills they need to participate in the digital economy. This is vital if we are to avoid a situation where millions of people are unable to participate in our brave new technology-driven world. […]   (643 words)

Cathy Smith, *The World Economic Forum* website, 2019

2 Multiple matching → WB p. 31/1–2

Match the subheadings (A–K) with the paragraphs (1–8) of the text. There are three subheadings more than you need.

- A A huge group that could benefit
- B Africa as the future of 4IR
- C A singular opportunity to improve incomes
- D Empowering the next generation
- E AI to fight government corruption
- F Making sure it is you
- G Fast changes in many areas are possible
- H A utopia that can be realised
- I Demographics show a potential that should be used
- J Overcoming small-scale farming
- K Learning from other successful models

3 Multiple choice

Choose the most suitable option.

1. Which is true? (paragraph 1)
   A 4IR has started to turbocharge the socio-economic development of Africa.
   B Africa's development has passed a crucial tipping point.
   C The huge number of young people in Africa is a potential to be used.
   D Thanks to sensible decisions, Africa is on a bold new way to prosperity.

2. The general tone of paragraph 2 is …
   A factual.
   B critical.
   C cautious.
   D enthusiastic.

3. According to paragraph 3, which statement is wrong?
   A AI can help governments to improve the lives of their people.
   B Apart from health and education, AI can also help people exercise their democratic rights.
   C The infrastructure deficit slows down the efficient use of 4IR technologies.
   D The beauty of 4IR technologies is that you can realise new digital approaches fast.

4. What is not mentioned in paragraph 4?
   A 70 % of African men work in small-scale agriculture.
   B Modern technologies can enable more efficient use of soil and water.
   C Improved food production reduces the need to import food.
   D New digital approaches can make farms profitable, i.e. overcome subsistence farming.

5. The author refers to India …
   A as an example of successful use of AI in healthcare system.
   B to stress the benefits of digital identification systems.
   C to explain the advantages of a high-performing digital ecosystem.
   D to show how digital platforms change student study patterns.

6. On the whole, the text …
   A is neutral and objective about the potential of AI for Africa.
   B focuses mainly on the potential of AI for farmers, healthcare and education.
   C is quite optimistic about possibilities of AI and 4IR for Africa.
   D considers AI as a chance for Africa but focusses on the obstacles.

4 Mediation

Beantworten Sie folgende Fragen auf Deutsch.

1. Welche Chancen für Politik und Wirtschaft nennt der Absatz von Zeile 15–26?
2. Welche finanziellen Vorteile bringt KI für die Menschen laut Zeilen 27–36? Wie?
3. Erklären Sie aus dem Kontext, was mit „the beauty of 4IR's technologies" (Zeile 37–38) gemeint ist.
4. Welches Problem kann KI im Bereich Gesundheitswesen lösen?
5. Worum geht es bei dem indischen Aadhaar System? Welchen Vorteil hat die Einzelperson?
6. Welches Problem nennt der letzte Absatz? Warum wird hier dringend eine Lösung benötigt?

3 TEXT C

5 Gapped summary

Complete the summary with the most suitable words from the corresponding sections (1–3) of the text. Give the line numbers for the words that you used.

> The entire African continent, particularly the societies and economies of the different countries, faces a ■ 1 of challenges ranging from establishing ■ 2 that actually work to providing better education and healthcare, and above all, clean ■■ 3. But how can you ■ 4 the development of a continent and get Africa on the road towards ■ 5? 4IR's technologies, AI and the IoT might be the answer. They can give us a new ■ 6 of a future with innovation and growth as the technical opportunities are limitless. More importantly, these technologies can work despite Africa's enormous ■■ 7. They empower developing countries to ■ 8 and improve critical areas such as farming or education. We have reached a tipping point in Africa's development. It is up to us to make the ■■ 9.

6 Focus on words

a Copy the table and complete it with adjectives and adverbs used in the text. Do they have a positive or negative connotation? Write down the context they are used in.

adjective/adverb	connotation	context
revolutionary (l. 1)	positive	referring to the effect new technologies will have in Africa

b Find die matching words in the text (lines 1–59) for the following definitions. Give the line numbers.

1. doing something well and thoroughly with no waste of time, money or energy
2. having the capacity to develop further
3. the state of being successful, especially in making money
4. extremely important because a future situation will be affected by it
5. the basic systems and services necessary for a country to run smoothly
6. companies or businesses
7. to change
8. to make better
9. supplying or making available
10. whole or complete

7 Focus on analysis → S 9

a Decide whether the text is more formal or informal. Give reasons for your answer.

b Use the table in exercise **6** to analyse the author's use of adjectives and adverbs and the effect this has on the reader.

c Analyse how the language used brings out the author's attitude to these technologies. Give quotes and examples.

8 A step further → S 10.3

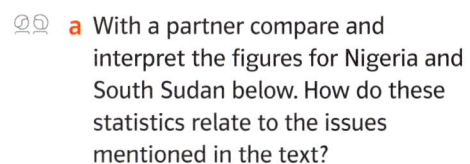

a With a partner compare and interpret the figures for Nigeria and South Sudan below. How do these statistics relate to the issues mentioned in the text?

b Get together in small groups. Do some research on the UN sustainable development goals (SDGs). Look at the diagram again. Which specific problems in Africa are connected to SDGs and what specific measures might be taken to achieve these SDGs?

c In your group, discuss how the SDGs and the ideas of the text could be relevant in other parts of the world. Each group can look at a specific group of countries / a continent / one SDG. Present your views in class and discuss them.
→ S 15 1-minute presentation

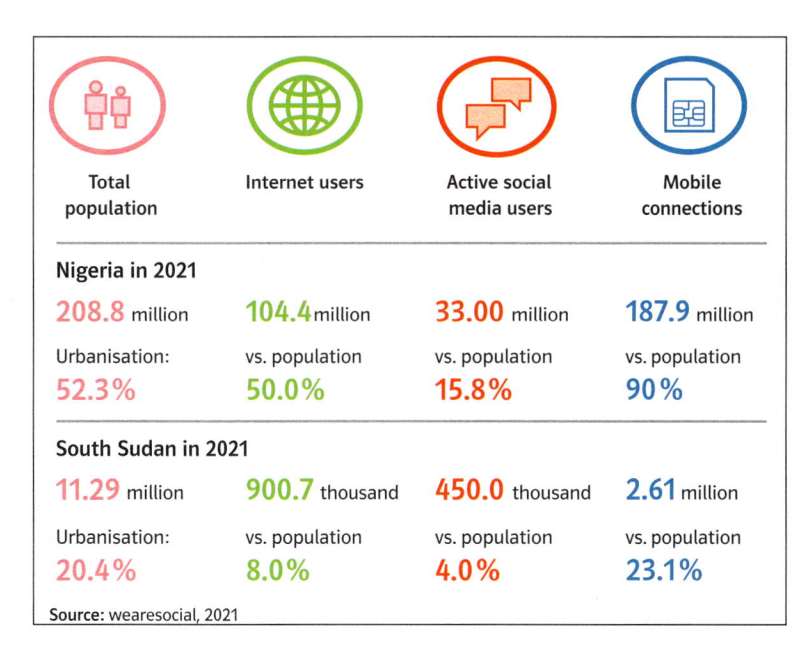

	Total population	Internet users	Active social media users	Mobile connections
Nigeria in 2021	208.8 million	104.4 million	33.00 million	187.9 million
	Urbanisation: 52.3 %	vs. population 50.0 %	vs. population 15.8 %	vs. population 90 %
South Sudan in 2021	11.29 million	900.7 thousand	450.0 thousand	2.61 million
	Urbanisation: 20.4 %	vs. population 8.0 %	vs. population 4.0 %	vs. population 23.1 %

Source: wearesocial, 2021

GOOD TO KNOW

Nigeria and South Sudan
Nigeria is located on the western coast of Africa and is the most populous of all African countries. South Sudan is located in Eastern Africa.

3 TEXT D

D Genetic engineering

1 Before you read

Look at the image and discuss with a partner how this and the information in the GOOD TO KNOW box relate to the issue of genetic engineering. Use the following keywords to help you. Present your results in class. → S15 1-minute presentation

Genetically modified plants | Genetically modified animals | Genetically modified foods

animal testing | cloning/curing diseases | decoding | designer babies | combating world hunger | genome | research and development | health and safety

GOOD TO KNOW

CRISPR stands for Clustered Regularly Interspaced Short Palindromic Repeats and is the basis for a revolutionary genome-editing technology that allows scientists to make very precise modifications to DNA.

1 **lab-grown** im Labor gezüchtet
1 **hybrid** Mischform; Zwitter
2 **marvel** Wunder
2 **misstep** Fehltritt
6 **womb** Mutterleib
8 **ectogenesis** Ektogenese
9 **hatchery** Brutstätte; Brutbetrieb
10 **nutrient** Nährstoff; Nährpräparat
10 **fetus** Fötus
20 **mammal** Säugetier
30 **chimera** Schimäre
32 **fraught** belastet
34 **to outweigh** aufwiegen; wettmachen
39 **scrutiny** Prüfung, Überprüfung
40 **in vitro fertilization** künstliche Befruchtung
45 **petri dish** Petrischale; Laborschale
58 **require** erfordern
59 **scale** hier: Ausmaß; Größenordnung
64 **to deploy** nutzen; anwenden

Lab–grown embryos and human–monkey hybrids: Medical marvels or ethical missteps?

In Aldous Huxley's 1932 novel "Brave New World," people aren't born from a mother's
5 womb. Instead, embryos are grown in artificial wombs until they are brought into the world, a process called ectogenesis. In the novel, technicians in charge of the hatcheries manipulate the
10 nutrients they give the fetuses to make the newborns fit the desires of society. [...] Huxley's imagined world of functionally manufactured people is no longer far-fetched.
15 On March 17, 2021, an Israeli team announced that it had grown mouse embryos for 11 days – **1** – in artificial wombs that were essentially bottles. Until this experiment, no one had grown a
20 mammal embryo outside a womb this far into pregnancy. Then, on April 15, 2021, a U.S. and Chinese team announced that it had successfully grown, **2**, embryos that included both human and monkey cells in
25 plates to a stage where organs began to form.
As both a philosopher and a biologist I cannot help but ask how far researchers should take this work. While creating
30 chimeras – the name for creatures that are a mix of organisms – might seem like the more ethically fraught of these two advances, ethicists think the medical benefits far outweigh the ethical risks.
35 However, ectogenesis could have far-reaching impacts on individuals and society, and the prospect of babies grown in a lab has not been put under nearly the same scrutiny as chimeras. [...]
40 When in vitro fertilization first emerged in the late 1970s, the press called IVF embryos "test-tube babies," **3**. These embryos are implanted into the uterus within a day or two after doctors fertilize
45 an egg in a petri dish.
Before the Israeli experiment, researchers had not been able to grow mouse embryos outside the womb for more than four days – providing the embryos with enough
50 oxygen had been too hard. The team spent seven years creating a system [...] that simulates the placenta and provides oxygen.
This development is a major step toward
55 ectogenesis, and scientists expect that it will be possible to extend mouse development further, **4**. This will likely require new techniques, but at this point it is a problem of scale – being able to
60 accommodate a larger fetus. This appears to be a simpler challenge to overcome than figuring out something totally new **5**.
The Israeli team plans to deploy its techniques on human embryos. Since
65 mice and humans have similar

developmental processes, it is likely that the team will succeed in growing human embryos in artificial wombs.

To do so, though, members of the team need permission from their ethics board. CRISPR – a technology that can cut and paste genes – already allows scientists to manipulate an embryo's genes after fertilization. Once fetuses can be grown outside the womb, 6, researchers will also be able to modify their growing environments to further influence what physical and behavioral qualities these parentless babies exhibit. Science still has a way to go before fetus development and births outside of a uterus become a reality, 7. The question now is how far humanity should go down this path. [...]

Human–monkey hybrids might seem to be a much scarier prospect than babies born from artificial wombs. But in fact, the recent research is more a step toward an important medical development than an ethical minefield.

If scientists can grow human cells in monkeys or other animals, it should be possible to grow human organs too. This would solve the problem of organ shortages around the world for people needing transplants.

But keeping human cells alive in the embryos of other animals for any length of time has proved to be extremely difficult. In the human-monkey chimera experiment, a team of researchers implanted 25 human stem cells into embryos of crab-eating macaques – a type of monkey. [...]

[...] at the end of the 20-day experiment, three embryos still contained human cells [...]. For scientists, the challenge now is to figure out how to maintain human cells in chimeric embryos for longer. [...]

Some ethicists have begun to worry that researchers are rushing into a future of chimeras without adequate preparation. Their main concern is the ethical status of chimeras that contain human and nonhuman cells [...]. What rights would such creatures have?

However, there seems to be an emerging consensus that the potential medical benefits justify a step-by-step extension of this research. Many ethicists are urging public discussion of appropriate regulation to determine how close to viability these embryos should be grown. [...] Given that researchers don't plan to grow these embryos beyond the stage when they can harvest rudimentary organs, I don't believe chimeras are ethically problematic 8.

Few ethicists have broached the problems posed by the ability to use ectogenesis to engineer human beings to fit societal desires. [...] for now, scientists lack the techniques to bring the embryos to full term. However, without regulation, I believe researchers are likely to try these techniques on human embryos – just as the now-infamous He Jiankui used CRISPR to edit human babies without properly assessing safety and desirability. Technologically, it is a matter of time before mammal embryos can be brought to term outside the body.

While people may be uncomfortable with ectogenesis today, this discomfort could pass into familiarity 9. But scientists and regulators would do well to reflect on the wisdom of permitting a process that could allow someone to engineer human beings without parents. As critics have warned in the context of CRISPR-based genetic enhancement, pressure to change future generations to meet societal desires will be unavoidable 10, regardless of whether that pressure comes from an authoritative state or cultural expectations. In Huxley's imagination, hatcheries run by the state grew a large number of identical individuals as needed. That would be a very different world from today.

(960 words)

Sahotra Sarkar, *University of Texas*, 2021

102 **to implant** einpflanzen; einsetzen
102 **stem cell** Stammzelle
103 **macuaque** Makake (Affenart)
123 **viability** Lebensfähigkeit
129 **to broach** anschneiden; ansprechen
131 **societal** gesellschaftlich; sozial
138 **to edit** verändern
147 **to permit** erlauben
148 **to engineer** entwickeln
151 **enhancement** Erweiterung; Anreicherung

GOOD TO KNOW

Sahotara Sarkar is an Indian-American professor at the University of Texas at Austin. He is one of the founders of conservation biology.

3 TEXT D

2 Multiple matching → WB p. 32/1–2

Match the phrases (A–L) with the gaps (1–10). There are two phrases more than you need. → S 15 Think-pair-share

A as in Huxley's world
B compared with the true test-tube babies of Huxley's world
C but researchers are getting closer
D like supporting organ formation
E as happened with IVF
F for the first time
G about half of the gestation period
H that was firmly the stuff of science fiction
I creating tools for modifying individual genes
J though they are nothing of the sort
K and dangerous
L possibly to full term outside the womb

3 Short-answer questions

Answer the following questions. You may use words from the text (lines 27–142).

1. The introduction describes two different uses of genetic engineering. Which is the ethically more problematic one? Why are ethicists nonetheless in favour of it?
2. What initially set a time limit in the mouse experiment?
3. What is the next step envisioned by the Israeli research team?
4. What do scientists hope to achieve with human-monkey hybrids?
5. What should proper regulation of techniques related to ectogenesis avoid?

4 Mediation

Beantworten Sie folgende Fragen auf Deutsch.

1. Was ist im Text mit „Huxley's imagined world of functually manufactured people" (Zeilen 12–13) gemeint?
2. Welche Debatte wird von der Ethik gefordert?
3. Warum sollte man mit der Genehmigung elternlose Menschen zu erschaffen vorsichtig sein?

5 A step further → S 10.3

a Analyse the diagram. What are the key points it illustrates?

b Gene editing and genetic engineering is a highly contentious issue. In small groups, look at the points mentioned in the text and the diagram again. Create a poster presenting the pros and cons of genetic engineering. You can add further information and examples from online sources.

c Present your posters in class. Discuss the information and arguments from the posters.
→ S 15 Gallery walk

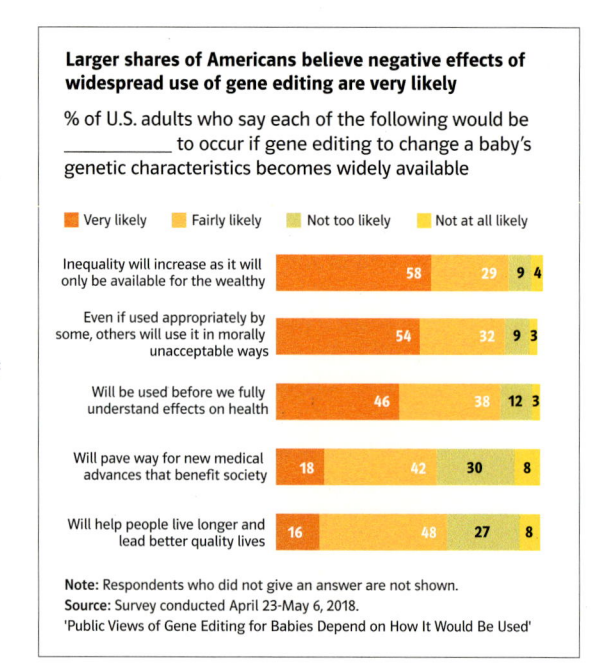

Larger shares of Americans believe negative effects of widespread use of gene editing are very likely

% of U.S. adults who say each of the following would be _____ to occur if gene editing to change a baby's genetic characteristics becomes widely available

Legend: Very likely | Fairly likely | Not too likely | Not at all likely

Statement	Very likely	Fairly likely	Not too likely	Not at all likely
Inequality will increase as it will only be available for the wealthy	58	29	9	4
Even if used appropriately by some, others will use it in morally unacceptable ways	54	32	9	3
Will be used before we fully understand effects on health	46	38	12	3
Will pave way for new medical advances that benefit society	18	42	30	8
Will help people live longer and lead better quality lives	16	48	27	8

Note: Respondents who did not give an answer are not shown.
Source: Survey conducted April 23-May 6, 2018.
'Public Views of Gene Editing for Babies Depend on How It Would Be Used'

WRITING 3

Living with AI and androids → S 6.2 → S 10.3 → WB p. 33/1

Androids such as C3PO or R2D2 in *Star Wars* and Adam in *Machines like me* are all fictional. Yet, robots and androids are increasingly becoming a part of our daily reality. Against this background write a composition on the following topic:

'Artificial intelligence (AI) and androids – what should they be used for and what should be their limits?'

Write a composition of at least 300 words. Include <u>all</u> the materials provided.

Material 1

Material 2

The real risk with AI isn't malice but competence. A superintelligent AI will be extremely good at accomplishing its goals, and if those goals aren't aligned with ours, we're in trouble.   *Stephen Hawking, British physicist and author (1942–2018)*

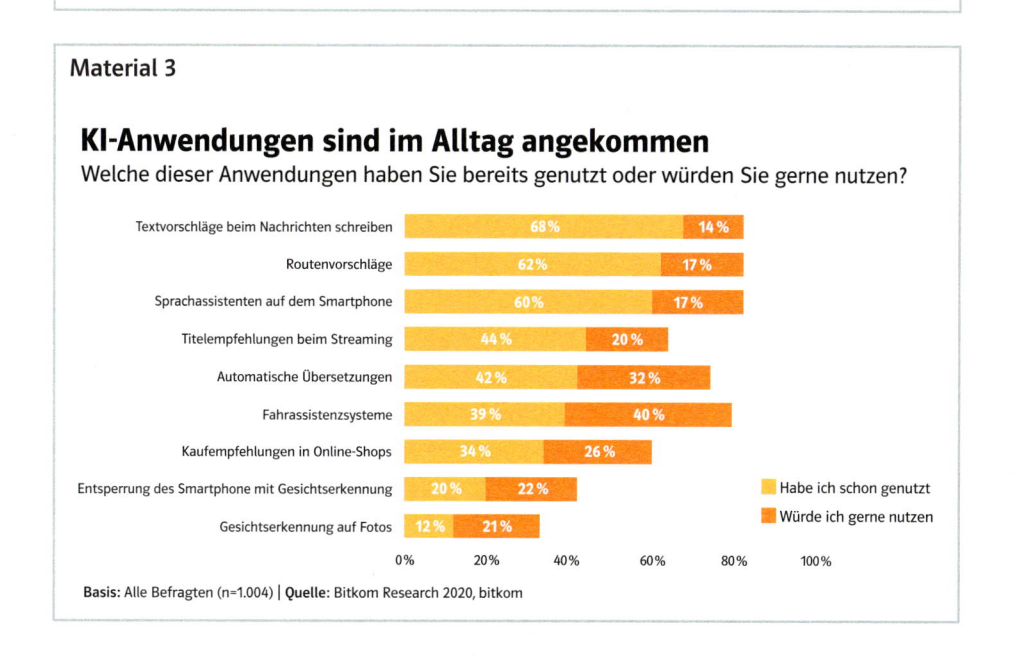

Material 3

KI-Anwendungen sind im Alltag angekommen
Welche dieser Anwendungen haben Sie bereits genutzt oder würden Sie gerne nutzen?

Anwendung	Habe ich schon genutzt	Würde ich gerne nutzen
Textvorschläge beim Nachrichten schreiben	68 %	14 %
Routenvorschläge	62 %	17 %
Sprachassistenten auf dem Smartphone	60 %	17 %
Titelempfehlungen beim Streaming	44 %	20 %
Automatische Übersetzungen	42 %	32 %
Fahrassistenzsysteme	39 %	40 %
Kaufempfehlungen in Online-Shops	34 %	26 %
Entsperrung des Smartphone mit Gesichtserkennung	20 %	22 %
Gesichtserkennung auf Fotos	12 %	21 %

Basis: Alle Befragten (n=1.004) | **Quelle:** Bitkom Research 2020, bitkom

3 MEDIATION

In love with my car → S 6.1

Für das Projekt „Fewer cars for a better future" bereiten Sie eine Übersicht vor. Verfassen Sie einen zusammenhängenden englischen Text (ca. 150 Wörter) unter Verwendung des Artikels unten.

Gehen Sie dabei auf folgende Aspekte ein:

1. Die Bedeutung des Autos seit 1945 als Transportmittel und als Statussymbol (2 Aspekte)
2. Die psychologische und soziale Bedeutung des Autos (2 Aspekte)
3. Die statistische Veränderung der Autokäufe und eine mögliche Ursache
4. Wie und warum sich die Rolle des Autos laut Katrin Dziekan ändern wird.

Weniger Gefühle für das Auto?

[...] *Die Werbung hat Autos schon immer mit vielen Emotionen verbunden. Doch immer mehr Leute sehen Autos inzwischen nüchterner und denken eher praktisch.* [...]
Bis vor 100 Jahren gingen die meisten Menschen zu Fuß, oder nutzen Pferd, Eisen- oder Straßenbahn. Erst um 1910 kauften reiche Bürger die ersten Autos. Mit der Massenproduktion waren sie nach dem zweiten Weltkrieg für immer mehr Menschen erschwinglich und Autos wurden ein Symbol für Wohlstand. [...]
Die Bedeutung des Autos als Statussymbol sei aber auch heute noch sehr groß und vor allem in den ländlichen Regionen von Europa deutlich. [...]
Inzwischen ist das Auto in vielen Ländern das wichtigste Transportmittel. In Deutschland werden „57 Prozent aller Wege mit dem Auto zurückgelegt und 75 Prozent aller Personen-Kilometer", sagt die Verkehrsexpertin und Psychologin Katrin Dziekan vom Umweltbundesamt. Wichtig sei für viele Menschen aber nicht nur der reine Transport. „Das ist eine Art Kostüm. Man kann sich durch ein Auto von anderen unterscheiden, es fungiert als soziales Signal nach außen mit Eigenschaften wie Freiheit, Stärke und Kontrolle." Für viele sei wichtig „das Lenkrad selbst in der Hand zu haben, selbst aktiv zu sein. Das ist ein positiver Effekt für das Selbstbewusstsein. Der Fahrer, die Fahrerin hat das Geschehen selbst in der Hand." [...]

Autos spielen in vielen Filmen eine wichtige Rolle. Fahrten mit Rad, Zug oder Bus sind dort eher die Ausnahme, das Auto ist am meisten präsent. Das sei eine problematische Verzerrung der Wirklichkeit, betont Dziekan. [...]
2017 wurden weltweit 80 Millionen PKW neu zugelassen, mehr als je zuvor. 2019 waren es sechs Prozent weniger und 2020, im ersten Jahr der Corona-Pandemie, sogar 20 Prozent weniger. Prognosen [...] gehen davon aus, dass [...] in Europa jedoch langfristig weniger PKW verkauft werden als früher. Vor allem in europäischen Städten beobachtet Gössling ein Umdenken. „38 Prozent der Haushalte in den deutschen Großstädten haben kein Auto mehr. Das ist eine freiwillige Wahl. Da ist das Auto eher eine Belastung geworden."
Der 59-jährige Volker Marten ist einer von ihnen, seit 2015 hat er kein eigenes Auto mehr. [...] „Das Auto war für mich selbstverständlich und ich bin gerne Auto gefahren. Durch das Bewusstsein für die Umwelt habe ich dann umgedacht", erzählt Marten [...]. „Wir wollten ausprobieren, ob es ohne Auto geht und es hat super geklappt. Wir sparen eine Menge Geld. Im Vergleich zu früher haben sich unsere Kosten etwa halbiert." [...]
Autos werden [...] künftig an Bedeutung verlieren und andere Verkehrsmittel zugleich aufgewertet. Auch werde der eigene Autobesitz durch Carsharing-

Angebote und autonome Fahrdienste unattraktiver. «Die Rolle des Autos wird sich so etwas verschieben», prognostiziert Dziekan. «Ein Auto wird dann eher als ein Transportmittel gesehen und ist nicht mehr so stark mit Gefühlen aufgeladen.»

(448 Wörter)
Gero Rueter, *Deutsche Welle*, 2022

A smart town for all

There are many documentaries with titles such as 'Building smart homes of the future' or 'Space elevators and smart machines: Life in the year 2100'. Which use of technology and technical devices is acceptable or desirable is a controversial issue.

The council of your hometown has invited young people to present their ideas on how smart devices and technology in general can improve the life and participation of senior citizens and people with disabilities and impairments. The ideas and suggestions should not focus on private homes but on the public spaces of your hometown.

You can discuss the following questions:
- Which problems do senior citizens and people with impairments face in your hometown?
- Where is help needed?
- How could technology be used to alleviate these problems?
- Which smart devices might be useful to improve the lives of senior citizens and people with impairments?
- Could technology and smart devices cause more problems than they solve?
- Is there a risk of too much technology? Should there be limits? Consider why or why not.
- How do you want to present your ideas to the town council?

a Present one or two of your ideas. (about one minute)

b Discuss and explain your ideas and views. Be precise about which problem / technology / device you are talking about.

c Each of you has to give a short statement that sums up the discussion for you. Try to come to a conclusion.

BLINDNESS OR VISION LOSS

DEAFNESS OR HEARING LOSS

ELECTRONIC ACCESSIBILITY

4 GETTING STARTED

Society now and then

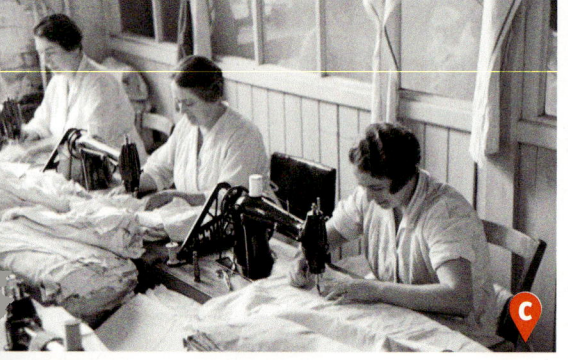

1 Working with pictures → S 10.1
→ WB p. 36–37/1–4; 38/1–2

a Which photo awakens your interest to find out more about that particular aspect of society now or in the past? Describe it to your partner and explain why you have chosen it.

b Use the following key words to talk about social changes that you associate with the pictures:

family life | gender roles | technology | working condition | consumerism

c Find photos to illustrate one further example of social change in the world of work. Present them in class.

> Technology enables us to work every minute of every day from any place on the planet.
> *Carl Honoré, Canadian journalist*

GETTING STARTED 4

2 Working with a quotation

a In small groups, discuss the quotation on page 74. Consider how it relates to aspects in your own or your families' lives.

b Compare the message of the quotation to what you said about the pictures on page 74, and any extra pictures you chose. Which ones does the quotation relate to best?

c Discuss the pros and cons of technological developments in the context of the quote.

A5 3 Listening → S 3

a Listen to the podcast "Different ways of shopping".

b Copy the table and take notes on the attitudes of the speakers concerning shopping.

	Typical shopping habit	Reasons for shopping behaviour
Speaker 1		
Speaker 2		
Speaker 3		
Speaker 4		

c In small groups, discuss each speaker's habit and attitude. Collect further arguments for and against their shopping behaviour. Present your results in class. → S 15 1-minute presentation

4 Creating a poster

a Create a word web on the topic of 'social change.' Include any words you encountered while completing tasks **1** and **2**, as well as ones of your own.

b Choose one of the following topics. Discuss what life will be like in 2070 with regards to your topic. Consider both potentials and challenges. Add keywords to your word web.

world of work | transport | social life | health | the dual education system | gender roles | consumerism

c Create a poster on your topic and present it in class in a gallery walk. → S 15 gallery walk

---

USEFUL PHRASES

Presenting a poster
Before I start, I'd like to give an overview of …
Our poster is divided into … parts.
I'll start with … / Next …
Finally, I'll present our results regarding …
I hope this explains the situation for you.
If you have any questions, please don't hesitate to ask.

Talking about social change
A tendency that can be observed is …
There's reason to assume that by 2070, …
Given the evidence of current developments, it can be predicted that …
One prospect is that …
In 2070, we will probably …
It is not likely that … will continue as we know it.

75

4 TEXT A

A A changing nation

1 Before you read

a Make a list of important changes that you know of in the history and society of the USA.

b Compare your list with a partner.

c Using the internet for help, put the changes you have collected into chronological order.

American poet and activist Amanda Gorman was only 22 years old when she recited her poem, *The Hill We Climb*, at the inauguration of President Joe Biden in January 2021. She grew up in Los Angeles and was recognised early on for her poetry. In 2017, she became the first person to be named National Youth Poet Laureate.

---

4 **to wade** waten
9 **to weather** überstehen
14 **pristine** unberührt
16 **to forge** schmieden
22 **arms** Waffen

The Hill We Climb
by Amanda Gorma

When day comes, we ask ourselves: Where can we find light in this never-ending shade?
The loss we carry, a sea we must wade.
5 We've braved the belly of the beast.
We've learned that quiet isn't always peace,
And the norms and notions of what "just is" isn't always justice.
And yet, the dawn is ours before we knew it.
Somehow we do it. Somehow, we've weathered and witnessed
10 A nation that isn't broken, but simply unfinished.
We, the successors of a country and a time where a skinny Black girl,
Descended from slaves and raised by a single mother,
Can dream of becoming president, only to find herself reciting for one.
And yes, we are far from polished, far from pristine.
15 But that doesn't mean we're striving to form a union that is perfect.
We are striving to forge our union with purpose,
To compose a country committed
To all cultures, colors, characters, and conditions of man.
And so we lift our gazes not to what stands between us, but what stands before us.
20 We close the divide, because we know to put our future first, we must first
Put our differences aside.
We lay down our arms so that we can reach our arms out to one another.
We seek harm to none, and harmony for all.
Let the globe, if nothing else, say this is true:

That even as we grieved, we grew, That even as we hurt, we hoped,
That even as we tired, we tried. That we'll forever be tied together. Victorious,
Not because we will never again know defeat, but because we will never again sow division.
Scripture tells us to envision that: "Everyone shall sit under their own vine and fig tree,
And no one shall make them afraid."
If we're to live up to our own time, then victory won't lie in the blade, but in all the bridges we've made.
That is the promised glade, the hill we climb, if only we dare it:
Because being American is more than a pride we inherit –
It's the past we step into, and how we repair it.
We've seen a force that would shatter our nation rather than share it,
Would destroy our country if it meant delaying democracy.
This effort very nearly succeeded.
But while democracy can be periodically delayed,
it can never be permanently defeated.
In this truth, in this faith, we trust.
For while we have our eyes on the future, History has its eyes on us.
This is the era of just redemption. We feared it at its inception.
We did not feel prepared to be the heirs of such a terrifying hour.
But within it we found the power to author a new chapter, to offer hope and laughter to ourselves. So while once we asked: How could we possibly prevail over catastrophe?
Now we assert: How could catastrophe possibly prevail over us?

We will not march back to what was, but move to what shall be:
A country that is bruised but whole, benevolent but bold, fierce and free.
We will not be turned around, or interrupted by intimidation, because we know our inaction and inertia will be the inheritance of the next generation.
Our blunders become their burdens. But one thing is certain:
If we merge mercy with might, and might with right,
Then love becomes our legacy, and change, our children's birthright.
So let us leave behind a country better than the one we were left.
With every breath from our bronze-pounded chests,
We will raise this wounded world into a wondrous one.
We will rise from the gold-limned hills of the West!
We will rise from the windswept Northeast, where our forefathers first realized revolution! We will rise from the lake-rimmed cities of the Midwestern states!
We will rise from the sun-baked South! We will rebuild, reconcile, and recover,
In every known nook of our nation, in every corner called our country,
Our people, diverse and dutiful. We'll emerge, battered but beautiful.
When day comes, we step out of the shade, aflame and unafraid.
The new dawn blooms as we free it,
For there is always light, if only we're brave enough to see it,
If only we're brave enough to be it.

(716 words)

---

29 **Scripture** die heilige Schrift
29 **to envision** sich vorstellen
29 **vine** Weinrebe
29 **fig tree** Feigenbaum
31 **blade** Klinge; Messer
33 **glade** Lichtung
43 **redemption** Erlösung
43 **inception** Beginn
44 **heir** Erbe/Erbin
46 **to prevail** sich durchsetzen
49 **benevolent** gütig; wohlwollend
50 **intimidation** Einschüchterung
51 **inertia** Trägheit
52 **blunder** Fehler; Dummheit
53 **mercy** Barmherzigkeit
56 **bronze-pounded** bronzen; mit Bronze beschlagen
56 **gold-limned** *hier:* goldgelb
60 **lake-rimmed** von Seen umrandet
61 **to reconcile** versöhnen
62 **nook** Ecke; Winkel

4 TEXT A

2 Short-answer questions → WB p. 39/1–2

Answer the following questions. You may use words from the first part of the poem (ll. 1–28):

1. Where does Gorman allude to the occasion for which the poem was written?
2. In line 1, Gorman asks "Where can we find light in this never-ending shade?" How does she start to answer the question?
3. How does Gorman refer to herself in the poem?
4. Where does Gorman use alliteration to describe an inclusive society?
5. According to Gorman, what has to be done if a harmonious future is to be achieved?

3 Multiple matching

Match possible sub-headings (A–H) with the correct section from the second part of the text (ll. 29–67). There are two sub-headings more than you need.

A Biblical quotation and positive outlook
B Courage needed to bring about change
C Dangers averted
D Different regions of the USA
E Early days of the USA
F Moving towards an improved country
G A broken nation
H Turning history around with strength

1 lines 29–33
2 lines 33–41
3 lines 42–47
4 lines 48–55
5 lines 56–63
6 lines 64–67

4 Mediation

Beantworten Sie die folgenden Fragen auf Deutsch.

1. Wie beschreibt Amanda Gorman in Zeilen 22–28 ihre positive Vision für die Zukunft?
2. Was sagt Gorman in Zeilen 34–40 über die amerikanische Geschichte und über die Demokratie?
3. Wie drückt Gorman in Zeilen 48–55 ihr Verantwortungsgefühl für die nächste Generation aus?
4. Was sind die Hauptaussagen in den Zeilen 55–67?

5 Words matter → S 11.3

Look at these words and expressions from the poem and match them with their synonyms.

A pristine (l. 14)
B to strive (l. 16)
C to grieve (l. 25)
D to envisage (l. 29)
E to assert (l. 47)
F might (l. 53)
G battered (l. 63)
H aflame (l. 64)

1 beaten
2 burning
3 immaculate
4 to be very sad
5 strength
6 to claim
7 to do one's best
8 to imagine

TEXT A   **4**

6 Analysing the poem

a Find the video of Gorman reading the poem online or read it out loud. Then describe what effect it has on you.

b Amanda Gorman uses language in many different ways to create this effect. Find three examples of each of the following stylistic devices in the poem. → S 7

alliteration | (internal) rhyme | repetition or anaphora | contrast or opposites | word play

c Find at least one example of a metaphor or symbol used to express the following:
- a problematic present
- a better future
- overcoming challenges
- reconciliation, ending a fight

d Write a short text and summarise how Gorman uses language to bring her message across. Say why you think Gorman chose this particular form of poetry for the poem to be recited at Joe Biden's inauguration.

7 A step further

a The roots of Hip Hop and rap go back to the 1970s, when young black people in the Bronx found a new way of expressing themselves. Their message was political and a cultural response to being largely excluded from American society. Look for Hip Hop or Rap songs with a political message and choose one you both like.

b Compare the lyrics with Amanda Gorman's poem. Where do you find similarities, where are there differences?

c In a small group, choose one of the topics below or one that interests you more and write a short rap or poem.

poverty | racism | exclusion | diversity | climate change | social justice

d Present your rap or poem to the class. → S15 Gallery walk

> **GOOD TO KNOW**
>
> **Amanda Gorman's** poem *The Hill We Climb* is an example of spoken word poetry, a form of poetry that is performed orally and is often experienced in poetry slams. Its style is related to Rap and Hip Hop in that it typically features stylistic devices such as end rhyme and internal rhyme, alliteration, repetition and word play.

79

TEXT B

B What do we really need?

1 Before you read

a Describe the picture and say how the person may feel.

b Discuss with a partner: What kinds of things do you own? Are there things that you do not have but would like to own? How does possessing your own things make you feel?

> The following text is taken from the preface to the book *How much is enough? Money and the Good Life* by the economist Robert Skidelsky and his son Edward Skidelsky, who is a philosopher.

How much is enough?
by Robert Skidelsky & Edward Skidelsky

How much is enough? A reply to our critics

Why do we work? Work, the standard view goes, is the cost of getting things we want. As people get richer – able to afford more of the things they want – they will work less. This in a nutshell was the theme of Keynes's essay 'Economic Possibilities for our Grandchildren', published in 1930. Keynes thought that about a hundred years hence – i.e. not far off from now – developed countries would be about four times richer on average than they were in 1930, and that therefore their inhabitants, on average, would work only a quarter as long, say fifteen hours a week rather than fifty or sixty. The demand for leisure would increase proportionately with income. In fact, though Keynes was not wrong in his forecast of economic growth, hours of work have fallen much less than he thought they would. We now work about forty hours a week and have been stuck there since the 1980s. To be sure, people have more leisure, but not nearly as much as he thought they would want.

So our book is really an enquiry into why Keynes got it wrong. He thought people would work only enough to enable them to live 'wisely, agreeably, and well' – to enjoy what we call 'the good life'. They seem to work much more than this. What did he miss? [...]

In the book we highlight two interlocking reasons for the continued dominance of the work ethic: one psychological, the other institutional.

The psychological explanation appeals to the perennial facts of human nature, particularly to the relative character of human wants. It is not just that we want more but that we want *more than others*, who at the same time want more than us; this fuels an endless race. [...] Human wants are insatiable because they are relative. And the more goods we want, the more we have to work to earn the money to acquire them.

Economic insatiability is as old as money itself, but it has been greatly exacerbated by the institutions of capitalism. [...] Capitalism promises us the moon – provided we work hard! It brings an increasing range of goods and services under the sway of money exchange, thus inflaming the love of money itself. [...]

---

6 **in a nutshell** in aller Kürze
7 **a hundred years hence** *hier:* hundert Jahre später
11 **proportionately with** proportional zu; entsprechend
16 **enquiry** Recherche
19 **interlocking** ineinandergreifend
20 **work ethic** Arbeitsmoral
21 **perennial** immerwährend
24 **insatiable** unersättlich
25 **to acquire** erwerben
26 **exacerbated** verschärft; verschlimmert
28 **to bring sth under the sway of sth** etwas unter die Herrschaft von etwas bringen
29 **to inflame sth** etw entfachen

TEXT B **4**

30 The thesis of our book is that the pursuit of money as an end in itself is bad not just because it is detrimental to happiness or the environment (though it may be to both these things) but because it is absurd. It rests on a misunderstanding of the nature and function of money. Money is essentially a means to the good; to treat its accumulation as an ultimate goal is to fall victim to delusion.

35 So what can we do to free ourselves from this delusion? The problem has two aspects, one intellectual, the other political.

The intellectual problem is to try to recover an idea of what money is for, because it is only in relation to such an idea that it makes sense to talk about 'having enough'. What money is for is, we argue, 'the good life', which can be broken down into the seven basic
40 goods of health, security, respect, personality, harmony with nature, friendship and leisure. To possess a sufficient quantity of these seven basic goods is to live well; to lack a sufficient quantity of one or more of them is to be deprived. If this account holds up, then the question 'how much is enough?' has a non-vacuous answer: it is 'enough for the good life.' Of course, precise figures are going to vary widely according to age,
45 circumstance and temperament. The needs of a twenty-year-old student are not those of a forty-year-old householder. But at least we have something more than the shifting fortunes of 'the Jones's' to guide us.

The political problem is to organize our collective existence so as to make it easier for people actually to live the good life. The state has a positive role to play here; it should
50 not pretend to be 'neutral' between rival conceptions of the good. In the last part of our book, we outline a number of policies for bringing this about, including working hour regulation, work-sharing, stricter controls on advertising, an unconditional basic income and – drawing on the work of the economist Robert Frank – a progressive consumption tax. An unconditional basic – or 'citizens' income – equivalent to the
55 'unearned' income enjoyed in the past by small minorities only – is probably the most important of these, as opening up individual choice between work and leisure. [...]

(770 words)

---

30 **pursuit** Streben
30 **as an end in itself** als Selbstzweck
31 **detrimental** nachteilig; schädlich
33 **accumulation** Anhäufung
34 **to fall victim to delusion** einer Täuschung zum Opfer fallen
42 **deprived** sozial benachteiligt; verarmt
43 **non-vacuous** hier: eindeutig
47 **the Jones's** from the expression "keeping up with the Jones's"= Nachbarn, mit deren Besitz man stets den eigenen vergleicht und mit denen man mithalten möchte
52 **unconditional basic income** bedingungsloses Grundeinkommen
53 **progressive consumption tax** progressive Verbrauchssteuer

2 Multiple choice → WB p. 40/1–3

Choose the most suitable option. You'll find the answers in the first part of the text (ll. 1–34).

1. It is generally assumed that we work …
   A to cover our costs.
   B to fulfil our material wishes.
   C to be eventually able to work less.
   D to get richer and richer.

2. Keynes predicted that one hundred years from the time of writing his essay, people would …
   A have to work more to have the same wealth.
   B be wealthier and therefore work less.
   C work the same for the same wealth.
   D not have to work at all any more.

3. Keynes was right in predicting …
   A the increase in general wealth.
   B the degree to which we work less now.
   C the amount of additional need for leisure.
   D the number of hours people worked in the 1980s.

4 TEXT B

4. In contradiction to Keynes' predictions, people now …
   - A work just enough to lead 'the good life.'
   - B do not want to live 'the good life.'
   - C work less than they need for 'the good life.'
   - D work more than they need to to lead 'the good life'.

5. People are never satisfied because they want to have …
   - A enough to lead 'the good life.'
   - B more than other people.
   - C as much as they can possibly get.
   - D more than their relatives.

6. What is wrong according to the text?
   - A Economic insatiability can cause harm to the environment as well as to people's well being.
   - B Capitalism has had the effect that people crave to have money for its own sake.
   - C People work less when they have enough money to fulfil their basic needs.
   - D People's needs vary according to their age and status.

3 Gapped summary

Complete the summary with the most suitable words from the second part (ll. 35–56) of the text. Give the line numbers of the words you used.

> The second part of the text discusses two ways of ridding ourselves of the ■ 1 that money is more than a means to an end. For one, we need to ■ 2 a sense of the true purpose of money, namely, to allow us to lead 'the good life.' What we need for this is a ■ 3 ■ 4 of seven basic goods, such as, among others, health and security, without which we consider ourselves ■ 5. On the other hand, the authors claim that the state has to play a role in enabling people to really live 'the good life' by introducing certain ■ 6 for instance a ■ 7 of working hours, work-sharing, stricter controls on advertising and an ■ 8 basic or citizen's income. The latter is the most important because it is instrumental in ■ 9 up the possibility for people to decide whether they want to work more, or to enjoy more ■ 10 time.

4 Focus on words → S 11.1

Find the corresponding verbs, nouns or adjectives for, or opposites of, the following words from the text (as indicated).

1. perennial (opposite) (l. 21)
2. insatiable (opposite, noun) (l. 24)
3. to acquire (noun) (l. 25)
4. accumulation (verb, adjective) (l. 33)
5. sufficient (opposite, noun, verb) (l. 41)
6. deprived (verb, noun, opposite) (l. 42)

5 Mediation

Beantworten Sie folgende Fragen auf Deutsch.

1. Was hat sich laut Absatz 1 (Zeilen 1–18) in Bezug auf unsere Arbeitswelt in den letzten 40 Jahren nicht verändert?
2. Wie erklären die Autoren in Absatz 2 (Zeilen 19–29), dass die Bedürfnisse der Menschen unersättlich sind?
3. Welche grundsätzliche Funktion hat Geld laut Absatz 3 (Zeilen 30–34)?
4. Was sind die wichtigsten Elemente, die „the good life" (Zeile 39) ausmachen?
5. Welche politische Maßnahme ist laut dem letzten Absatz die wichtigste, damit es leichter für alle wird, ein gutes Leben zu führen?

TEXT B **4**

6 Focus on grammar → G 2 → WB p. 44–45/1–2

a Use the ideas from the table to formulate arguments for a discussion about work-sharing and an unconditional basic income. Use conditional sentences. Decide whether you think that the condition is likely to become real (if-clause type 1), or whether it is unlikely (if-clause type 2).

Example: If job-sharing becomes the norm, people will have more time for their families or their hobbies.

Condition	Consequence
– It becomes normal that two people share one job. – Parents who have the same qualification share one job. – Job-sharing becomes the norm. – Everybody receives a certain amount of money, irrespective of their wealth or income. – An unconditional basic income is introduced. – Everyone has just enough money to get by.	– Unemployment is reduced drastically. – People have more time for their families or their hobbies. – There are fewer stress-related illnesses. – There is no one there to do unpopular jobs. – The infrastructure collapses. – People are much happier because they can choose whether they want to work or live a modest life doing what they want to do. – No one works any more. – People still work because the income paid by the state is too little to afford any luxuries. – The state is bankrupt within months.

b Read the text again. Think about what would have happened if Keynes's predictions had come true and complete the sentence using conditional type 3 clauses. You can also use your own ideas.

Example: If Keynes had got it right, weekly working hours would have dropped to about 15.

If Keynes's predictions had got it right, …
– Weekly working hours drop to about 15.
– People stop seeing the accumulation of money as an end in itself.
– Industry stops producing more than is needed.
– People understand what it means to have enough.
– People learn to be content with living the good life.

7 A step further

Two of the suggestions made by the Skidelskys directly concern how people work. They suggest that the state should support work-sharing and introduce an unconditional or universal basic income. In groups, choose one question and find arguments for and against each position. Hold a discussion.

– Should work-sharing be made the standard, wherever possible?
– Should each person get a basic income that is just enough to get by, no matter how much or how little money they own?

4 TEXT C

C Closing the gender gap

1 Before you read

a Using a dictionary, find out what is meant by the term 'boardroom' (often just called 'board'). → S 11.3

b Describe and analyse the cartoon. → S 10.2

c In small groups, discuss what, in your opinion, can be done to increase the number of women in leading positions in large companies.

"I heard they spent all day arguing whether to let women into the boardroom."

Gender diversity reforms have helped UK company boards, but they are failing in other countries – new research explains why

It may take close to 300 years to achieve gender equality and the empowerment of all women and girls, according to a UN progress report on its sustainable development goals (SDG), Gender Snapshot 2022. This is way off the 2030 deadline set when the SDGs were adopted by UN member states in 2015.

Closing the gender gap in the corporate world will contribute to meeting these goals. This means not only boosting women's participation in the workforce, but ensuring that women are represented equally in positions of power and leadership within companies. However, global progress has advanced at different rates, with some countries lagging far behind.

Worldwide corporate governance reforms have encouraged changes in the composition of boards of directors for the last two decades. While they vary in scale and severity, gender diversity regulations generally aim to increase the pool of female talent at companies and to make boards more independent in terms of how their members are chosen and appointed.

And for good reason. A gender diverse and independent board can help a company in several ways. Research shows that boards which are gender diverse can boost company performance and lower the probability of corporate fraud, for example. (…)

Gender diversity regulations that apply to companies' boards of directors are either voluntary – that is, entirely at a company's discretion – or enforced through legal quotas. But research I recently published with my colleagues shows that voluntary gender diversity regulations often don't work.

Progress on gender reforms

Norway was the first country to introduce a proportional gender quota for listed and state-owned companies in 2003. Other countries followed suit in trying to boost gender equality, either by also establishing board-level gender quotas or by making recommendations of a voluntary nature in codes of good corporate practice.

Since investors are likely to appreciate companies following good corporate governance practice, voluntary gender regulation can be an incentive to appoint more women to corporate boards. These recommendations are non-binding, however, and tend to be vague in setting a target for board diversity. This might promote a "one and done" approach, where compliance is achieved with the appointment of a single female director. (…)

By contrast, gender quotas set at 30%–40% of board composition achieve higher female board representation faster. Certainly, many countries – including European states such as France, Germany, Italy, the Netherlands and Spain – have dropped voluntary regulations altogether, in favour of legislative quotas. Gender quotas may also force companies to look

---

1 **company board** Vorstand; Firmenvorstand
4 **empowerment** Stärkung; Mitwirkungsmöglichkeit
6 **sustainable development goals (SDG)** Ziele für nachhaltige Entwicklung
11 **gender gap** Ungleichheit; Ungleichbehandlung
13 **to boost** stärken; verstärken
19 **to lag behind** hinterherhinken; zurückbleiben
25 **severity** Ernsthaftigkeit
29 **to appoint** bestimmen; ernennen
35 **corporate fraud** Unternehmensbetrug
39 **at discretion** nach Belieben; nach Gutdünken
49 **to follow suit** mitziehen; dem Beispiel folgen
53 **code** Code; Kodex
57 **incentive** Ansporn; Anreiz
63 **compliance** Regelbefolgung; Regelkonformität

84

externally in search of more talent to fulfil the required targets, creating a more independent board.

Ineffective voluntary regulations

Our research also found that voluntary gender diversity regulations are particularly ineffective in countries with a strong familial culture, such as Mexico. This kind of culture is associated with societal attitudes and expectations that establish the role of women as carers and men as breadwinners. In such countries, women might have to overcome barriers to reach a board appointment because of stereotyped perceptions about their advisory and leadership abilities.

In countries with a strong familial culture, we found that female director appointments are likely to be symbolic and are predominantly based on relationships. To publicly demonstrate commitment towards the voluntary reform, companies don't tend to draw from the pool of externally available talent, which means they don't get the corporate benefits of board gender diversity. (…)

Mexico introduced a voluntary gender quota regulation for company boards in 2018, making the basic recommendation of "incorporating women on the board of directors". After two years, the proportion of women on company boards of directors voluntary quota introduced in 2018 had increased from 7.3% to 9%.

This is an improvement, but at a much slower pace than, for example, the UK, which saw female directors on boards increase from 9.5% to 17.4% two years after establishing a similar voluntary regulation in 2011. And by 2020, the UK had no more "one and done" boards – women now make up around 40% of non-executive directors on the boards of FTSE 350 companies.

In this way, the UK performed as well as other countries that have quotas, such as Norway and France, where seats held by women on boards in 2021 were about 42% and 43%, respectively.

The independence element has been particularly difficult to achieve in Mexico's familial culture, with the percentage of female directors with no previous ties to a company growing from 0.9% of all directors in 2018 to only 1.9% in 2020.

This research shows the benefits of legal gender quotas over voluntary regulations. But as a first step towards addressing this gender diversity issue, particularly in countries with a strong familial culture, voluntary regulations could be made more specific.

In the case of Mexico, even a tweak to current recommendations to specify the appointment of women who are independent to boards of directors could go a little way towards increasing board gender diversity. For more significant progress towards global gender equality goals, however, legal quotas seem to be the best way forward. (847 words)

Jannine Poletti-Hughes,
The Conversation, 2022

86 **breadwinner** Hauptverdiener/-in
90 **advisory** Berater-; beratend
98 **pool** *hier:* Gruppe
100 **benefit** Vorteil; Nutzen
116 **one and done** einmalig
124 **respectively** jeweils
138 **tweak** Korrektur

2 Short-answer questions → WB p. 41/1–2

Answer the following questions. You may use words from the text (ll. 1–77).

1. How does the original goal set forth by the UN in terms of gender equality compare with a recent projection by the UN?
2. What is the expected consequence of closing the gender gap in large companies?
3. What advantages are named with respect to company boards in which women and men are represented equally, and whose members are chosen independently?
4. Which two types of gender diversity regulations are mentioned in the text?

4 TEXT C

3 Multiple matching

Match the information (1–6) with the most suitable country or countries mentioned in the text (A–H). Some pieces of information can be matched with more than one country, and one country can be matched with multiple pieces of information.

A France	C Italy	E The Netherlands	G Spain
B Germany	D Mexico	F Norway	H The UK

1. earliest adoption of a gender quota for certain companies
2. replaced voluntary quotas with legally binding ones
3. fixed gender roles barring women from entering corporate leadership
4. women on company boards usually because of relationship with the company
5. percentage of women on company boards more than doubling after introduction of voluntary quota
6. percentage of women on company boards amounting to 40 % or slightly above

4 Mediation

Beantworten Sie folgende Fragen auf Deutsch. Sie beziehen sich auf den zweiten Teil des Textes (Zeilen 78–146).

1. Welche gesellschaftlichen Einstellungen und Erwartungen tragen zu den Hindernissen bei, mit denen Frauen in manchen Ländern konfrontiert werden?
2. Welche Gefahr besteht bei einer freiwilligen Regulierung zur Erhöhung des Frauenanteils in Firmenleitungen?
3. Wie unterscheiden sich die Resultate der freiwilligen Regulierungen in Mexiko und im Vereinigten Königreich, und wie wird dieser Unterschied erklärt?
4. Wie könnten die freiwilligen Regelungen in Mexiko verbessert werden, um die Geschlechtervielfalt in Firmenführungen zu erhöhen?
5. Welche Schlussfolgerung wird gezogen bezüglich freiwilliger und gesetzlich bindender Regelungen zur Erhöhung des Frauenanteils in den Führungsetagen?

5 A step further

a With a partner, summarise the information from the graph. → S 10.3

b Do some online research and find out what measures the individual countries apply to work towards closing the gender gap. Work in groups and concentrate on one country per group. Present your results to the class.

c In small groups, discuss which measures you consider the most effective. Find arguments that speak for and against those measures.

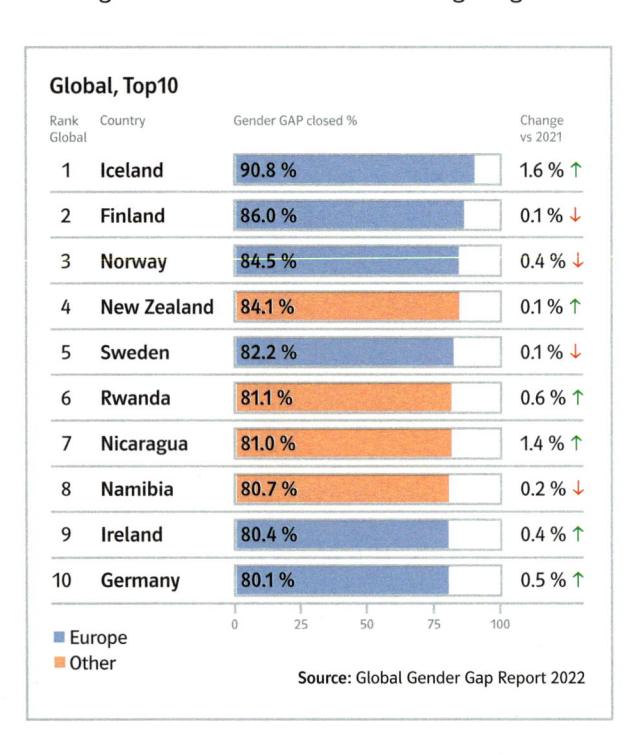

Global, Top 10

Rank Global	Country	Gender GAP closed %	Change vs 2021
1	Iceland	90.8 %	1.6 % ↑
2	Finland	86.0 %	0.1 % ↓
3	Norway	84.5 %	0.4 % ↓
4	New Zealand	84.1 %	0.1 % ↑
5	Sweden	82.2 %	0.1 % ↓
6	Rwanda	81.1 %	0.6 % ↑
7	Nicaragua	81.0 %	1.4 % ↑
8	Namibia	80.7 %	0.2 % ↓
9	Ireland	80.4 %	0.4 % ↑
10	Germany	80.1 %	0.5 % ↑

■ Europe
■ Other

Source: Global Gender Gap Report 2022

D Identity in a diverse world

1 Before you read

a Discuss with a partner: How would you define the word 'other'? Who in our society could be considered to be the 'other?'

b What do you think the term 'othering' refers to?

'Othered' in America – an old story still playing out daily

CHICAGO – Activist Hoda Katebi rarely takes a break from organizing. As tensions between the U.S. and Iran escalated in recent weeks, she became even busier.

On a recent Sunday afternoon, the 25-year-old Iranian American sat in her Chicago apartment shifting between monitoring her Twitter feed, taking phone calls and texting via encrypted messaging: She and other organizers had word that an Iranian student was being detained at O'Hare International Airport.

"This past week, I think I slept one night," she said.

Across the U.S., Iranian Americans – many of whom have family in Iran – said they are experiencing renewed anxiety since an American drone strike killed a top Iranian general last month and Iran retaliated by launching ballistic missiles at U.S. forces in Iraq. They say they are concerned both about the safety of family members abroad and about Iranians who live in the U.S. facing extra scrutiny at airports as they return. At least 10 students have been sent back to Iran upon arrival at U.S. airports since August.

For many young Iranian Americans, this is a mobilizing moment: They are embracing their Iranian identity and beginning to identify as people of color in the U.S. as part of a larger struggle alongside other ethnic minorities.

For minorities in the United States – from Latinos to African Americans to Muslims and beyond – being viewed with suspicion is something that can happen at any time in a number of ways. A citizenship status questioned. A hate crime committed. Even simply a passing comment made that implies they aren't welcome in the U.S., or deserving of the same treatment as white Americans.

Activists say the episodes make minorities feel separated – "othered," as the recently coined verb puts it.

The concept of "otherism" is hardly new. It has lingered in the U.S. for decades – centuries, even.

Irish, Germans and Italians were sometimes viewed as "others" when they became new Americans during 19th- and early 20th-century immigration. Many were deported. The Chinese Exclusion Act of 1882 prevented Chinese laborers from immigrating to the U.S. Following the attack on Pearl Harbor during World War II, Japanese Americans were forced from their homes and sent to internment camps, despite trying to prove their loyalty to the U.S.

After the 9/11 attacks, Muslim Americans faced increased government surveillance and were viewed largely with suspicion. For black Americans, the legacy of chattel slavery lingers today in housing discrimination, mass incarceration and everyday instances of discrimination. Native Americans were forced to relocate to reservations in the West following the Indian Removal Act of 1830.

---

10 **encrypted messaging** verschlüsselte Nachrichtenübermittlung
12 **to detain** festnehmen; festhalten
18 **anxiety** Angst; Angstzustände
21 **to retaliate** zurückschlagen
25 **scrutiny** Prüfung
30 **to embrace** umfassen; etwas annehmen
37 **suspicion** Verdacht
48 **to coin** prägen
50 **to linger** bleiben; verweilen
61 **internment camp** Internierungslager
65 **surveillance** Beobachtung
67 **legacy** Erbe; Vermächtnis
67 **chattel slavery** Leibeigenschaft
69 **incarceration** Inhaftierung

TEXT D

84 **withering** vernichtend
87 **to disparage** verächtlich machen
88 **coarse** grob; vulgär
93 **dormant** ruhend
113 **to marginalize** ausgrenzen

In each of these examples, both government policies and public perception served the function of "othering" particular ethnic communities. More recently, many activists say the problem has grown since President Donald Trump was elected in 2016. And while European immigrants have become more accepted in American society, those from other parts of the world still face sometimes <u>withering</u> scrutiny. This was highlighted in Trump's own remarks in an Oval Office meeting with lawmakers in 2018 when he <u>disparaged</u> Haiti and some African countries with <u>coarse</u> language and questioned why the U.S. would accept more immigrants from them rather than places like Norway. "Trump has opened up a Pandora's box of racism and bigotry that had been <u>dormant</u>," said Domingo Garcia, president of the League of United Latin American Citizens, the nation's oldest Latino civil rights organization.

"Now I see no difference from attacks on synagogues to an Iranian student being detained for 10 hours to a migrant baby from Central America being taken from her mother," Garcia said. "It all originates from the same hatred and fear."

Destiny Harris, 19, an African American student from Chicago, said the "othering" goes beyond the Trump era. She was pulled into activism years ago after then-Chicago Mayor Rahm Emanuel, a Democrat, closed a number of under-enrolled schools in the city, primarily affecting black and brown students. "As someone who is black, poor, queer and a woman, being a part of those <u>marginalized</u> communities is the very definition of being 'other' in this country, in terms of who belongs here and who doesn't and who deserves to be treated with equality and who doesn't," Harris said.

Much of the inspiration for Katebi's work stems from her identity. Her Twitter bio reads, in part: "angry daughter of immigrants." She was born and raised in Oklahoma and, as a practicing Muslim who also wears the hijab, or headscarf, found herself having to constantly explain her identity to others.

"No one knew what I was," Katebi said, describing growing up in a post-9/11 America as "politicizing."

"When the U.S. invaded Afghanistan, I was Afghan. When it invaded Iraq, I was Iraqi. Every time, I had to answer to all these identities. So I started researching and learning so that I could respond and have something to say, for my own protection and safety."

She added: "The more you learn, the more you get angry." (794 words)

Noreen Nasir and Russell Contreras, *AP News*, 2020

2 Multiple choice → WB p. 42/1–2

Choose the most suitable option.

1. Hoda Katebi's work involves …
   A organising demonstrations.
   B writing letters and petitions.
   C giving speeches.
   D using different means of communication.

2. Tensions between the USA and Iran have grown after …
   A Iran attacked a US camp in a drone strike and the USA hit back.
   B the USA killed an Iranian general after an Iranian attack.
   C the USA killed an Iranian general and then Iran hit back.
   D Iran killed an American general and the USA hit back.

3. At airports, Iranians returning to the USA …
   A are controlled more carefully than usual.
   B have to produce extra documents.
   C are not let in at all any more.
   D are not allowed to talk about their family members.

4. Which of these statements is not true?
   A Iranian Americans are beginning to identify with other ethnic minorities in the USA.
   B Iranian Americans are becoming more aware of their identity and are therefore setting themselves apart from other ethnic minorities in the USA.
   C Iranian Americans are getting more involved in activism for ethnic minorities.
   D Iranian Americans are developing a sense of their own ethnic identity and are joining other minorities in the USA.

5. Members of ethnic minorities in the USA have in common that they …
   A feel welcome in the USA.
   B are treated the same as white Americans.
   C enjoy unquestioned citizenship status.
   D experience hatred and discrimination.

6. 'Othering' is a …
   A new word for a new concept.
   B new concept described by a word that has been around for a long time.
   C word and concept that have existed for a long time.
   D new word for a concept that has existed for a long time.

3 Short-answer questions

Copy the table and complete it with information from the text (ll. 52–73).

Ethnic group	Time in history	Situation as being 'othered'
Irish, Germans, Italians		
Chinese		
Japanese Americans		
Muslim Americans		
Black Americans		
Native Americans		

4 Working with words

a Make a list of the verbs in the sentences relating to othering in ll. 35–73. What do you notice with regard to voice (active vs. passive)? → G 3

b Find the missing word in the text to complete the collocation.

1. … scrutiny
2. embrace …
3. being viewed …
4. … the function
5. become …
6. treated with …
7. … stems from
8. … to these identities

4 TEXT D

5 Gapped summary

Complete the summary with the most suitable words from the text (ll. 74–136). Give the line numbers of the words that you used.

> The final part of the text deals with the problem of ■ 1, which has become worse in recent years. While some groups are now better ■ 2, others face increased ■ 3 and bigotry especially after Donald Trump publicly announced that he would prefer to accept ■ 4 from places like Norway as opposed to Haiti and some African countries. ■ 5 ■ 6 activist Domingo Garcia claims that any form of discrimination ■ 7 from negative feelings towards minorities, such as hate and fear. Hoda Katebi, who was ■ 8 and grew up in the USA, is a practising Muslim, wearing a headscarf. She is often taken for being from whatever Muslim country is in the news at the time and feels the need to ■ 9 her true origin. This situation is making her increasingly ■ 10.

GOOD TO KNOW

Psychological explanations for 'us' vs. 'them'
Competition: When we find ourselves in competition with another group, especially over a limited resource, we are likely to feel hostile to members of the other group.
Identity and self-esteem: Even in the absence of competition we tend to categorise people into 'us' and 'them' and behave favourably towards 'us' because if we feel good about our group, we feel good about ourselves.

A6 🔊 6 Listening → S 3

a Listen to Prof. John A. Powell's talk and make a list of the groups mentioned in the talk that are being 'othered.' What do they have in common? What has this got to do with power?

b Outline the scope of 'othering'.

c Explain the shortcoming Powell sees regarding 'inclusion.'

7 A step further

a Brainstorm categories people use to differentiate between 'us' and 'them.'

b Use the information given in the GOOD TO KNOW box to explain why we categorise people into 'us' and 'them.'

c Use your results to analyse and explain the message of the cartoon below. → S 10.2

Freedom vs. security? → S 6.2 → S 10.3

The fight against terrorism has often been given as a reason to limit individuals' liberties. More recently, massive restrictions were imposed on people around the world to combat the Corona pandemic. These limitations of personal liberties were responded to with fierce protests.

What is your opinion? Does protecting people from danger justify the limitation of personal freedom? Write a composition of at least 300 words. Include <u>all</u> the material provided.

Material 1

When security impinges on freedom
The purpose of a state's security apparatus is to protect the citizens and the stability of the state. Human rights demand reasonable limits on the power of security forces and security laws so that while citizens are protected from danger and chaos, their other rights are not impinged. However, what are 'reasonable limits' depends very much on the culture, history, and politics in a given country. What is acceptable interference by the government in one country may be unacceptable in another. And, there are some levels of interference – regardless of the culture or politics of the region – that are always violations of human rights.

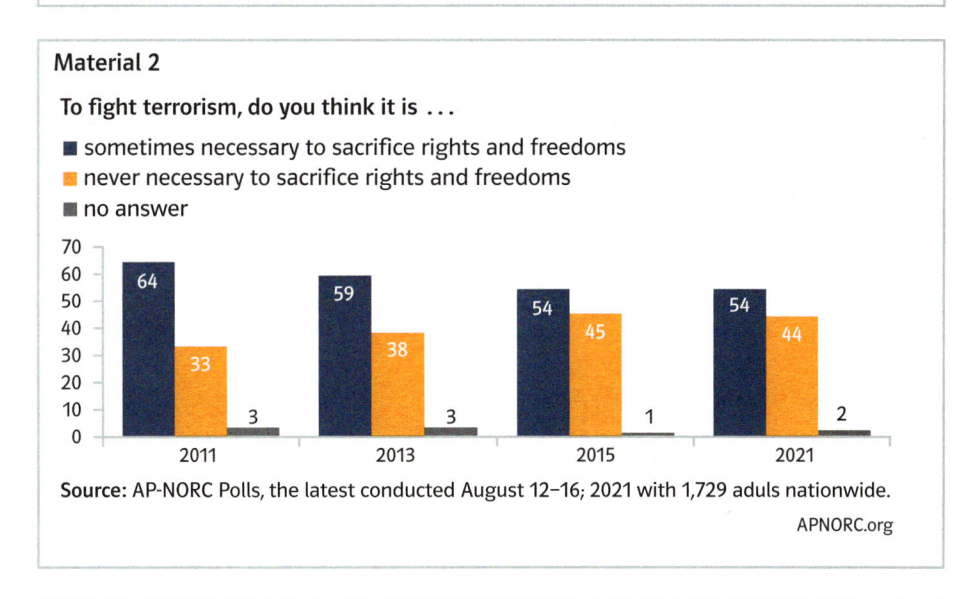

Material 2

To fight terrorism, do you think it is ...

- sometimes necessary to sacrifice rights and freedoms
- never necessary to sacrifice rights and freedoms
- no answer

Year	sometimes necessary	never necessary	no answer
2011	64	33	3
2013	59	38	3
2015	54	45	1
2021	54	44	2

Source: AP-NORC Polls, the latest conducted August 12–16; 2021 with 1,729 adults nationwide.
APNORC.org

Material 3

> Im Kampf gegen terroristische Anschläge sind Menschen- und Bürgerrechte an vielen Orten der Welt außer Kraft gesetzt worden. Das Prinzip von der Unteilbarkeit und Allgemeinheit der Menschenrechte, einst das Hohe Lied der westlichen Demokratien, hat im Krieg gegen den Terror Schaden genommen.
>
> *Jutta Limbach, deutsche Rechtswissenschaftlerin*

4 MEDIATION

Green cities → S 6.1 → WB p. 43/1

Verfassen Sie unter Verwendung der Quellen einen zusammenhängenden englischen Text (ca. 150 Wörter) zu „Sozialer Zusammenhalt in Städten und Gemeinden".
Gehen Sie dabei auf folgende Aspekte ein:
1. Konzept und Zielsetzung des Gemeinschaftsgartens
2. Weitere Ansätze zur Förderung des Zusammenhalts im Stadtteil.

Erdinger Gemeinschaftsgarten: Warten auf die ersten Tomaten

Auf einer Wiese im Bereich der Flurstraße stehen seit einiger Zeit kreuz und quer hellbraune Holzkisten herum. Sie sind bis zum Rand mit Erde gefüllt und warten darauf, bepflanzt zu werden. Am vergangenen Samstag war es soweit: Oberbürgermeister Max Gotz (CSU) gab die Hochbeete des künftigen Gemeinschaftsgartens „Eden für Jeden" zum Säen und Bepflanzen frei. [...] Seit November 2020 gibt es in Erding Klettham-Nord das vom Bund-Länder-Städtebauprogramm „Sozialer Zusammenhalt" geförderte Quartiersmanagement. Inzwischen gibt es zahlreiche Projekte, darunter auch die Hochbeete, die die Stadt Erding zur Verfügung stellt. Inzwischen gibt es auf der rund 1100 Quadratmeter großen Blumenwiese in der Nähe des Sportheims von Rot-Weiß Klettham auch eine Gießkannenstation und Bänke. [...]
OB Max Gotz ging am Samstag mit gutem Beispiel voran und setzte einen Beerenstrauch in die Erde des Gartens „Eden für Jeden". Auch die Beet-Paten legten los. Kräuter- und Blumensamen für die erste Aussaat hatte das Quartiersmanagement verteilt. Wer wollte, konnte sein Beet mit einer beschrifteten Steinplatte kennzeichnen. Im Anschluss stand ein Vortrag von Alice Dobersalske vom Fachbereich Gemeinschaftsgärten des Vereins Green City auf dem Programm über das richtige Anpflanzen für eine erfolgreiche Ernte. [...]
Eines der Ziele des auf mehrere Jahre ausgelegten Städtebauförderprogramms „Sozialer Zusammenhalt" für Kletthams Norden ist, dem Stadtteil eine neue Mitte zu geben. Einen Ort, an dem sich die Bewohner wohlfühlen, an dem sie sich gerne aufhalten, sich treffen können. Der Gemeinschaftsgarten ist dafür bestimmt bestens geeignet.

Regina Bluhme, *Süddeutsche Zeitung*, 2022

Stadtentwicklung: In Klettham wächst was zusammen

Das Erdinger Viertel feiert am Samstag sein erstes interkulturelles Stadtteilfest. Es wird richtig bunt. Angefangen von Seemannschor bis zur Afrikanischen Trommlergruppe.

In Klettham findet am Samstag, 23. Juli, zum ersten Mal das interkulturelle Stadtteilfest statt. Das Programm [...] umfasst eine Bilder-Schau mit historischen Aufnahmen von Klettham, Aktionen für Besucher aller Altersgruppen, Infostände und Kunsthandwerk, Musik, Tänze und Chöre sowie Speisen und Getränke aus den Küchen verschiedener Nationalitäten. Wer will, kann sich auch ansehen, wie der Gemeinschaftsgarten „Eden für Jeden" gediehen ist. [...] Aus manchen [Beeten] wächst jetzt, Mitte Juli, durchaus die eine oder andere Zucchini, Tomate und Grünpflanze. Einige der im Mai eingesetzten Gemüse- und Blumensamen sind aber leider nicht aufgegangen oder die Pflanzen sind vertrocknet. Aller Anfang ist nun mal schwer, manchmal braucht es eben ein paar Versuche, bis es klappt.

Regina Bluhme, *Süddeutsche Zeitung*, 2022

DISCUSSION 4

Skills for the 21st century

An international group of educators and politicians have got together to discuss what the school of the future needs to look like in order to meet the changing demands of the world of work.

In order to involve the people who are most directly concerned by these changes, a group of students have been invited to contribute to the discussion. The students are asked to formulate a statement that summarises the most important thoughts on the issue.

The key question is: 'What does school need to teach young people to make them fit for the world of work in the 21st century?'

a Read the excerpt of the P21 Framework which has the goal of formulating skills that are considered relevant for 21st century education. Choose one or two of these skills and give a short presentation on why you consider them particularly important (about one minute).

> **The P21 Framework**
>
> **Learning and Innovation Skills**
> Learning and Innovation Skills are those skills that separate students who will be able to deal with an increasingly complex society in 21st century, and students who won't be able to do it, such as Critical Thinking, Creative Thinking, Collaborating and Communicating.
>
> **Information, Media, and Technology Skills**
> In a society based on technology and media, students must learn how to properly use them in order to be able to evaluate the abundance of information they get in contact with, becoming attentive citizens and workers. The skills to develop are Information Literacy, Media Literacy and Technology Literacy.
>
> **Life and Career Skills**
> To deal with complex life and work environments, students need to develop thinking skills, content knowledge, social and emotional competencies like Flexibility, Initiative, Social Skills, Productivity and Leadership.

b Discuss your ideas in the group and decide on a set of five or six skills that you consider essential, as well as ideas on how schools could be organised to best convey these skills.

c Formulate a joint statement to present to the group of experts and politicians.

5 GETTING STARTED

Global challenges

> It is time to draw the economy anew, embedding it within society and within nature, and powered by the sun.
> — *Kate Raworth, British economist*

> Global challenges also require global solutions, and few indeed are the situations in which the United States or any other country can act completely alone.
> — *Shashi Tharoor, Indian politician*

> Climate change does not respect border; it does not respect who you are - rich and poor, small and big. Therefore, this is what we call 'global challenges,' which require global solidarity.
> — *Ban Ki-moon, South Korean diplomat*

1 What is globalisation? → WB p. 46–47/1–5; 48/1

a Make a mind map for globalisation and the issues linked to it. Use the words and phrases below and add your own words. Then share your results in class.

economy | trade | supply chain | communications | technological advances | local business | resources | investment | institutions | growth | climate change | exploitation | human rights

b Write a definition of the term 'globalisation'. Compare your definition with a partner's. Then check it online.

94

GETTING STARTED 5

2 Working with pictures → S 15 Think-pair-share

a Choose two of the pictures and note down the challenges they illustrate.

b Find a partner who chose a pair of different pictures. Exchange your results from **a** and make a list of all the challenges represented.

c In class, discuss what the most pressing global challenges are at this point in time. Collect ideas on how we as individuals can contribute to finding solutions.

> **USEFUL PHRASES**
>
> **Talking about challenges**
> To my mind, one of the most important issues/challenges … | We have to take responsibility for … | I think you have to consider what this means for … | We shouldn't over-/underestimate … | There could be grave/fatal/dire consequences if … | It's important to set goals if …

3 Working with quotes

a Read the quotes on page 94. Choose two of the quotes and paraphrase them. Which global issues are highlighted by the ones you chose?

b Think of real-life examples that demonstrate the main points of your chosen quotes. Take notes and discuss your examples with a partner.

4 Listening → S 3 → WB p. 48/2

a Listen to the first part of the podcast "Globalisation" by Kathleen Whitehead. Copy the table and take notes on the positive and negative aspects of globalisation mentioned.

Positive effects	Negative effects
Free trade …	Tax evasion …

b Now listen to the second part of the podcast. Add further aspects to your table.

c Listen again to both parts of the podcast and answer the following questions.

1. Why do many global players have a bad image?
2. What has the UN achieved so far?
3. Which arguments are given by those who deny a collective spirit of globalisation?
4. How could globalisation become fair according to Kathleen Whitehead?

5 Creating a poster

a In small groups, agree on one aspect of globalisation that you are particularly interested in. Find pictures, quotations and statistics to illustrate your choice.

b Present your poster in class. → S 15 Gallery walk → S 15 Tip - top

5 TEXT A

A Doughnut economy

1 Before you read

a Describe the diagram and explain in simple terms which economic goal it aims to illustrate.
→ S 10.3

b In small groups, use a dictionary to find out what the economic terms below mean.

capital goods | consumer price index | gross domestic product | inflation | liquidity | recession | trade deficit | unemployment rate

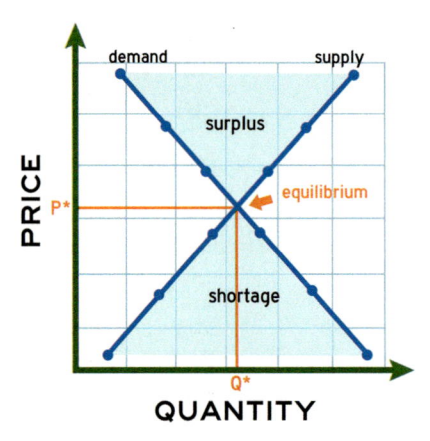

c Write example sentences using each of the terms.

"Doughnut Economic" model arrives in California

If a doughnut isn't the first thing that pops into your head when you think about saving the planet and fixing the economy, I wouldn't blame you. But, as it turns out, a doughnut might be just what we need right now.

As the world continues to crumble around us, communities and cities have been turning to an economic model known as "Doughnut Economics." The "doughnut" is an idea that was first presented by renegade economist Kate Raworth in her bestselling 2017 book, "Doughnut Economics: Seven Ways to Think Like a 21st-Century Economist." The idea is based on an image that contains two rings. The inner ring represents our social foundation and the outer ring represents our ecological ceiling. The goal of the "doughnut" model is to get humanity into the doughy center — the space where we are meeting our economic needs while remaining within planetary boundaries. The most prominent image that is associated with economics is probably the supply and demand curve. And while useful in certain contexts, Raworth wants to replace this image with that of a doughnut. Her vision is one which rejects our current attachment to endless economic growth while making sure that humanity is thriving.

"What is the goal of the economy?" Raworth says. "The old diagram that told us that the goal of the economy was that of GDP growth, which is just an ever rising line going up and up – this deeply rooted notion that forward and up is good. But we know that GDP growth and growth itself is not bringing all the wellbeing that we want in the world. The process we have now is leading to extraordinary environmental degradation and extraordinary inequalities as well."

By creating policies and frameworks which reject blind, endless growth – policies that lie within the doughnut's sweet spot, Raworth believes that we can structure our societies in a way that provides communities with the economic securities they need while maintaining a habitable planet.

"The doughnut is trying to represent a vision of the world in which we can meet the needs of all within the means of our planet," Raworth says. "That is the vision of human wellbeing that it's depicting. So that every person has the resources and

---

2 **to pop into one's head** jdm einfallen
5 **to blame** vorwerfen
8 **to crumble** zerbröckeln; zerfallen
13 **renegade** abtrünnig
22 **doughy** teigig
23 **to meet the needs** den Bedarf decken
24 **planetary boundaries** Grenzen des Planeten
33 **to thrive** gedeihen
38 **deeply rooted** tief verwurzelt
39 **notion** Idee; Vorstellung
44 **environmental degradation** Umweltzerstörung
46 **frameworks** Rahmenbedingungen
53 **habitable** bewohnbar

abilities to meet their needs and their rights to food, water, health, education, housing, community, connection, energy, and political voice."

And Raworth is not alone in her vision. Many communities and even entire cities have begun exploring the "doughnut" model as a goal for community and environmental wellbeing as well as for public policy. And although the goal is a global doughnut, all of them will not look the same.

The model is flexible and can be applied in a grassroots way by a diversity of communities, cities, states, and even countries. After realizing how much interest there was in the doughnut model, Raworth and co-founder Carlota Sanz launched the Doughnut Economics Action Lab, or DEAL to create a global network of communities that want to embrace doughnut economics.

Most recently, residents of the state of California have been gathering in Zoom meetings in an attempt to bring the "doughnut" model to their state. "I read Doughnut Economics when it came out and honestly it was the first glimmer of hope," Jared Ruiz Bybee told Shareable. "It brought together lots of different threads that I knew were important individually but didn't have a mental map for them being together. So when Kate Raworth and the DEAL team launched the DEAL platform and were making some of these tools and concepts available to people I was really hopeful that I could participate in something happening in California and later around the world." Bybee has been spearheading the efforts to bring the "doughnut" to his state.

"We are trying to stay really broad and open about what it might mean to apply Doughnut Economics in the state of California," Bybee told Shareable. "Whether that's at a very grassroots level or whether a statewide policy level. I'm most interested in statewide politics and policy, but other folks from the group are interested in much more grassroots type efforts. And we're hopeful to create a big enough tent that there's a space for each of those and everyone in between."

After setting up a Slack channel and amassing around 100 people, the group created different working groups that focus on the different dimensions of bringing the doughnut model to California, including the ecological dimension, the social dimension, and the business dimension.

"I'm hopeful that, like with a lot of things, California can take the lead," Bybee told Shareable. "That we can show other states and other places what is possible if there was political will to think about economics and to think about our economy in more holistic ways." (804 words)

Robert Raymond, *Shareable*, 2021

Line	Word	Translation
69	public policy	öffentliche Ordnung
73	grassroots	basisdemokratisch
81	to embrace	*hier:* zu eigen machen
87	glimmer of hope	Hoffnungsschimmer
89	thread	Strang; Faden
99	to spearhead the efforts	an der Spitze der Bemühungen stehen
108	folks	*(infml)* Leute
114	to amass	ansammeln
122	to take the lead	die Führung übernehmen
127	holistic	ganzheitlich

2 Mediation → WB p.49/1–2

Beantworten Sie folgende Fragen auf Deutsch.

1. Welche Vision liegt dem „doughnut economic model" zugrunde?
2. Wie flexibel ist das Modell und für wen kann es angewendet werden?
3. Mit welchem Ziel wurde DEAL gegründet?
4. Warum setzt sich Jared Ruiz Bybee für das Modell ein?

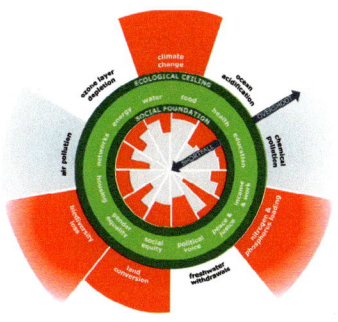

Source: Raworth, K. (2017), *Doughnut Economics: Seven Ways To Think Like a 21st Century economist*, London: Penguin Random House.

5 TEXT A

3 Multiple matching

Match the statements (A–H) with the correct person or service (1–4) from the text. You can use a person or service up to three times.

1 Robert Raymond (author)   2 Kate Raworth   3 DEAL   4 Jared Ruiz Bybee

A I developed this model because I don't believe that the supply and demand curve reflects our current needs.
B Our team is here to assist you in implementing our new economic model.
C Being willing to take a more all-inclusive look at economics is a first step in setting a good example and that's why I'm so active.
D I initially had a hard time making the connection between a breakfast food and economics.
E The goal of the platform is to connect individuals, communities and organisations that all share the same vision.
F The internet offers so many tools for getting people to meet and work together and it makes our job of organising a lot easier.
G I like to explain it like this: The model illustrates how we can satisfy people's basic needs without overtaxing the earth.
H I'm leading a group that wants to establish the doughnut model where we live.

4 Multiple choice

Choose the most suitable option.

1. Kate Raworth is …
   A a popular author of economics books.
   B a renegade who writes novels.
   C a baker who wrote a doughnut book.
   D an economist who wrote a book.

2. She uses the model of a doughnut to …
   A explain the supply and demand curve.
   B outline grassroots policies.
   C illustrate her new economic model.
   D define the planetary boundaries.

3. Why does Raworth reject blind, endless growth?
   A It hurts the environment.
   B It doesn't follow the demand and supply curve.
   C It causes insecurities.
   D It's a weak framework.

4. What does she include in her list of basic needs and rights?
   A collaboration
   B vacation
   C education
   D equation

5. The doughy part of the doughnut is where …
   A there's great growth and nature is protected.
   B our needs are met and we aren't harming the earth.
   C everyone gets what they want.
   D people are in harmony with nature.

6. Which of these statements about California is not true?
   A Residents have got together online to discuss the model.
   B California is often leading the way introducing new policies.
   C California uses Slack channels in all communications with its residents.
   D The state wants to accommodate different kinds of interest groups.

TEXT A 5

5 Words matter

a Find the following metaphors and concepts used in the article and explain their meanings. With a partner, discuss what helped you understand them: the context or the visuals that come to mind?

  1. renegade   2. doughy   3. grassroots   4. to spearhead   5. tent

b Look for more economic metaphors and explain three of them. → S15 Round robin

6 A step further

a Dairy milk or soy milk? This decision seems to be purely about food preferences, not about global impact. However, looking at the doughnut model, you can see that other areas can be affected by this decision. List the areas and explain your choice.

b Look again at the information collected here and at the model. Based on this information, what would you recommend to a friend?

Soy milk:
- good source of protein, calcium and iron
- has fewer calories than cow milk
- all nine essential amino acids
- no problem if you're lactose intolerant
- can reduce blood pressure and cholesterol levels
- US and Brazil biggest suppliers
- 'beany' taste
- some people are allergic
- carbon footprint high if grown on land converted from forest

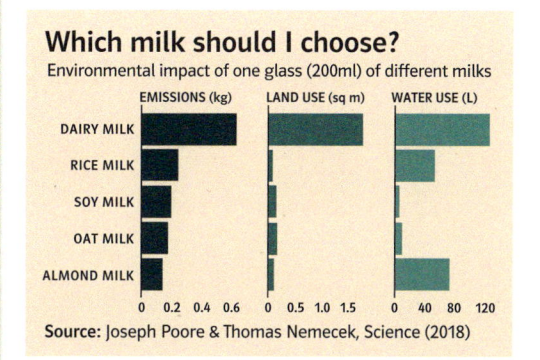

Which milk should I choose?
Environmental impact of one glass (200ml) of different milks

EMISSIONS (kg) | LAND USE (sq m) | WATER USE (L)

DAIRY MILK
RICE MILK
SOY MILK
OAT MILK
ALMOND MILK

0 0.2 0.4 0.6   0 0.5 1.0 1.5   0 40 80 120

Source: Joseph Poore & Thomas Nemecek, Science (2018)

Dairy milk:
- high in calcium, vitamin B12 improves memory power
- good source of protein
- strengthens immune system
- all the amino acids and nutrients make it a complete meal
- nitrous oxide – a by-product of cow manure – depletes the ozone layer
- may reduce blood pressure and risk of heart disease

c With a partner, choose another everyday aspect and discuss the pros, cons and alternatives. Examine where the aspect you have chosen fits into the doughnut model.

d Write a recommendation (about 150 words) for a friend based on your research. → S 6.3

e Exchange your recommendation with a partner. → S 15 Peer correction

USEFUL PHRASES

Based on the doughnut economic model, …
This aspect fits well into …
In addition, the amount of emissions …
One possible alternative is …

Take into account the transport from …
The main argument for me is that …
I believe I can compensate for …
Nevertheless, my recommendation is …

5 TEXT B

B The USA and the world

1 Before you read

a In small groups, discuss the role of the USA in the world, both in the past and today. What changes have occurred in the American economy and in relations to other countries in recent years?

b Compare your ideas in class.

> Joseph R. Biden Jr. became president of the USA in January 2021. He is a member of the Democratic Party and considered to be a moderate Democrat. From 2009 to 2017 he was vice president under Barack Obama. Biden, who was born in 1942, was the oldest politician to become president and the first to have a female vice president.

GOOD TO KNOW

Isolationism and interventionism
The foreign policy of the USA has had a long history of shifting between isolationism and interventionism – either in an attempt to abstain from any involvement in other countries and their conflicts or with the aim of forming alliances and even taking on a policing role in other countries' conflicts.

Remarks by President Biden on America's Place in the World

[…] [T]he message I want the world to hear today: America is back. America is back. Diplomacy is back at the center of our foreign policy.

1 As I said in my inaugural address, we will repair our alliances and engage with the world once again, not to meet yesterday's challenges, but today's and tomorrow's. American leadership must meet this new moment of advancing authoritarianism, including the growing ambitions of China to rival the United States and the determination of Russia to damage and disrupt our democracy.

We must meet the new moment […] – accelerating global challenges – from the pandemic to the climate crisis to nuclear proliferation – challenging the will only to be solved by nations working together and in common. We can't do it alone.

2 That must be this – we must start with diplomacy rooted in America's most cherished democratic values: defending freedom, championing opportunity, upholding universal rights, respecting the rule of law, and treating every person with dignity. That's the grounding wire of our global policy – our global power. That's our inexhaustible source of strength. That's America's abiding advantage.

Though many of these values have come under intense pressure in recent years, even pushed to the brink in the last few weeks, the American people are going to emerge from this moment stronger, more determined, and better equipped to unite the world in fighting to defend democracy, because we have fought for it ourselves. […]

3 Over the past two weeks, I've spoken with the leaders of many of our closest friends – Canada, Mexico, the UK, Germany, France, NATO, Japan, South Korea, Australia – to [begin] reforming the habits of cooperation and rebuilding the muscle of democratic alliances that have atrophied over the past few years of neglect and, I would argue, abuse.

America's alliances are our greatest asset, and leading with diplomacy means standing shoulder-to-shoulder with our allies and key partners once again. By leading with diplomacy, we must also mean engaging our adversaries and our competitors diplomatically, where it's in our interest, and advance the security of the American people. That's why, yesterday, the United States and Russia agreed to extend the New START Treaty for five years to preserve the only remaining treaty between our countries safeguarding nuclear stability. […]

And we'll also take on directly the challenges posed by our prosperity,

---

7 **inaugural address** Ansprache zur Amtseinführung
16 **to disrupt** stören; durcheinanderbringen
18 **to accelerate** beschleunigen
20 **proliferation** Verbreitung; Weitergabe
24 **rooted** verwurzelt; verankert
25 **to cherish** (wert)schätzen
26 **to champion** sich einsetzen für
29 **dignity** Würde
29 **grounding wire** (fig) Erdung(skabel)
31 **inexhaustible** unerschöpflich
32 **abiding** bleibend; dauerhaft
35 **to push to the brink** an den Rand drängen
48 **to atrophy** verkümmern
51 **asset** Vermögen
56 **adversary** Kontrahent/-in

security, and democratic values by our most serious competitor, China. [...] We will compete from a position of strength by building back better at home, working with our allies and partners, renewing our role in international institutions, and reclaiming our credibility and moral authority, much of which has been lost. That's why we've moved quickly to begin restoring American engagement internationally and earn back our leadership position, to catalyze global action on shared challenges.

4 On day one, I signed the paperwork to rejoin the Paris Climate Agreement. We're taking steps led by the example of integrating climate objectives across all of our diplomacy and raise the ambition of our climate targets. That way, we can challenge other nations, other major emitters, [...] to up the ante on their own commitments. I'll be hosting climate leaders – a climate leaders' summit to address the climate crisis on Earth Day of this year. America must lead in the face of this existential threat. And just as with the pandemic, it requires global cooperation.

We've also reengaged with the World Health Organization. [...] We've elevated the status of cyber issues within our government, including appointing the first national – Deputy National Security Advisor for Cyber and Emerging Technology. We're launching an urgent initiative to improve our capability, readiness, and resilience in cyberspace. [...]

We also face a crisis of more than 80 million displaced people suffering all around the world. The United States' moral leadership on refugee issues was a point of bipartisan consensus for so many decades when I first got here. We shined the light [...] of liberty on oppressed people. We offered safe havens for those fleeing violence or persecution. And our example pushed other nations to open wide their doors as well. So today, I'm approving an executive order to begin the hard work of restoring our refugee admissions program to help meet the unprecedented global need. [...]

5 There's no longer a bright line between foreign and domestic policy. Every action we take in our conduct abroad, we must take with American working families in mind. [...] When we invest in economic development of countries, we create new markets for our products and reduce the likelihood of instability, violence, and mass migrations.

When we strengthen health systems in far regions of the world, we reduce the risk of future pandemics that can threaten our people and our economy.

When we defend equal rights of people the world over – of women and girls, LGBTQ individuals, indigenous communities, and people with disabilities, the people of every ethnic background and religion – we also ensure that those rights are protected for our own children here in America. [...] (837 words)

Joe Biden, *The White House*, 2021

78 **to catalyze** beschleunigen
83 **objective** Ziel
87 **to up the ante** den Einsatz erhöhen
92 **existential threat** Existenzbedrohung
96 **to elevate** anheben; erhöhen
103 **resilience** Belastbarkeit
111 **haven** Zufluchtsort
112 **persecution** Verfolgung
118 **unprecedented** beispiellos
121 **conduct** *(fml)* Auftreten
134 **indigenous** einheimisch; indigen

2 Gapped summary → WB p. 50/1–2

Complete the summary of the text. Fill in the gaps with the most suitable words from the corresponding sections (ll. 3–94) of the text. Give the line numbers of the words that you used.

President Biden's first promise in his speech was to reinstate ■ **1** to the way his country deals with other countries. For him, this means working on rebuilding ■ **2** and once again interacting with the rest of the world. He talks about the different challenges facing the leaders of the US and the world and expressly names two countries whose ■ **3** is a threat. However, he again emphasises that the world can only ■ **4** these challenges if everyone works together. America is well-prepared to take on a leadership

5 TEXT B

role because it has an advantage that is ■ 5 in its long history of democracy. But diplomacy means not only working with partners but also with ■ 6 – renewing treaties and addressing competition. Biden offers concrete examples of how his country can rejuvenate its international ■ 7. The first example has to do with adding ■ 8 to all levels of diplomacy because the climate crisis and the threat it poses is already ■ 9.
The second example is the country becoming involved with the WHO again. Thirdly, he addresses the ■ 10 necessity of assisting refugees on a global scale and explains how, historically, the US took a position of moral leadership that set an example for other countries.

3 Multiple matching

Match the subheadings (A–H) with the paragraphs (1–5) of the text. There are three subheadings more than you need.

A Actions abroad are actions at home
B Welcoming America back
C Friends and enemies
D Democratic values
E Steps to re-enter the leadership role
F A hurting nation
G Facing challenges
H Eliminating competition

4 Multiple choice

Choose the most suitable option.

1. President Biden believes that America draws its strength from …
   A its rivalry with China.
   B its own free will.
   C the democratic values it treasures.
   D the power it holds over the world.

2. Having to fight for democracy …
   A makes you strong and determined.
   B pushes people to the edge.
   C is of little value in America.
   D is important for emerging economies.

3. The New START Treaty between the USA and Russia is so important because it …
   A is only valid for five years.
   B supports diplomatic competition.
   C is the only treaty between them.
   D regulates the use of nuclear arms.

4. Which of these is a new government priority for the US according to Biden?
   A signing a climate agreement
   B more resilience to cyber attacks
   C promoting world health
   D reestablishing global power

5. Which of these statements does not reflect Biden's plans?
   A The USA will address the refugee problem with a renewed admission program.
   B Environmental issues will be given priority and cooperation with other nations is back on the agenda.
   C He will concentrate on domestic measures to improve the economic situation.
   D Diplomatic relations with European countries will be strengthened.

6. According to Biden, it is difficult to separate …
   A foreign and domestic policy
   B instability and violence
   C health and pandemics
   D ethnicity and religion

5 A step further

Listen to, watch or read President Biden's inaugural address of January 20th 2021 online. What was the focus of that speech compared to the one on page 101?

TEXT C 5

C Business and responsibility

1 Before you read

a With a partner, look at these words and phrases. Write a definition for each of them.

to file a law suit | to give a deposition | plaintiff | to be liable | to settle outside court | defendant | to reach a verdict | to present evidence | to allege | to sue sb

b One stereotype about Americans is that they file a lot of lawsuits for all kinds of reasons. One example of this was a lawsuit filed against a fast food restaurant by a woman who had dropped her coffee on her legs and suffered third-degree burns. Discuss who you think should take responsibility for her suffering.

Empire of Pain is a non-fictional book by Patrick Radden Keefe, who is a writer at *The New Yorker*. One of the richest families in the world, the Sackler family is famous for their philanthropy. They donated millions to science and the arts. Keefe shows how their empire was built on the marketing and sales of pain killers that played a major part in the opioid crisis.

Empire of Pain: The Secret History of the Sackler Dynasty
by Patrick Radden Keefe

THE NEW YORK HEADQUARTERS of the international law firm Debevoise & Plimpton
5 occupy ten floors of a sleek black office tower that stands in a grove of skyscrapers in midtown Manhattan. […]
One bright, cold morning in the spring of 2019, as reflected clouds slid across the black glass of the facade, Mary Jo White entered the building, ascended in an elevator to the Debevoise offices, and took up position in a conference room **1**. […] White sometimes
10 joked that her specialty was the "big mess" business: she wasn't cheap, but if you found yourself in a lot of trouble, **2** she was the lawyer you called. […]
The conference room was teeming with lawyers […] The occasion for which this small army of attorneys had assembled was the deposition of a reclusive billionaire, **3** who was now at the center of a blizzard of lawsuits alleging that the accumulation of those
15 billions had led to the deaths of hundreds of thousands of people. […]
The lawyer who would be posing the questions that morning was a man in his late sixties named Paul Hanly […], a class-action plaintiff's lawyer. **4**, White's clients were "arrogant assholes."
The billionaire being deposed that morning was a woman in her early seventies, a
20 medical doctor, **5**. […] Her lawyers had fought to prevent this deposition, and she did not want to be there. She projected the casual impatience, one of the lawyers in attendance thought, of someone who never waits in line to board an airplane.
"You are Kathe Sackler?" Hanly asked.
"I am," she replied.
25 Kathe was a member of the Sackler family, **6**. A few years earlier, Forbes magazine had listed the Sacklers as one of the twenty wealthiest families in the United States, **7**. […] The Sackler name adorned art museums, universities, and medical facilities around the world. […]

---

5 **to occupy** belegen
5 **sleek** elegant; stylisch
5 **grove** (Baum-)Gruppe
8 **to ascend** *hier:* hochfahren
12 **teeming with** wimmelnd von
13 **reclusive** zurückgezogen; öffentlichkeitsscheu
14 **to allege** behaupten
17 **class-action** Sammelklage
19 **to be deposed** unter Eid befragt werden

103

5 TEXT C

Vocabulary:
- 29 **to leave a mark** prägen; Spuren hinterlassen
- 30 **foundation** Stiftung
- 32 **patronage** Unterstützung; Mäzenatentum
- 41 **surgical residency** chirurgische Facharztausbildung
- 43 **drug manufacturer** Arzneimittelhersteller
- 43 **subsequently** *hier:* in der Folge; später
- 46 **generosity** Großmut; Großzügigkeit
- 48 **to scour** durchsuchen; absuchen
- 51 **groundbreaking** bahnbrechend; innovativ
- 51 **opioid** Opioid (stärkstes verfügbares Schmerzmittel)
- 52 **to herald** ankündigen; verkünden
- 53 **revenue** Umsatz
- 54 **rash of** Ausbruch von
- 57 **to transition to** übergehen auf
- 58 **staggering** schwindelerregend
- 62 **quintessentially American** uramerikanisch
- 63 **metric** Kennzahl

Over the previous six decades, Kathe Sackler's family had <u>left its mark</u> on New York City
30 [...] "I grew up," Kathe told Hanly, "with my parents having <u>foundations</u>." They contributed, she said, to "social causes."
One museum director likened the family to the Medicis, **8** whose <u>patronage</u> of the arts helped give rise to the Renaissance. But whereas the Medicis made their fortune in banking, the precise origins of the Sacklers' wealth had, **9**, been more mysterious. [...]
35 [T]o the casual observer, it could be difficult to connect the family name with any sort of business that might have generated all this wealth. [...]
"You graduated from NYU undergraduate in 1980," Hanly said. "True?"
"Correct," Kathe Sackler replied.
"And from NYU Medical School in 1984?"
40 "Yes."
And was it true, **10**, that after a two-year <u>surgical residency</u> she had gone to work for the Purdue Frederick Company?
Purdue Frederick was a <u>drug manufacturer</u>, which <u>subsequently</u> became known as Purdue Pharma. Based in Connecticut, it was the source of the vast majority of the
45 Sackler fortune. Whereas the Sacklers tended to insist, through elaborate "naming rights" contracts, that any gallery or research center that received their <u>generosity</u> must prominently feature the family name, the family business was not named after the Sacklers. In fact, you could <u>scour</u> Purdue Pharma's website and find no mention of the Sacklers whatsoever. But Purdue was a privately held company entirely owned by Kathe
50 Sackler and other members of her family. In 1996, Purdue had introduced a <u>groundbreaking</u> drug, a powerful <u>opioid</u> painkiller called OxyContin, which was <u>heralded</u> as a revolutionary way to treat chronic pain. The drug became one of the biggest blockbusters in pharmaceutical history, generating some $35 billion in <u>revenue</u>. But it also led to a <u>rash of</u> addiction and abuse. By the time Kathe Sackler sat for her
55 deposition, the United States was seized by an opioid epidemic in which Americans from every corner of the country found themselves addicted to these powerful drugs. Many people who started abusing OxyContin ended up <u>transitioning</u> to street drugs, like heroin or fentanyl. The numbers were <u>staggering</u>. According to the Centers for Disease Control and Prevention, in the quarter century following the introduction of
60 OxyContin, some 450,000 Americans had died of opioid-related overdoses. Such overdoses were now the leading cause of accidental death in America, accounting for more deaths than car accidents – more deaths, even, than that most <u>quintessentially</u> American of <u>metrics</u>, gunshot wounds. In fact, more Americans had lost their lives from opioid overdoses than had died in all of the wars the country had fought since World
65 War II. (776 words)

2 Multiple matching → WB p. 51/1–2

Match the phrases (A–L) with the gaps (1–10) in the text section ll. 7–42. There are two sentences more than you need.

- **A** the noble clan in fifteenth-century Florence
- **B** a longtime client of Mary Jo White's
- **C** earlier in her career
- **D** and you happened to have a lot of money,
- **E** a prominent New York philanthropic dynasty
- **F** In his view,
- **G** over the centuries
- **H** for a long time
- **I** though she had never actually practiced medicine
- **J** that was buzzing with subdued energy
- **K** with an estimated fortune of some $14 billion
- **L** Hanly asked

TEXT C 5

3 Short-answer questions

Answer the following questions. You may use words from the text.

1. How did people learn that the Sacklers are one of the richest families in the USA?
2. What was Paul Hanly's function at the deposition?
3. What caused the Sackler fortune to grow in the mid 1990s?
4. Why was the Sackler name well known in the arts scene?
5. What were the negative effects of the introduction of OxyContin?
6. How did many people who were addicted to OxyContin die?

4 Gapped summary

Complete the summary of the text. Fill in the gaps with the most suitable words from the corresponding sections (ll. 43–65) of the text. Give the line numbers of the words that you used.

> Even though the Sackler family's ■ 1 came from the company Purdue Pharma, you would never know this by looking at the company ■ 2 or any other information. The name is nowhere to be found. This ■ ■ 3 company had a big breakthrough in 1996 when its new ■ 4 came onto the market. The drug was considered to be ■ 5 in the field of treating chronic pain, ■ 6 billions of dollars for Purdue Pharma. However, it also had a downside. After being prescribed the drug, a great number of people became ■ 7 to it. In many cases, this led to severe ■ 8. In the 25 years after OxyContin was introduced, about 450,000 deaths in the US were linked to ■ 9 with opioids. In fact, deaths resulting from opioid consumption the most common ■ 10 of unintentional fatalities in the US.

5 Mediation

Lesen Sie die letzten zwei Absätze. Beantworten Sie die folgenden Fragen auf Deutsch.

1. Wodurch hat die Sackler Familie ihr Vermögen erworben?
2. Was verlangte die Sackler Familie von den Organisationen und Institutionen, die sie förderten?
3. Wieso kann man OxyContin als Einstiegsdroge bezeichnen?
4. Warum ist die Anzahl der Todesfälle, die mit Opiaten zusammenhängen so bemerkenswert?

6 A step further

a With a partner, brainstorm ideas for a letter to Kate Sackler in which you express your opinion regarding her family's role in the US opioid epidemic.

b Write your letter to Kate Sackler.

c Exchange your letter with a partner and give each other feedback.
  → S 15 Peer correction
  → S 15 Tip-top

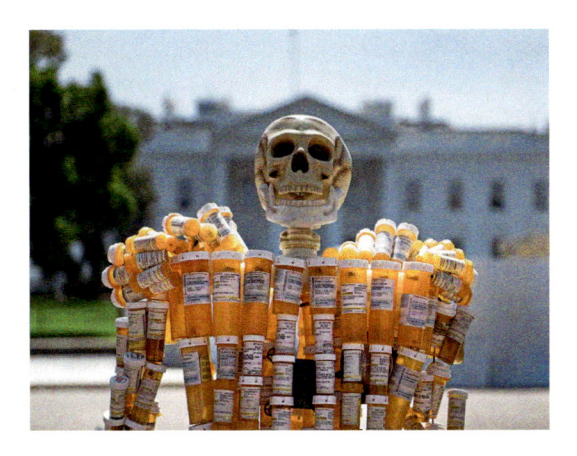

105

5 TEXT D

D Facing climate change

1 Before you read

a Describe the picture and explain the message on the sign.

b With a partner, discuss what forms of change the sign may want to encourage.

c What do you know about global warming? Take notes and give at least three examples of the effects of climate change on the world and on your own lives.
→ S15 Think-pair-share

GOOD TO KNOW

The Paris Agreement was signed by almost all countries of the world during the annual international climate conference (COP) held in Paris in 2015, pledging to work towards keeping the increase of global temperature levels to a maximum of 2°C – ideally below 1.5°C – compared to pre-industrial levels.

---

1 **court ruling** Gerichtsentscheid; Rechtsprechung
6 **to violate** verletzen
13 **to target** zielen auf; anpeilen
17 **to slash** reduzieren; streichen
21 **to appeal** *hier:* Berufung einlegen
27 **to offset** kompensieren; ausgleichen
36 **improbably** unwahrscheinlich
40 **exploration** Erforschung; Erkundung
41 **to ramp up** steigern; erhöhen
43 **carbon capture** Kohlendioxidabscheidung
49 **ledger** Konto; Bestand
53 **liquefied** verflüssigt
58 **to up** erhöhen; hinaufschieben
59 **to slash** kürzen

What a Dutch court ruling means for Shell and Big Oil

Climate lawyers are preparing to take on more fossil-fuel companies after a Dutch court ordered Royal Dutch Shell Plc to cut its emissions faster than planned, on the grounds that the oil giant is violating human rights by contributing to global warming. It was a turning point for climate court cases, which boomed after the Paris Agreement on global warming was reached in 2015. Initially, many cases challenged governments' plans, but litigators are increasingly targeting companies.

1 [...]
A Dutch court ruled on May 26 that Shell should slash its greenhouse gas emissions [by] 45 % by 2030 compared with 2019 levels, forcing the company to make some hard choices. The oil giant expects to appeal. [...]

2 [...]
A big part of Shell's existing plans for cutting carbon rely, to some extent, on so-called nature-based solutions – planting trees, reforesting and restoring land to offset industrial emissions. Shell has a 2050 net-zero plan using natural offsets for about 120 million tons a year of carbon dioxide. Scientists and environmental groups are skeptical of such practices and argue companies should focus first on cutting emissions and offset only those that can't be eliminated. In Shell's case, opponents say it would have to plant an improbably large number of trees. The oil major's energy transition plans involve producing less oil, more gas and spending as much as $3 billion a year on renewables and business of exploration and production. It also plans to ramp up the emissions it puts in the ground using carbon capture and storage projects in North America and Europe.

3 [...]
If the ruling is upheld, the equivalent of 740 million tons a year of carbon dioxide, more than the emissions of Germany, will have to be removed from Shell's ledgers by the end of the decade. To hit the court-ordered emissions target, Shell would have to cut output of both oil and pipeline gas by 3 % a year, keep liquefied natural gas production flat and cut oil product sales by 30 % from 2020 levels, according to RBC Capital Markets analyst Biraj Borkhataria. Like many of its European peers, over the last year Shell has upped its targets to slash its carbon emissions and ultimately become a "net-zero" company by the middle of the century.

4 [...]
The ruling can be appealed, a process that could last many years. The decision was in line with the Paris Agreement to limit global warming. But it was countries, not companies, that signed up to that accord.

Eric De Brabandere, a professor of international dispute settlement at the University of Leiden, said he understands the verdict as it currently stands, but would also see why another judge could reach another conclusion. While the Dutch government signed up to the Paris Agreement, Shell's existing targets don't violate Dutch law. [...]

5 [...]

Companies headquartered in the Netherlands could face similar cases, while those that have a subsidiary in the country can only be held responsible for their Dutch branches. Oil companies, or other big polluters, based in other countries may face similar cases; Milieudefensie is in touch with other nonprofit organizations and it expects the approach it took in this case will be replicated by others across Europe, its leader said. Jurisdictions differ, however, and the Dutch system provides more space for interpretation by the judge than most.

6 [...]

Two landmark cases have taken place in the Netherlands. In [another] case the Dutch government was told to step up its efforts to adhere to the Paris Agreement, while in the Shell case a similar verdict was applied to a corporation. Both cases were built on a 'duty of care' clause in the Dutch system which provided judges some liberty to interpret unwritten rules and consider links to human rights and the effect climate change has on the right to a healthy environment. A lawyer involved in both cases was Roger Cox, who wrote a book about judicial intervention and climate change, "Revolution Justified."

(668 words)
Diederik Baazil and Laura Millan Lombrana, *Bloomberg*, 2021

69 **dispute settlement** Streitschlichtung; Beilegung
71 **verdict** Urteil
80 **subsidiary** Tochtergesellschaft
88 **to replicate** vervielfältigen
89 **jurisdiction** Rechtssystem; Rechtsprechung
94 **landmark case** Grundsatzurteil

2 Multiple matching → WB p. 52/1–2

Match the questions (A–H) with the paragraphs (1–6). There are two questions more than you need.

- A Why are Dutch courts leading on climate?
- B Which legal options does Shell have?
- C What was the Shell verdict?
- D When did the courts turn around?
- E How could Shell comply with the court ruling?
- F What about Shell's long-term targets?
- G How many trees are enough?
- H What does it mean for other companies?

3 Short-answer questions

Answer the following questions. They only refer to ll. 1–44 and ll. 77–108. You may use words from the text.

1. What brought about a lot of climate court cases?
2. How do they differ from the cases that are brought to court nowadays?
3. Which goal does *Shell* want to reach by 2050?
4. Why is there skepticism about nature-based solutions?
5. Who were the signatories of the Paris agreement?
6. In which ways do Dutch judges have more freedom compared to other EU countries?

5 TEXT D

4 Multiple choice

Choose the most suitable option.

1. The verdict in the Dutch case against Shell …
   A will have no effects on other companies.
   B could cause oil companies to shut down.
   C has encouraged climate lawyers in similar cases.
   D has consequences for the Dutch government.

2. The ruling of the Dutch court …
   A should help reduce greenhouse gases.
   B goes into effect in 2030.
   C offers Shell different choices.
   D aims at returning to 2019 levels.

3. So-called nature-based solutions …
   A can eliminate industrial emissions.
   B include carbon capture.
   C cost about $3 billion every year.
   D don't actually reduce emissions.

4. 'Offsetting' means …
   A cutting emissions.
   B planting trees to make up for emissions.
   C producing less oil.
   D promoting renewables.

5. Carbon dioxide emission levels in Germany …
   A are as high as what Shell must eliminate.
   B will never hit the court-ordered target.
   C are affected by Shell oil product sales.
   D are getting close to making it a net-zero country.

6. In order to be net zero by 2050 …
   A the courts have cut output.
   B Shell's ledgers have to be removed.
   C gas pipelines have to be cut.
   D oil companies have raised their targets.

5 A step further

a Your class is going to take part in an online conference on climate issues. A number of people have been asked to give a keynote speech to provide discussion topics. Look at the tips for writing a good speech. Copy the table and add at least two items to each aspect.

Structure	Audience	Language	Delivery
– The speech should have a clear beginning – …	– Connect to your audience – …	– Think of <u>how</u> and not just what you are going to say	– Rehearse … – …

b Using the information given in the text, write a speech on one of the following topics. Include quotations from the text in your speech.

1. Shared responsibilities: governments, companies and individuals.
Or:
2. Avoiding or offsetting? – How best to reduce CO2 emissions.

c Find a partner with a different topic than yours. Listen to each other's speeches and give feedback. → S15 Tip-top

Global players → S 6.2 → S 10.2 → S 10.3 → WB p. 53/1

One aspect of globalisation is the fact that big multinational companies with a worldwide presence and brand recognition play a big role. These companies are often also called global players. They are world leaders in their industries through technology, quality and innovation.

'Do you think that global players have a positive or negative effect on the world economy?'

Write a composition of at least 300 words. Include <u>all</u> the material provided.

Material 1

"WHEN EUROPEAN WORKERS ARE LOSING THEIR JOBS BECAUSE OF AN ASIAN STOCK MARKET CRASH – THAT'S THE MEANING OF 'GLOBALIZATION'".

Material 2

Outsourcing and globalization of manufacturing allows companies to reduce costs, benefits consumers with lower cost goods and services, causes economic expansion that reduces unemployment, and increases productivity and job creation.

Larry Elder, American radio host

Material 3

Armutsgefährdungsquote von Erwerbstätigen 2021 in %
in ausgewählten Staaten der Europäischen Union

Land	%
Rumänien (EU-Max)	15,6
Spanien	12,7
Griechenland	11,3
Bulgarien	10,0
EU (27 Länder)	8,9
Polen	8,9
Deutschland	8,6
Frankreich	7,0
Schweden	6,6
Slowenien	5,0
Tschechien	3,5
Finnland (EU-Min)	2,8

Source: Eurostat, 2021

5 MEDIATION

Terrorism and media → S 6.1

Verfassen Sie einen zusammenhängenden englischen Text von ca. 150 Wörtern für ein Projekt im Rahmen eines Medienkompetenzprogramms an Ihrer Schule. Gehen Sie dabei auf folgende Aspekte ein:

1. Wie überlappen sich Realität und Fiktion in Filmen zum Thema Terrorismus?
2. Warum ist die Serie Teheran besonders brisant im Hinblick auf die politische Situation im Nahen Osten?
3. Warum dürfen die Schauspieler und Schauspielerinnen keine politischen Fragen bentworten?
4. Wie beurteilt der Autor die Serie „Teheran"?

Ecstasy beim Erzfeind

Eine Mossad-Agentin in Iran zwischen Party und Schattenkrieg: Die Serie „Teheran" [...] soll die nächste Erfolgsproduktion aus Israel werden.

Anfang Juli meldeten die Nachrichtenagenturen eine Reihe von Explosionen in iranischen Militärbasen und Nuklearanlagen. Experten vermuten, dass der israelische Geheimdienst Mossad hinter den Attacken steckt. Kurz zuvor liefen bei einem israelischen Sender die ersten Folgen von „Teheran", einer Serie, in der eine junge Mossad-Agentin undercover in der iranischen Hauptstadt ihren ersten großen Einsatz hat: Sie soll einen Anschlag auf ein Atomkraftwerk vorbereiten.

„Teheran" ist das jüngste Beispiel dafür, wie frappierend sich in israelischen Serien Fiktion und Realität überlagern; wie psychologische Thriller von der Konfrontation im Nahen Osten erzählen – und von den damit verbundenen Themen Identität und Loyalität. [...]

Die Serie „Teheran" [...] treibt das Konfrontationsszenario auf die Spitze: Tamar Rabinyan (Niv Sultan), eine Mossad-Agentin mit iranisch-jüdischen Wurzeln, wird unter falscher Identität in Iran eingeschleust. Das Land gilt als Erzfeind Israels, es gibt keinerlei diplomatische Verbindungen. Um in das Datennetz des Kraftwerks einzudringen, nimmt sie mit einem iranischen Hacker Kontakt auf, der in der Dissidentenszene aktiv ist. Auf dem Stützpunkt in Israel warten derweil Bomber auf das Zeichen zum nächtlichen Angriff.

[...] [B]ald lernt Rabinyan über den Hacker ein Iran kennen, in dem die Menschen auf illegalen Partys Ecstasy nehmen und ihre Sexualität frei ausleben, in dem die Intellektuellen freimütig über politische Theorien diskutieren. [...]

In einem Videochat schwärmt die Hauptdarstellerin Niv Sultan davon, wie Musik, Essen und Lifestyle die Menschen miteinander verbänden und dass „Teheran" die Metropole in einem Licht zeige, wie man sie noch nie im Fernsehen gesehen habe. Über schwierigere Themen darf sie leider nicht sprechen, [der Streamingdienst] ist da sehr strikt. Direkt vor dem Gespräch mahnt aus dem Off eine Stimme: „Keine politischen Fragen!" Wirklich? Da erwirbt [ein] Streamingdienst [...] als erste ausländische Produktion eine Serie, die vom Schattenkrieg Israels im Nahen Osten handelt, aber das politische Weltgeschehen darf bei der Promotion keine Rolle spielen? Das zeigt, wie nervös die Chefs [des Streaming-Ambieters] sind [...].

Die Unruhe mag auch mit der hohen Investition in „Teheran" zu tun haben. [Der Streaming-Anbieter] soll für „Teheran" eine Million Dollar pro Folge für die internationalen Rechte gezahlt haben. Die Angst davor, politisch anzuecken, zeigt einen großen Schwachpunkt der mit massiven Kapitalströmen aus den USA vorangetriebenen Streaming-Industrie. Die großen Player sind zwar darauf aus, mit brisanten Stoffen global größtmögliche Aufmerksamkeit zu erzielen und so die Konkurrenz auszustechen, zugleich scheuen sie es oft, sich zu politischen Fragen zu äußern. Stromlinienförmigkeit regiert das Streaminggeschäft. Was gerade angesichts konfliktgeladener israelischer Serien im Programm absurd wirkt. In der hochpolitischen Konfrontation dieser Geschichten liegt ja gerade ihre Besonderheit. Ideologien und Religionen treffen hier meist mit voller Wucht aufeinander. [...]

(449 Wörter)
Christian Buß, *Der Spiegel*, 2020

A sustainable café

Your school wants to open a student-run, sustainable coffee shop and café on campus. It should be as local and organic as possible but still stay within the school's small budget. The students have been invited to brainstorm and submit their ideas to the planning committee. Today your group has come together to discuss your ideas and suggestions. In the meeting, you can discuss the following ideas.

- What will you be selling at the coffee shop?
- Which supplies are needed?
- Where can they be optained?
- How can students and staff be persuaded to use the coffee shop?
- Which things are the most important to spend money on?
- Where can you compromise if the budget is very tight?
- Which problems could occur while trying to get everything ready in time?
- Which difficulties could arise later on?

a Introduce the topic and one or two of your ideas about products you plan to sell (about 1 minute).

b Discuss the following issues in more detail.

local versus global | sustainability | quality versus price | budget | time management

c Sum up the most important points and decide what your coffee shop should look like and what you'd like to sell. Plan your first steps and write down your ideas to be given to the planning committee.

6 GETTING STARTED

A global community

Global village
by Judy Small

I have seen the global village
And it looks just like LA
Where the baseball caps reverse
And the smog defines the day
There's a little hope of sunshine
For the hungry and the poor

And life's a colliseum
Where the crowd that bays for more.
You cannot see the line but if you
Step on it you die when money
Speaks in volumes and the
Limit is the sky

1 What is a global village? → WB p. 56–57; 58/1

a What do we understand by the term 'global village'? Brainstorm about the concept and create a mind map.

b To what extent do the pictures (A–D) illustrate the concept of a 'global village'? Complete your mind map with concepts from the pictures.

GETTING STARTED 6

2 Working with song lyrics

a Read the lyrics from the song "Global village" recorded in 1995. Look up any unknown words in a dictionary.

b Outline the aspects of a life in a global village as the singer sees them and describe the atmosphere of the song.

c In small groups, discuss the message of the song in relation to your mindmap. Are there any aspects you did not consider?

A8 3 Listening → S 3 → WB p. 58/1

a Communication and transportation are two factors that advance the 'global village'. In the podcast "Global migration" Simon Ronay and and Professor Hemlington talk about a further factor – migration. Listen and decide whether the statements are true or false and correct the false ones.

1. Refugees normally leave their country because they are looking for jobs elsewhere.
2. 'Brain drain' occurs because other countries offer greater benefits to intellectuals.
3. Social change has always been influenced by migration.
4. According to Professor Hemlington, the volume of recent immigration from the South to the North is steadily increasing.
5. The majority of African immigrants to Europe are highly educated but have a poor financial background.

b With a partner, take notes on the following aspects.

1. the meaning of the terms 'migrant', 'refugee' and 'asylum seeker'
2. migration of Europeans to oversea territories over the centuries
3. Professor Hemlington's view on migration flows

c Compare your notes and complete them.

4 Creating a poster

a What if the world was represented by 100 people? Do some research and find out who would live there. You might want to include the following aspects.

average age | origin | access to water and sanitation | literacy | internet access | religion | education | income | adequate housing

b In small groups, share your findings and decide which aspects you would like to show on your poster. Find pictures and statistics to illustrate your aspects.

c Present your poster in class. → S 15 Gallery walk → S 15 Tip-top

d Compare and discuss the posters. What do the statistics say about the 'global village'? Is it a fair place? Is it a safe place? Would you like to live in this village?

6 TEXT A

A The importance of trees

1 Before you read. → S 15 Placemat

a Do a survey in class. What do you think is the most pressing environmental problem today? Global warming? Pollution? Overpopulation? Other? Take notes.

b Work in groups of four. Copy the placemat, and in your corner, write down which habits you yourself would be willing to change to support the environment.

c Discuss what each of you has written and suggest some actions in the middle of the placemat.

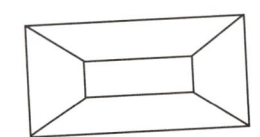

Richard Powers is an American novelist and winner of many literary awards, among them the 2019 Pulitzer Prize for Fiction for *The Overstory*. His novels mainly deal with the effects of science and technology on society. In *The Overstory*, he follows nine Americans whose experiences have brought them together and who are now fighting the destruction of forests. Patricia Westerford, one of the nine, is writing a novel called *The Secret Forest* which mirrors the books of German author and forester Peter Wohlleben.

The Overstory
by Richard Powers

THE AUDITORIUM is dark and lined with redwood <u>questionably</u> obtained. Patricia looks out from the podium on hundreds of experts. She keeps her eyes high above the
5 <u>expectant</u> faces and clicks. Behind her appears a painting of a naïve wooden <u>ark</u> with a parade of animals <u>winding up</u> into it.
"When the world was ending the first time, Noah took all the animals, two by two, and loaded them aboard his escape craft for evacuation. But it's a funny thing: He left the plants to die. He failed to take the one thing he needed to rebuild life on land, and
10 concentrated on saving the <u>freeloaders</u>!"
[…]
"The problem was, Noah and his kind didn't believe that plants were really alive. No intentions, no vital <u>spark</u>. Just like rocks that happened to get bigger."
[…] "Now we know that plants communicate and remember. They taste, smell, touch,
15 and even hear and see. […] We've begun to understand the <u>profound ties</u> between trees and people. But our separation has grown faster than our connection."
She clicks, and her slide changes. "Here's a satellite view of North America at night, 1970. And here, we are, a decade later. And another. And another. One more, and done." Four clicks, and light screams across the continent, filling the blackness from sea to sea. […]
20 "In this state alone, a third of the forested acres have died in the last six years. […] **1** Whole ecosystems are <u>unraveling</u>. Biologists are <u>scared senseless</u>.
[…] Out from her hip pocket comes [a] <u>glass vial</u>. "And these are plant extracts I found while walking around this campus yesterday. My goodness, this place is an <u>arbor</u>. A little paradise!"
25 She cups the vial in both hands and puts it on top of the podium. "You see, a lot of folks think trees are simple things, incapable of doing anything interesting. But there's a tree for every purpose under heaven. Their chemistry is astonishing. Waxes, fats, sugars.

---

1 **overstory** Überständer (die höchste Stufe der Bäume im Regenwald)
3 **questionable** fragwürdig; zweifelhaft
5 **expectant** erwartungsvoll; gespannt
5 **ark** Arche
7 **to wind up** sich hochwinden; sich einen Weg bahnen
10 **freeloader** Schmarotzer
13 **spark** Funke
15 **profound ties** tiefe Verbundenheit
21 **to unravel** aus den Fugen / ins Wanken geraten
21 **scared senseless** zu Tode erschrocken
22 **glass vial** Glasfläschchen
23 **arbor** Laube; Gartenlaube

Tannins, sterols, gums, and carotenoids. […] They're learning to make whatever can be made. And most of what they make we haven't even identified." […]

30 "Life has a way of talking to the future. It's called memory. It's called genes. To solve the future, we must save the past. My simple rule of thumb, then, is this: when you cut down a tree, what you make from it should be at least as miraculous as what you cut down." She can't hear if her audience laughs or groans. […]

"My whole life, I've been an outsider. But many others have been out there with me. We
35 found that trees could communicate, over the air and through their roots. Common sense hooted us down. We found that trees take care of each other. Collective science dismissed the idea. **2** Outsiders discovered that trees sense the presence of other nearby life. That a tree learns to save water. That trees feed their young and synchronize their masts and bank resources and warn kin and send out signals to wasps to come and
40 save them from attacks.

"Here's a little outsider information, and you can wait for it to be confirmed. A forest knows things. They wire themselves up underground. There are brains down there, ones our own brains aren't shaped to see. Root plasticity, solving problems and making decisions. Fungal synapses. What else do you want to call it? Link enough trees together,
45 and a forest grows aware. […] Trees want something from us, just as we've always wanted things from them. This isn't mystical. The 'environment' is alive—a fluid, changing web of purposeful lives dependent on each other. […] Flowers shape bees as much as bees shape flowers. Berries may compete to be eaten more than animals compete for the berries. A thorn acacia makes sugary protein treats to feed and enslave the ants who
50 guard it. Fruit-bearing plants trick us into distributing their seeds **3** " […]

"Trees are doing science. Running a billion field tests. They make their conjectures, and the living world tells them what works. Life is speculation, and speculation is life. What a marvelous word! It means to guess. It also means to mirror.

"Trees stand at the heart of ecology, and they must come to stand at the heart of human
55 politics. Tagore said, *Trees are the earth's endless effort to speak to the listening heaven.* But people – oh, my word – people! People could be the heaven that the Earth is trying to speak to.

"[…] **4** If we could understand green, we'd learn how to grow all the food we need in layers three deep, on a third of the ground we need right now, with plants that protected
60 one another from pests and stress. If we knew what green wanted, we wouldn't have to choose between the Earth's interests and ours. They'd be the same!" […]

She takes up the vial of tree extracts from where she set it down on the podium. […]

"I've asked myself the question you brought me here to answer. I've thought about it based on all the evidence available. I've tried not to let my feelings protect me from the
65 facts. I've tried not to let hope and vanity blind me. **5** *What is the single best thing a person can do for tomorrow's world?*" A trickle of extract hits the glass of clear water and turns into tendrils of green.

(942 words)

28 **tannin** Tannine (pflanzlicher Gerbstoff)
28 **sterol** Sterol (Naturstoff aus der Obergruppe der Steroide)
28 **carotenoid** Carotenoid (natürlich vorkommendes fettlösliches Pigment)
31 **rule of thumb** Faustregel
36 **to hoot sb down** jdn niederbrüllen
39 **kin** Verwandte
42 **to wire oneself up** sich verdrahten; sich verkabeln
43 **plasticity** Plastizität; Formbarkeit
44 **fungal** Pilz-
49 **thorn acacia** Dornenakazie
49 **treat** Leckerbissen; Süßigkeit
51 **conjecture** Annahme; Hypothese
59 **layer** Schicht
64 **evidence** Beweis; Beleg
65 **vanity** Eitelkeit; Selbstgefälligkeit
67 **tendril** Ranke; Blattranke

2 Multiple matching → WB p. 59/1–3

Five phrases have been cut from the text. Match the most suitable sentences (A–H) with the gaps (1–5). There are three sentences more than you need.

A Our brains evolved to solve the forest.
B If we could see what green was doing, we'd never be lonely or bored.
C Forests are falling to many things – drought, fire, and plain old felling for farms and subdivisions.
D Outsiders discovered how seeds remember the seasons of their childhood and set buds accordingly.

6 TEXT A

E This tree grows from Colombia to Costa Rica.
F They've seen this exploding light show too many times before.
G We've shaped and been shaped by forests for longer than we've been Homo sapiens.
H I've tried to see this matter from the standpoint of trees.

3 Short-answer questions

Answer the following questions on the first part of the text (ll. 3–29). You may use words from the text.

1. What does Patricia Westerford criticise about Noah's evacuation?
2. Which visual does she use to illustrate the lack of forests?
3. What makes a tree's chemistry astonishing?

4 Gapped summary

Complete the summary with the most suitable words from the corresponding sections of the text (ll. 34–57). Give the line number of the words that you used.

Patricia Westerford considers herself an ■ 1, but feels that this attribute helped her and others in science. Because they had a nonconformist viewpoint, they ■ 2 things about trees that ■ 3 science thought to be impossible. Some of the abilities that trees have are sensing the ■ 4 of other life forms in their vicinity, figuring out how to ■ 5 water in times of drought or even transmitting warning ■ 6 when there is danger. Westerford compares trees' root systems to human ■ 7, but also emphasises that humans aren't able to understand the complexity of trees. She believes that roots are flexible and resilient and because they have a sense of awareness, they can form ■ 8 connections with other trees. She goes on to stress the interconnectedness of all living beings because in this web of life, every being is ■ 9 – from flowers to bees to berries and beyond. She makes a final appeal to include trees not only in ecology but also in ■ 10 as this is the way to combine the interests of nature and humans.

5 A step further

a Do some research on charities for planting trees. You can look for national and international organisations. With a partner, select four that interest you and take notes. Consider the following.

- When was the organisation founded?
- Who were the founders? What was their motivation?
- Which country or countries does the organisation operate in?
- What is their main aim?
- How are they financed?

b Write a blog post recommending your favourite charity to your friends. Write about 180 words. → S 6.4

B Cultural identity

1 Before you read

a Look up the terms 'culture' and 'identity' in a dictionary and write down keywords for each term. → S 11.3

b With a partner, compare your keywords and come up with a definition of the term 'cultural identity'.

c Which factors or experiences in your life have determined or still determine your cultural identity? Make a list.
→ S 15 Think-pair-share

Examples: family traditions, social clubs, …

Why I loved being an expat child – and what I've learned

1 As an expat child, or 'Third Culture Kid', I had a delightfully unstable upbringing. From the age of three, I moved
5 from Windsor to Florida to London to Indiana and – for the grand finale – back to the Big Smoke. […] Caught between two (arguably four) cultures, my childhood forced me to create a culture of my own.
10 One that combined sunshine frivolities with capital-dwelling cynicism, and everything in between. With almost no effort, growing up as a global citizen helped me become an extraordinarily self-
15 aware, resilient, empathetic and travel-driven adult. These are my lessons learned – and why they proved so important.

2 I was referred to as the 'The American Girl', 'The British Girl' and 'The New Girl'
20 (even years after arriving at a new school, ironically) throughout my childhood. To other children I was continually something new and confusing. Easily marked by either where I had come from
25 or where I stood 'in the pack'. […] "What neighbourhood do you live in?" "Why do you talk like that?" "Do you have two parents?" "Why did you move here?" "Do you want to go to church with my family?"
30 The more questions I was asked, the more I put my answers under a microscope.

I knew my differences made people uneasy, and I get it; when a Third Culture Kid enters a classroom filled with boys and girls who have grown up together 35 (often next-door to each other), their differences will be scrutinized. But nobody wants to be defined by things out of their control.
Because of this, I developed an enormous 40 capacity for introspection. When someone tried to put me in a box, I questioned the labels. I questioned my character, my feelings, my motives and my desires. Then I questioned how the answers might help 45 me do and be the kind of person I would hope to become. Outside of a single culture's expectations or assumptions.
In an odd way, having my identity challenged so regularly laid the 50 groundwork for a confident, assured and self-aware adult. A person that, however imperfect, I'm very proud to be.

3 Third Culture Kids are noticeably different to those around them. And 55 children are quick to notice. It's no fault of theirs, really. Even adults find it challenging to accept or understand things they aren't familiar with. But it can turn the simplest exchange into a 60 battlefield for an expat child.

---

1 **expat** Auswanderer/-in; Person, die im Ausland lebt
4 **upbringing** Erziehung
6 **grand finale** stören; durcheinanderbringen
7 **the Big Smoke** Bezeichnung für London (wegen des Smogs in den 50er Jahren des letzten Jahrhunderts)
10 **frivolities** Leichtfertigkeiten
11 **capital-dwelling** in einer Hauptstadt wohnend
14 **self-aware** selbstbewusst
15 **resilient** widerstandsfähig
33 **uneasy** unbehaglich; unruhig
37 **to scrutinize** genau prüfen
41 **capacity** hier: Vermögen; Fähigkeit
41 **introspection** Selbstbeobachtung
44 **desire** Wunsch; Verlangen
48 **assumption** Annahme
50 **to lay the groundwork** die Grundlagen schaffen
51 **assured** gefestigt
61 **battlefield** Schlachtfeld

TEXT B

66 **misconception** falsche Vorstellung; Irrglaube
69 **target** Ziel
70 **circumstance** Umstand
79 **affinity** Verbundenheit; Zugehörigkeit
82 **to send shivers down sb's spine** kalt den Rücken hinunterlaufen
87 **hilarious** witzig
90 **to loath** verachten
100 **to set up** austatten
101 **penchant** Vorliebe
105 **hidden gem** verstecktes Kleinod; *hier:* Geheimtipp
106 **to spur** den Anstoß geben

Settling into a new country, school and culture – even with the stark similarities of my own British/American upbringing – can be painful. Kids will have misconceptions of the 'type' of person you are (typically led by their parents' cultural illusions). They may see you as an easy target for bullying (no friends, no support system). Whatever the circumstance, they will take far more time to accept your arrival than another kid's continued presence. In time, you get used to it. And it gives you a perspective that will serve you for life. […]

4 Expat children often see varying degrees of intolerance that contrast with those in the other cultures they've been a part of. But nothing gives you an affinity for outsiders like being an outsider.
The proud, gay communities I grew up around in London would have sent shivers down the spines of many of my Midwestern peers. To me, they were just nice people with incredible clothes.
Being cared for by the family of my best friend in Florida – a hilarious and super-smart Indian girl named Hanna – left me with zero tolerance for the immigrant-loathing racists who 'campaigned' down the high street of my next home, in the UK.
I was incredibly lucky to grow up around so many different types of people. I now have open-minded instincts, always try to learn from others (rather than judge them), and make a point to connect with anyone who seems as though they might be out of place.

5 Naturally, a life spent travelling set me up with a penchant for places undiscovered. Whether I leave a place in love or indifferent, many of my best memories are linked to the discovery of new cultures, foods and hidden gems.
It was wanderlust that spurred the decision to study French, German and English, take four months out to travel America by plane, sleeper train and car (welcoming new friends on the journey every step of the way), and even move to Bangkok on the edge of my twenty-first birthday.
Today, a life well-travelled continues to teach me to value people, kindness and experiences above everything else.

(763 words)
Lela London, *The Telegraph*, 2019

2 Multiple matching → WB p. 60/1–3

Match the correct subheadings (A–H) with the paragraphs from the text (1–5). There are three more subheadings than you need.

- **A** Finding your identity
- **B** Growing up globally
- **C** Cultural expectations
- **D** Being bullied
- **E** Exploring different cultures
- **F** Developing resilience
- **G** Empathy and open-mindedness
- **H** Campaigns against racism

3 Mediation

Beantworten Sie die folgenden Fragen auf Deutsch. Sie beziehen sich auf die Teile 2, 3 und 4.

1. Wie reagierte die Autorin, wenn man sie in eine Schublade stecken wollte?
2. Warum kann man schmerzhafte Erfahrungen machen, wenn man in ein neues Land kommt, selbst wenn es große Übereinstimmung zwischen den Kulturen gibt?
3. Was bildete die Basis für die positive Entwicklung der Autorin zu einer selbstbewussten Persönlichkeit?
4. Wie beeinflussen ihre persönlichen Erfahrungen das Verhalten der Autorin anderen Außenseitern gegenüber?

4 Multiple choice

Choose the most suitable option.

1. How many times did the author move as a child?
   - A five times
   - B four times
   - C three times
   - D six times

2. Being asked a lot of questions made the author …
   - A feel confused.
   - B scrutinise others.
   - C take a closer look at herself.
   - D feel out of control.

3. The author finds it is difficult …
   - A for people to accept unfamiliar things.
   - B especially for kids, to accept new kids.
   - C to combine her British and American upbringing.
   - D to grow up in a community like London.

4. What does the author think is good about being an outsider?
   - A You can choose where you grow up.
   - B It helps you understand other outsiders.
   - C You can wear incredible clothes.
   - D Nobody has misconceptions about you.

5. What was a result of moving around so much as a child?
   - A She became indifferent to travelling.
   - B She had bad memories of childhood.
   - C She only had four months to travel.
   - D She developed a love of travelling.

6. What is not mentioned in section 5?
   - A discovering new cultures
   - B living in France and Germany
   - C travelling by train
   - D moving to Asia

5 A step further

a With a partner, analyse the cartoon and discuss the irony and the message it contains.
→ S 10.2

b Read the text on pages 117–118 again. How do you think the author of the text, Lela London, would respond to this situation?

c Discuss what we as individuals can do to make third culture people welcome in our society.

6 TEXT C

C Global water

1 Before you read

a Do some research online for non-governmental organisations that are active worldwide and deal with inequality and poverty. Make a list in class.

b With a partner, prepare a short presentation about one of the organisations and include the basic facts (who, what, when, where, why and how). Present it to the class.
Then discuss which organisation you think has the most powerful impact.
→ S15 1-minute presentation

Women helping women

Women Helping Women [...] is a Voss Foundation campaign that has raised nearly $950,000 in Europe and the United
5 States to build clean water access points and sanitation facilities in Kenya, the Democratic Republic of the Congo, Liberia, and Swaziland.
Water is disproportionately a women's
10 burden in Africa. Rural women and girls are responsible for their families' daily water needs, often sacrificing their own health, education, and futures to do so. Providing women with facilitated access
15 to clean water is an important part of Voss Foundation's Ripple Effect, creating an engine for growth that spurs change in a family, community, region, and country. [...] Water sources are often far from the
20 village, and women must walk for hours to fetch water daily. Some families even keep their daughters at home so that they can help collect water. Instead of going to school, these girls follow their mothers and walk, on average, at least 10 miles 25 every day. While walking to get water, particularly when they must walk alone before or after daylight hours, women are vulnerable to rape and other violent attacks. 30
The journey also requires them to carry buckets of water weighing over 40 pounds on their heads. Carrying such a heavy load over long distances has detrimental health effects, including back and 35 chest pains, developmental deformities, arthritic disease, and miscarriages.
Drinking the water in Sub-Saharan Africa is often just as hazardous as retrieving it. Women are not only at risk of sickness 40 themselves, but are also responsible for taking care of family members who fall ill after drinking contaminated water.

---

5 **access point** Entnahmestelle
9 **disproportional** unverhältnismäßig
12 **to sacrifice** opfern; aufgeben
16 **ripple effect** Sogwirkung; Kreise ziehen
34 **detrimental** (gesundheits-)schädlich
36 **deformity** Fehlbildung; Verkrüppelung
37 **miscarriage** Fehlgeburt
40 **to be at risk** gefährdet sein
43 **contaminated** verseucht

Furthermore, they may then have to take on the labor of the sick family member, on top of their own labor, while they nurse their loved ones back to health.

Just as women and girls in Africa shoulder a disproportionate amount of the world's water burden, they also stand the most to gain from clean water projects. [...]

When we build a well:

- Employment statistics go up immediately: we employ local laborers to build the projects, local cooks to provide them with food while they're working, and we train local individuals to maintain and secure the well in the future.
- Mothers can give birth in clean healthcenters with a much lower chance of getting an infection.
- Children do not die from diarrhea, cholera, or other water-borne illnesses.
- More children can go to school: In the village of Latawken, Kenya, where we built a water system, local authorities had to build a bigger school because there were more students after there was clean water.
- More of these students are girls who no longer are removed from school to help their mothers carry water when their families get too big: In Kalebuka, in the Democratic Republic of the Congo, we've built a well at the area's first all-girls school.
- Children can grow without developmental problems that they otherwise incur from carrying such heavy loads on their backs and heads at such a young age.
- Women now have the time to pursue their own education and earn an income: In Pel, Mali, where we built 5 wells, one of them is at a garden owned by a local women's cooperative. This co-op functions like a sort of savings-and-loan organization, whereby the women pool and save their money altogether. We've helped them grow healthy vegetation for themselves and, in the process, helped them double their income.
- With money comes power: once women are contributing to their families' income, they begin to achieve parity.
- Women also gain political power through their positions on newly-created water management committees. Each of our projects creates a local council to oversee the well or water system. Every water management committee must be composed of at least 50% women. (621 words)

Voss Foundation, New York – Oslo, 2020

48 **to shoulder a burden** eine Last schultern
62 **diarrhea** Durchfall
63 **water-borne illness** durch Wasser übertragene Krankheit
77 **developmental** entwicklungsbedingt
79 **to incur sth** etwas erleiden; sich etwas zuziehen
82 **to pursue** nachgehen; verfolgen
87 **savings-and-loan organization (AE)** Spar- und Darlehenskasse
89 **to pool** zusammenlegen; bündeln
96 **parity** Parität; Gleichstellung

2 Gapped summary → WB p. 61/1–3

Complete the summary with the most suitable words from the text sections (ll. 1–47) of the text on page 120–121. Give the line numbers of the words that you used.

Focusing on countries in Africa, the campaign Women Helping Women works to improve access to clean water and ■■ **1**. The money that the organisation ■■ **2** is used for building projects. In many African countries the responsibility of providing water for the family falls ■ **3** on the shoulders of women and girls. Because they often have to walk many miles every day to reach ■■ **4**, they are disadvantaged in many ways. First of all, their ■ **5** suffers from the loads on their heads. The ■ **6** weights can not only cause such serious problems as miscarriages but they can also be ■ **7** to their bodily development. Secondly, girls cannot receive an education if they are required to stay home and help. Indeed, they are ■ **8** their right to go to school. Thirdly, the walk to get water can be dangerous and the women are ■ **9** to violence. However, the water itself is a risk for anyone who drinks it because it can be ■ **10** and cause sicknesses.

6 TEXT C

3 Multiple choice

Choose the most suitable option.

1. Not being able to easily access clean water is …
   A a problem that is being ignored.
   B a big problem for women in rural regions.
   C something that can't be changed easily.
   D a problem that only exists in Swaziland.

2. Carrying 40 pounds of water …
   A can cause severe health problems.
   B is a daily task for every woman.
   C results in strong back and chest muscles.
   D is a task that girls and boys help their families with.

3. What is the dual purpose of the garden cooperative in Pel, Mali?
   A a public pool and a hospital
   B healthy food and a kind of bank
   C a girls' school and a business
   D teacher training and a vegetable store

4. Who is responsible for well management once a project has been completed?
   A people from the Voss Foundation
   B trained men from the region
   C committees with 50% women
   D women's cooperatives

5. Which kinds of positive effects can be felt in the community as a result of the campaign?
   A lower unemployment and healthier foods
   B higher birth rates and bigger schools
   C better cooks and more equality
   D higher incomes and free education

6. What is not mentioned in the text?
   A improved education for women
   B new schools for boys
   C water that is not fit for consumption
   D women's cooperatives

4 Words matter

a Find the matching words for the following definitions in the text on pages 120–121. Give the line numbers.

   A to make sth happen faster
   B easily hurt or attacked
   C to keep in good condition through checking and repairing
   D a group of people who have the power to make decisions

b Explain the following phrases from the text in your own words.

   1. sanitation facilities (l. 6)
   2. just as hazardous (l. 39)
   3. to take on the labor of sb (ll. 44–45)
   4. to stand the most to gain (ll. 50–51)
   5. to give birth (l. 59)
   6. in the process (l. 92)

122

5 Mediation

Beantworten Sie die folgenden Fragen auf Deutsch. Sie beziehen sich auf die Zeilen 21–47 und 60–93.

1. Warum bekommen viele Mädchen keine gute Schulbildung?
2. Welche Aufgaben übernehmen Frauen in der Familie, wenn jemand krank ist?
3. Warum tragen Brunnen zur Senkung der Kindersterblichkeit bei?
4. Wodurch verbessert sich der Stand von Frauen in der Gesellschaft?

6 A step further

a The 2030 Agenda for Sustainable Development aims at ending poverty worldwide. But in 2020, the Covid pandemic pushed another 8 million working people into poverty. More than four years of progress against poverty had been erased. Look at the statistic from 2021, then try and find figures for the following years. What is the trend now?

Percentage of working people worldwide living on less than $1.90 a day

2019	2020	2021
6.7	7.2	6.9

b In small groups, search the internet for information about NGOs and other organisations that tackle some of the causes of poverty. Each group member chooses a different organisation and takes notes on the most important aspects of the project. Consider the following issues.

no or unreliable electricity | drought | lack of healthcare facilities | illiteracy | limited access to financial services

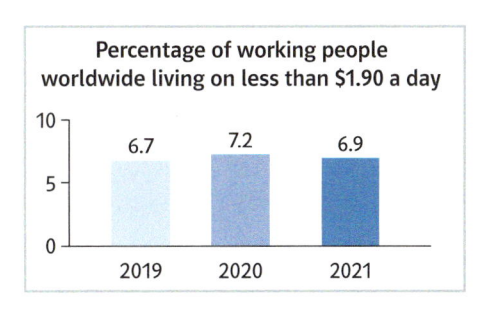

c Share your notes about the various projects in your group and agree on one project you like most.

d Present your project in class. Raise awareness for the issues it addresses and explain what makes your project special. → S 15 1-minute presentation

6 TEXT D

D Economic factors of migration

1 Before you read

a Look up the words in a monolingual dictionary and take notes on their meaning. → S 11.3

drought | famine | genocide | neediness | relocation | scarcity | persecution

b Reseach online to find factors that might drive people away from a location ('push') and factors that might draw people to a new location ('pull'). Make a list of these factors.

Debating Brain Drain, Part 1
by Gillian Brock

The basic needs of desperately poor people rightly command our normative attention. We are concerned not only about the fact that there is poverty and unmet need **1**, but also the scale of this neediness – so many in the world lack the basic necessities for a decent life. Some of these widespread, severe deprivations include lack of food, clean water, **2**, primary education, basic security, infrastructure, and an environment that can sustain and ensure secure access to these goods and services. An important part of enjoying the basic goods and services necessary **3** is the availability of skilled personnel able to provide these. Here there are severe shortages, especially in developing countries where needs are gravest. For instance, about 2 million more teachers and 4.25 million more health workers are needed to supply basic health and education for all. These shortages are exacerbated by high numbers of skilled personnel departing developing countries and seeking better prospects for themselves **4**. What, if anything, may developing countries defensibly do to stem the flow? This is the central question that orients my work in this book.

Before I can explain my approach to answering this question, further background is necessary. As noted, fueling the shortage of skilled personnel is the very high rate of emigration among those with the necessary skills, a problem commonly referred to as "brain drain." Though brain drain occurs in most sectors, brain drain among health professionals is particularly widespread **5**. These countries typically have poor health care resources anyhow, so the loss of trained healthcare workers is felt even more than it might be in places that are better resourced. In some cases, the departure of healthcare workers from developing countries threatens the viability of the healthcare systems in those countries, **6**.

Skilled workers often have good reasons for wanting to leave poor countries of origin. Inadequate remuneration, bad working conditions, lack of professional development opportunities, lack of security, and lack of funding are important factors in their decision to leave. Developed countries frequently appear to offer better pay and working conditions, or career and training opportunities that are not available in developing ones. Departure seems to be an entirely rational decision under such circumstances. Skilled workers, like everyone else, should have the right to exit countries in which

---

7 **unmet** unerfüllt
8 **neediness** Bedürftigkeit
9 **necessity** Notwendigkeit
10 **severe** ernst; schlimm
10 **deprivation** Entbehrung
14 **to sustain** erhalten; fortsetzen
21 **grave** gravierend; riesig
25 **to exacerbate** verschärfen; verschlimmern
30 **to stem the flow** sich dem Strom entgegenstemmen
35 **to fuel** anheizen; vorantreiben
47 **resourced** ausgestattet
50 **viability** Durchführbarkeit
54 **remuneration** Bezahlung

124

they no longer wish to live. But there are normative questions about citizens' responsibilities, fair terms of exit, and whether migration should be managed to ensure the burden of migration does not fall disproportionately on the world's worst off, so that those who benefit from movement across borders do not also impose impermissible severe losses on those who suffer disadvantage because of that movement.

As we discuss, these losses sometimes include significant reduction in educational and health services, poor health and educational attainment, public funds wasted on expensive tertiary training which does not benefit citizens, fiscal losses, and – more generally – loss of assets required for beneficial development. As I also discuss, there are various ways to ensure that movements work well for all significant stakeholders, but one such way, for which I argue, is that developing countries may permissibly tax citizens who depart under certain conditions. I also argue that they may reasonably expect citizens with relevant skills to assist fellow citizens for a short period of compulsory service under certain important conditions.

Compulsory service and taxation are two kinds of measures that developing countries may take to help reduce poverty in their countries.

While there has been considerable normative theorizing on the topic of immigration, most analyses have focused on the relation between the migrant or prospective migrant and the society she will join – issues of admission, accommodation, integration, and so forth. By contrast, in this work I focus on the more neglected relationship between the migrant and the society she will leave, and the normative implications of her departure. […] (666 words)

Sidebar vocabulary:
- 72 **disproportionate** unverhältnismäßig
- 75 **impermissible** unzulässig
- 81 **attainment** Leistung; Errungenschaft
- 84 **fiscal** steuerlich
- 85 **asset** Vermögen
- 88 **stakeholder** Interessenvertreter/-in
- 97 **taxation** Besteuerung
- 102 **to theorize** theoretisieren

2 Multiple matching → WB p. 62/1–3

Eight phrases have been cut from the text. Match the most suitable phrases (A–G) with the gaps (1–6) There are two phrases more than you need.

- **A** in developed ones
- **B** in the world today
- **C** especially in sub-Saharan Africa
- **D** underprivileged people
- **E** basic healthcare
- **F** in other job areas
- **G** for a decent life
- **H** and damaging for developing countries

3 Short-answer questions

Answer the following questions about lines 52–112. You may use words from the text.

1. Which other two words for 'salary' does the author use?
2. What advantages await healthcare professionals in developed countries?
3. What noun does the author use to describe a person who has a special interest in an issue?
4. Who does the author think should pay special taxes to support developing countries?
5. Which outcome does the author hope for from compulsory service?
6. Which aspect of migration does the author pay special attention to?

6 TEXT D

4 Multiple choice

Choose the most suitable option.

1. The author is not only concerned about poverty but also about …
   A widespread diseases.
   B the extent of neediness in the world.
   C protecting the environment.
   D creating new jobs.

2. If skilled workers aren't available, …
   A basic goods and services can't be provided.
   B new ones can be trained.
   C they have to be hired from other countries..
   D migration increases.

3. Which of these words is not a synonym for 'exacerbate'?
   A aggravate
   B provoke
   C intensify
   D improve

4. If a lot of healthcare workers leave a country, …
   A the healthcare system will remain stable.
   B the healthcare system develops more quickly.
   C the healthcare system could collapse.
   D the healthcare system has more room for new ones.

5. Which shortage does the author not address?
   A teachers
   B basic security
   C sanitation workers
   D skilled personnel

6. Which is a major reason for skilled personnel leaving developing countries?
   A too much competition
   B looking for better opportunities
   C education is unavailable
   D environmental concerns

5 A step further

a Research online for different examples of economic migration. You may look at economic migration to the US or to Europe. Then choose one example and find more information about it. Make sure you answer these important questions using different sources.

1. Who are/were the people migrating?
2. What caused them to migrate?
3. When did it happen?
4. Where did they migrate to?

b Prepare a short presentation with your findings from a. Choose one visual for your presentation: a picture, a cartoon, an object, a diagram.

c Share your presentation in class. → S15 1-minute presentation

d In class, discuss who profits from economic migration.

Different forms of citizenship → S 6.1 → S 10.2 → S 10.3

Every person is a citizen of the world and of a country. However, different factors make people feel more or less connected to their national or global identity. Write a composition discussing different attitudes of people towards their country and how they might be influenced by globalisation.

Write at least 300 words using all the material provided.

Material 1

"I like this slogan, it appeals to the customers' patriotism. Now we've got to find a way to explain why 95 % of your products are made in China."

Material 2
Most Patriotic Countries 2022

Country	% of People Thinking Their Country is the Best	2022 Population
United States	41.00 %	338,289,857
India	36.00 %	1,417,173,173
Australia	34.00 %	26,177,413
United Arab Emirates	27.00 %	9,441,129
Thailand	25.00 %	71,697,030
Saudi Arabia	25.00 %	36,408,820
Philippines	15.00 %	115,559,009
Indonesia	14.00 %	275,501,339
GB	13.00 %	67,508,936
…		
Germany	5.00 %	83,369,843

Source: YouGov plc. 2016

Material 3

Zwischen McWorld und Tribalismus

Unter Globalisierung der Kultur verstehen vor allem Globalisierungskritiker/innen eine Ausbreitung westlicher Wertvorstellungen und Lebensstile. Eine massive Verbreitung westlicher Werte findet vor allem über das Fernsehen und das Kino statt, aber auch Musik (MTV) und Mode (wie zum Beispiel die Krawatte) sowie die westliche Unternehmenskultur breiten sich weltweit aus – so die Sorge vieler. Neben der medialen Globalisierung trägt der Massentourismus in vielen Regionen – so eine weitere Befürchtung – zum Rückgang der lokalen kulturellen Traditionen bei, weil im Zuge einer wachsenden Abhängigkeit fast nur noch für die Touristen gelebt und gearbeitet werde. Befürworter/innen sehen in der Globalisierung eine Entwicklung zur weltweiten Verfügbarkeit von Elementen aller Kulturen (beispielsweise Restaurants deutscher Tradition in Afrika, afrikanische Musik in Deutschland, etc.). Die Verdrängung der einheimischen Kulturen spiele sich, sagen sie, häufig nur auf einer oberflächlichen Ebene ab. Einflüsse würden modifiziert und in die eigenen kulturellen Wertvorstellungen eingebunden. Außerdem verbessere sich die Situation von vielen Menschen bzw. Menschengruppen durch den Kontakt mit der westlichen Kultur (zum Beispiel Gleichberechtigung der Frau). Bislang lassen sich zwei gegenläufige Trends beobachten: das Phänomenen der kulturellen Vereinheitlichung einerseits, als auch eine neue Blüte regionaler Identitäten und Kulturen andererseits.

6 MEDIATION

Attracting foreign workers → S 6.1 → WB p. 63/1

Verfassen Sie einen zusammenhängenden englischen Text (ca. 150 Wörter) im Rahmen eines Projekts zum Thema Willkommenskultur an Ihrer Schule. Gehen Sie dabei auf folgende Aspekte ein:

1. Welche deutschen Verhaltensmuster sind für die ausländischen Fachkräfte befremdlich?
2. Warum kann es sich die deutsche Wirtschaft nicht leisten, die Kritik an der Willkommenskultur zu ignorieren?
3. Wie können kulturelle Hürden abgebaut werden?

Wenn die Griechin einlädt und kein einziger deutscher Kollege kommt

Deutsche Unternehmen sind zunehmend auf qualifizierte Fachkräfte aus dem Ausland angewiesen. Doch der internationale Vergleich offenbart, dass Neuankömmlingen die Eingewöhnung hierzulande besonders schwer gemacht wird.
Maria-Anastasia Andri ist in ihrem Leben schon öfter umgezogen. Aus ihrer Heimatstadt Athen ging es für die Griechin vor einigen Jahren nach Turin. Inzwischen ist sie in Bayern angekommen: […] Zu Beginn gab sie sich viel Mühe, ihre Kollegen besser kennenzulernen. Sie lud sie zu sich nach Hause ein und bereitete griechisches Essen vor – doch niemand aus dem Büro kam.
Beim Start in Italien sei das ganz anders gewesen: „Fast alle, die ich eingeladen habe, sind gekommen […]." Umso ernüchternder war dann die Erfahrung in Deutschland. Für die 35-Jährige ist inzwischen klar: „Die Deutschen brauchen viel Zeit, um andere Menschen zu integrieren und in ihren Freundeskreis aufzunehmen – wenn sie es denn überhaupt tun."
Wie schwer das Einleben in Deutschland für ausländische Fachkräfte ist, bestätigt die neue Ausgabe der regelmäßigen […] Umfrage […] unter rund 20.000 im Ausland arbeitenden Menschen. In der Kategorie „Eingewöhnung" landet Deutschland nur auf Platz 60 von 64. […]
Die Mängelliste ist lang: Mit der Kultur zurechtzukommen sei schwierig, die Deutschen seien „ganz versessen auf Regeln", bestätigt ein Befragter aus Malaysia ein gängiges Klischee. Wenn man die deutsche Sprache nicht sehr gut beherrsche, habe man fast keine Chance, ein persönliches Netzwerk aufzubauen, schreibt ein Ungar. Und ein Mexikaner kritisiert: „Die Deutschen sind Ausländern gegenüber nicht wirklich aufgeschlossen. Sie sagen zwar, dass sie diese integrieren möchten, aber meistens geschieht es dann doch nicht."
So altbekannt diese Kritik auch klingen mag: Sie vorschnell abzutun wird immer mehr zum Risiko. Denn der Bedarf an Fachkräften […] steigt immer weiter. Der Arbeitsmarktreport des Deutschen Industrie- und Handelskammertags (DIHK) aus diesem Jahr zeigt, dass rund die Hälfte der 23.000 befragten Unternehmen offene Stellen längerfristig nicht besetzen kann, weil sie keine passenden Kandidaten findet.
[…] Der Wettbewerb verschärft sich also; bei Gewinnung und Haltung von ausländischen Fachkräften gewinnen neben dem Gehalt weiche Faktoren an Relevanz. Diese Erfahrung hat auch Sabine Mesletzky gemacht. Sie ist bei der Industrie- und Handelskammer (IHK) Koblenz zuständig für den Bereich Fachkräftesicherung. „Vor wenigen Jahren haben ausländische Fachkräfte in den Belegschaften kaum eine Rolle gespielt", sagt sie. „Heute setzen 50 Prozent der

Unternehmen in Rheinland-Pfalz auf diese Zielgruppe." Immer stärker gehe es dabei um Menschen aus Nicht-EU-Ländern. Entsprechend größer sind die kulturellen Hürden.

„Da prallen oft Welten aufeinander", sagt die IHK-Expertin. „Pünktlichkeit und Eigenverantwortung sind teilweise unausgesprochene Regeln, die sich nicht auf den ersten Blick erschließen und bewusst angesprochen werden müssen", sagt sie. Das Thema Willkommenskultur spiele deshalb eine immer größere Rolle. „Deutschland gilt ja meist als streng und bürokratisch", sagt Mesletzky. „Daran zu arbeiten wurde jahrelang vernachlässigt. Wenn wir das aber tun, ist es eine riesige Chance für die Wirtschaft." [...]

(461 Wörter)
Christine Haas, *WELT*, 2019

Community volunteering

Your school has an annual 'Global Village Week' This year one of the proposed ideas is to have a community-wide day of volunteering during that week. The short-term goal of the day is that different people and different groups come in contact with each other by working together. The long term goal is that groups are formed that continue volunteering together in the future.

The following volunteer projects have been suggested:

1. Going to schools and reading to young children in different languages
2. Cooking ethnic foods together and distributing the food to homeless people
3. Offering professional support and advice (translating, tax preparation, legal issues, …) to people with language difficulties
4. Leading walking tours for new citizens through different parts of the city
5. Organising an exercise group for immigrant women

a Choose one of the suggested volunteer projects and explain why you think it's the best one for involving different people from your community (about 1 minute).

b Discuss the following questions:
   1. What are the benefits of the different volunteer projects and which project would be most beneficial to your community?
   2. What role should your school play?
   3. How many projects are feasible in one day?
   4. How could you organise the projects? Who would be involved?

c Agree on one project that you will do on the day of volunteering.

SKILLS FILES

S1	**Communication skills**	**S1.1**	Mastering communication situations	131
		S1.2	Giving a talk or presentation	
S2	**Group discussion**	**S2**	Preparing and having a discussion	135
S3	**Listening skills**	**S3**	Dealing with listening tasks	136
S4	**Reading skills**	**S4.1**	Mixed reading tasks	136
		S4.2	Reading techniques	
S5	**Writing skills**	**S5.1**	Dealing with writing tasks	139
		S5.2	Improve your writing	
S6	**Writing specific text types**	**S6.1**	Mediation German – English	140
		S6.2	Materials-based writing: Writing a composition	
		S6.3	Writing a comment	
		S6.4	Writing a blog post	
		S6.5	Writing an email	
		S6.6	Creating an information sheet	
		S6.7	Writing a story	
S7	**Analysing language**	**S7.1**	Stylistic devices	147
		S7.2	Style, tone and register	
S8	**Analysing fictional texts**	**S8.1**	Fictional text types	148
		S8.2	Analysing novels and short stories	
		S8.3	Narrative perspectives	
		S8.4	Narrative techniques	
		S8.5	Characterisation	
S9	**Analysing non-fictional texts**	**S9.1**	Non-fictional text types	153
		S9.2	Structure of non-fictional texts	
		S9.3	Analysing argumentative texts	
		S9.4	Analysing newspaper articles	
S10	**Analysing and using visuals**	**S10.1**	Analysing and using pictures and paintings	156
		S10.2	Analysing and using cartoons	
		S10.3	Analysing and using diagrams and statistics	
S11	**Vocabulary skills**	**S11.1**	Expanding your vocabulary	158
		S11.2	Guessing unkown words	
		S11.3	Working with a dictionary	
S12	**Making a video**	**S12**	Preparing a video	162
S13	**Online research and checking sources**	**S13.1**	Checking sources	163
		S13.2	Citing sources	
		S13.3	Quoting	
S14	**Preparing for an exam**	**S14**	Dealing with exam tasks	165
S15	**Cooperative learning**	**S15**	Methods	165

S1 Communication skills

S1.1 Mastering communication situations

Language has a huge variety of functions to offer: you can use it to make small talk, to have heated discussions, to write personal or business correspondence, to give instructions, to express feelings etc. The following phrases will help you to master key communication situations like these:

EXPRESSING OPINIONS

Stating your opinion
The point is … | Wouldn't you say that …? | If you ask me … | As I see it … | It seems to me that … | As far as I understand … | As far as I'm concerned … | In my opinion … | I am of the opinion that … | I take the view that … | From my point of view … | To my mind … | I would like to emphasise that … | I would like to mention/say that … | I'd like to point out that … | I strongly believe that … | I'm sure/convinced/certain that … | It is obvious that … | Obviously/Without a doubt, it is wrong/right to say that … | I reject the idea that … | It is completely/absolutely/totally wrong to argue that …

Expressing probability/predicting
Definitely: Of course, it'll … | It's going to … | There's no question that … | It's sure to say … | It's bound to …
Probably: It'll probably … | I expect it to … | I wouldn't be surprised if … | I bet it'll …
Perhaps: I guess it might … | There's a chance it'll …
Probably not: I doubt (if) it'll … | I don't think it'll …
Definitely not: Of course it won't … | There's no chance of it …-ing. | I'm absolutely sure it won't …

Emphasising
definitely | extremely | indeed | absolutely | positively | obviously | naturally | always | never | without a doubt | certainly

DISCUSSING

Persuading/objecting
That's a good idea, but … | That might be OK, but … | I really don't think so because … | Why don't you …? | I see what you mean, but … | That's true, but …

Giving reasons
because | since | therefore | consequently | accordingly | As there are … | As a result of … | Due to … | Because of …

Giving examples
for example | for instance | in another case | take the case of | to illustrate | as an illustration | to take another example | as shown by … | as illustrated by … | as expressed by …

Agreeing and disagreeing
Exactly. | I couldn't agree more. | That's just what I was thinking. | That's a good point. | I see where you're coming from, but … | I'm not sure if I agree … | Maybe, but don't you think that …?

Comparing and contrasting
Comparing: also | as well as | both | comparatively | in the same way | just as | like | similarly
Contrasting: although | besides | but | compared with | even though | however | in contrast to | instead | nevertheless | on the other hand | rather than | yet

Balancing pros and cons
On the one hand …, on the other hand … | although | however | We shouldn't forget that … | In contrast to … | On the contrary … | Weighing up the pros and cons …

STRUCTURING

Sequencing/structuring
I'm going to … | I would like to talk about … | I would like to point out/mention … | To begin with … | Now I want to describe … | There are three things to consider: Firstly … Secondly … Thirdly … | Finally …

Summarising/drawing a conclusion
All things considered … | Taking everything into account … | Briefly … | On the whole … | In short … | Finally … | That's why … | For this reason/these reasons … | Therefore … | As a result … | Consequently …

SKILLS FILES

HANDLING CONVERSATIONS

Speaking politely
Could you please …? | Would you …? | May I …? | Maybe you could …? | I was wondering if …? | Excuse me, could you …? | Thank you.

Getting more information
Could you tell me some more about …? | Would you mind telling me more about …? | I'd like to know more about … | Something else I was wondering about was …

Hesitating
Um … | Well … | Well, let's see now … | You see … | You know … | The thing is … | How can I put it?

Repeating
As I have (already) said … | As I have pointed out / mentioned …

Checking understanding
OK so far? | Are you with me? | Is that clear? | Do you see what I mean?

Interrupting politely
If I could just come in here … | Sorry to interrupt, but … | The way I see it … | Um … (repeat until the speaker lets you speak)

Preventing and handling interruptions
There are three points I'd like to make clear … | Could I just finish my point? As I was saying …

MAKING SMALL TALK

Introducing oneself/introducing others
Hi, I'm … | Let me introduce myself … | I don't think we've met. My name is … | I'd like to introduce myself. My name's … | Nice to meet you. | It's a pleasure to meet you. | I'd like you to meet someone. This is … | I'd like to introduce you to … | There's someone I'd like you to meet …

Saying goodbye/closing
That's it for today. | That's all for now. | Bye for now! | Thanks for …

Talking about likes and dislikes
What I like doing is … | I really/especially/particularly like …-ing | One of my biggest hobbies is …-ing. | My favourite pastime is …-ing. | What I really dislike is … | What I am really not a fan of is …-ing. | I just hate …-ing.

ASKING FOR UND GIVING HELP

Asking questions
I was wondering if you could help me. I'd like to know … | I wonder if you could tell me … | Excuse me, do you know …? | I'm sorry to bother you, but … | There's something you could help me with.

Asking for advice
What do you suggest/recommend? | What should I do? | What would you do if you were me?

Making suggestions/giving advice
I was wondering if you have ever thought of … | I think it might be a good idea to … | Have you ever thought of …? | Don't you think it might be a good idea to …? | If I were you I'd perhaps … | Why don't you …?

Asking for a favour
Would/Could you do me a favour? | Would you mind …-ing …? | May I …? | Could you please …?

Asking for permission
May I …? | Can I …? | Could I perhaps …? | Do you mind if I …? | Is it okay if …?

Refusing to help
I'm sorry, but … | I'd like to, but … | I'd really like to help you, but …

EXPRESSING FEELINGS

Apologising
I'm sorry for … | I'm sorry that … | I would like to apologise for … | Please accept my apologies. | It was my fault.

Thanking
Thanks a lot. | Thank you for … | That's very kind of you. | You're welcome. / My pleasure. (when someone thanks you)

SKILLS FILES

S 1.2 Giving a talk or presentation

The key to giving a good talk or presentation is to prepare well in advance. Think of a good structure for your talk or presentation and prepare prompt cards with keywords. Then you'll be ready to go!

A Preparing a talk or presentation

4 Prepare your introduction and conclusion
- Catch the listener's attention by starting with an interesting question or fact, a quote, a picture or a cartoon.
- Write a prompt card featuring your main points so you can give a brief outline of your talk or presentation at the beginning.
- Choose a final quote or example you'd like to use.
- Make a prompt card with the points you want to emphasise or summarise again.

3 Arrange your prompt cards in a logical order
Choose how you want to present your points:
- chronologically (presenting a person or historical events)
- contrasting (comparing different approaches or arguments)
- from least important to most important or vice versa (arguing for or against something)

2 Choose the points you want to talk about and make prompt cards
- Choose three main points or arguments for the main part of your talk/presentation.
- Prepare a prompt card with keywords and useful phrases for each part of your talk or presentation.
- Note down any examples or quotations.

1 Gather material on your topic
- Brainstorm ideas and organise them in a word web.
- Do research and collect information from relevant sources (online, library, newspapers, …).

---

1 Introduction
– *note down main points of talk*
– *keywords for initial joke / quote / example…*
– *note useful phrases*

4 Main point 3

3 Main point 2

2 Main point 1
– *one argument / point per card*
– *note keywords*
– *note useful phrases*

5 Conclusion
– *note down main points of talk*
– *keywords for final quote / example*
– *note useful phrases*

SKILLS FILES

Before your talk
- Practise your talk or presentation out loud in front of a mirror.
- Ask a friend/relative to listen to you and give feedback.
- Prepare a handout for your audience which briefly lists your main points or arguments.
- Use keywords and make sure you include your sources on the handout.
- Test any equipment you need (laptop/tablet/projector/speakers …) as early as possible.

B Speaking in front of other people

Follow these Dos to make your talk or presentation as successful as possible for both you and your audience:

👍 Dos for giving a talk or presentation

- Speak slowly and clearly.
- Use short, clear sentences.
- Use vocabulary that is known to your audience.
- Explain unknown terms or phrases.
- Vary your intonation so that you don't sound boring.
- For example, you could emphasise particularly important points by speaking a little more loudly.
- Look at your audience as often as possible and speak freely.
- Smile! (But don't laugh nervously!)
- Start by introducing yourself (if necessary) and your topic.
- Finish by thanking your audience for listening and asking if anyone has any questions.

USEFUL PHRASES

Introduction
Good morning/afternoon, (my name is …).|
My topic today is … /The title of my talk today is: …|
In my presentation today I want to talk about …|
I will begin by explaining/describing … and continue with … Finally, I will …

Main part/structuring ideas
Have you ever thought about …|
Did you know that …?|
I would like to cover three aspects in my talk: …
First of all … /Secondly … /Finally …|
Moving on to the next point, I would like to talk about …|
For this reason/Therefore, we can assume that …

Examples/quotes
In the words of … (name of person) "…" (quote).|
This example proves that …|
X once said that … /According to X …

Commenting on visuals
As we can see from the cartoon/photo …|
The statistics clearly show that a minority/a majority of …

Conclusion
I think we can safely say that …|
So in conclusion, I would like to sum up by …|
Thank you for listening. Are there any questions?

134

SKILLS FILES

S2 Group discussion

Preparing and having a discussion

The group discussion is the oral part of your exam. In small groups, you are going to discuss a given topic.

Preparation (exam – 20 minutes)	– Read the situation for the discussion and the tasks very carefully. – Look at the given material and make sure you understand it and are able to present and use it for your arguments. – Prepare arguments and aspects you would like to include in the discussion. – Note down single items only, no complete sentences. – Make a list of useful words and phrases. Use a dictionary. – Look up all the words you do not know. You can use a bilingual dictionary. – Sometimes you are asked to rank the provided material.
Introduction (exam – maximum one minute each)	Each student presents his/her point of view/proposal: – Do not interrupt each other or ask questions. – You may take notes while the others are talking. – Look at each other – not at your notes. – Use connecting words.
Discussion	– Defend your opinion, but stay polite and respectful towards the other participants. – Refer to the others' arguments when introducing a new argument. – Turn towards the others when referring to their argument or while they are talking. – Show that you are confident, but also interested in the others' arguments and their opinion. – Use the discussion phrases. – Help others, listen attentively to others. – Do not give up your idea/proposal/point of view too early. – Do not interrupt unless you feel it is really necessary. – Keep to the point. – Be open to compromise towards the end, especially if the task asks for a consensus. – Try to mediate between the others.
Exam (the end)	Exam (the end) – Give a final statement. – Summarise./Come to a conclusion. – Try to find a compromise/solution everyone is happy with. – It is also OK not to agree with each other at the end. – Look into the future – which steps are to be taken next? – Say how satisfied you are with the whole discussion. – You can state which 1–2 arguments/ideas of the others impressed/convinced you the most.

USEFUL PHRASES

Introducing the topic
(As you know,) Our discussion today is about … | Who'd like to start? | I'm going to start.

Structuring a talk
I'm going to look at … | I'd like to talk about/point out/mention … | There are three things to consider. Firstly … Secondly … Thirdly … | One point is … Another aspect is … | To begin with … | Now I want to describe … | Finally I'd like to …

Getting more information
Could you tell me more about …? | I'd like to know more about … | Something else I was wondering about was …

Agreeing and disagreeing
Exactly. I couldn't agree more. | That's just what I was thinking. | That's a good point. | I see what you mean, but isn't it also true that …? | I'm not sure if I agree with you about …

Asking questions
What I'd like to know is who/what …? | Why do you think that …? | Could you explain what you mean by …?

Checking that someone has understood you
Are you with me? | Do you see what I mean?

Hesitating
Well, let me see now … | How can I put it?

Interrupting/Being interrupted
I'm sorry to interrupt you, but … | Could I just finish my point? As I was saying …

SKILLS FILES

S 3 Listening skills

Dealing with listening tasks

Listening tasks assess your listening comprehension, which is your ability to listen to and understand what someone is saying.

In everyday life, pure listening situations are limited to radio programmes, podcasts, radio plays and audiobooks. Before you listen or watch, read through the assignments. It is often possible to predict what the speakers are going to talk about.

While listening, follow these steps:

Listening for the 1st time
- focus on the general topic
- get the overall picture
- identify the main points

Listening for the 2nd time
- concentrate on specific details and relevant information

As with all comprehension situations, it is important to first look out for keywords (e.g. names, times, numbers, places) and try to find out about the context (speakers, their situation and the type of conversation they are having).

Listen to English-speaking people as often as possible:
- The internet is a great source of free audio and video materials in English. Listen to audio clips or watch videos a couple of times. For video clips, turn on the subtitles if they are available.
- If you find an interesting online article, use a text-to-speech reader. Copy the article into the reader and have it read out loud to you.
- Listen to audiobooks.

S 4 Reading skills

In order to improve your reading skills, read as much as possible. Focus on aspects you find interesting, from football news to the latest film and fashion gossip – make reading a discovery.
While reading, be patient with yourself. Try not to read word for word, but instead focus on longer paragraphs. It is often enough just to get the basic idea of a paragraph.
In the long run, make a habit of reading English texts. Maybe checking an English news site every day/week might be a good start?

S 4.1 Mixed reading tasks

Reading tasks usually follow these three stages of the reading process:

- pre-reading
- while-reading
- post-reading

Pre-reading
Before you start reading, ask yourself the following questions:
– What will the text be about?
– What does the title reveal?
– Are there any subheadings or highlighted quotes?
– What kind of text is it?
– When was it published?
– Are there any pictures/diagrams?

While-reading
– Read the assignments first. Find out what type of information you are looking for and then choose the appropriate reading technique.
– Highlight the main ideas and make annotations. Marking and annotating a text helps you to focus while reading, as you are selecting and organising the most important information.

Post-reading
– Double-check your answers.
– You might be asked to do further tasks related to the text you have just read to make sure you have understood it correctly, e.g. looking at vocabulary or analysing characters.

Marking a text
Underline or highlight keywords, key phrases, examples etc. Use different styles:

- main ideas of the text
- key phrases
- author's opinion
- examples
- characterisation

Annotating a text
Make notes next to the text to help you find information quickly, e.g.
– defining vocabulary
– summarising/paraphrasing passages
– defining and understanding examples, quotes …
– identifying important moments in the plot
– commenting on characters

1 Multiple matching

– Read the complete text and try to get an overview of what it is about.
– Read the task carefully and find out whether you have to match
  – questions and answers,
  – people and statements,
  – paragraphs and headings,
  – beginnings and endings of sentences,
  – a gapped text and missing sentences.
– There are usually two separate lists of items to be matched.
– Check with the help of your dictionary that you have thoroughly understood all the options.
– There are usually more options than needed.
– Match the correct options to the appropriate items.
– Mark the options you have already used to save time.
– Check your results thoroughly and make changes where necessary.

SKILLS FILES

2 Short-answer questions

This type of exercise contains …
- either short comprehension questions, which should be answered with words or with a phrase from the text, or incomplete sentences, which should be completed with words taken from the text,
- or questions, which should be answered in note-form (sometimes in a table, mind map etc.). The key words or phrases should be taken from the text, but need not be given in complete sentences.
- Important!
  If not otherwise stated, you don't have to use your own words in these answers. You only have to find the correct passage in the text and take the appropriate word or words from there.

3 Multiple choice

Remember
- Only one answer is correct from the four answers given in the examination question.
- Look for the best possible answer from all four alternatives.
- The distractors (the wrong answers) are often partly true.

- Try to get an overview of the text and the questions.
- Don't panic if the text seems too difficult at first.
- Read the tasks carefully.
- Read the text a second time to find the answers to the individual tasks and mark the appropriate passages in the text.
- Only use your dictionary when necessary (especially when you cannot understand part of the multiple-choice questions).
- Do the tasks chronologically (normally the tasks refer to the text in a chronological order).

When sitting an exam:
- Don't spend too much time on "difficult" tasks.
- When in doubt, have a guess at the right answer (you won't be punished for a wrong answer).

4 Gapped summary

Remember
In this type of exercise you are presented with a summary of (a part of) the text. This summary is incomplete as certain key words are missing. It is your task to restore the missing words, and this can only be accomplished if you have both read and understood the main ideas of the original text. Make sure you write down the line number where you found the missing word.

- Mark the passage the summary is about.
- Important! Only use the exact words from the text to fill the gaps. In exams, you will not get any points for using your own words.
- Lines (or blocks) in the gaps indicate how many words are needed.
- First check by looking at the context which type of word is expected (adjective, verb, noun).

5 Mediation: English – German

In this type of exercise you are asked to reproduce the contents of certain text passages in German.
- Often you have to find specific information from the text and list this information in key points.
- Sometimes you are asked to explain certain aspects of the text or explain idiomatic expressions.
- Important!
  Mediation does NOT mean translation! It usually refers to text passages where a literal ("word-by-word") translation does not make any sense.

S 4.2 Reading techniques

Skimming	– Read the title, the introduction or the first paragraph, the first sentence of every paragraph and any headings and sub-headings. – Note any pictures, charts or graphs. – Pay attention to any words or phrases in italics or bold print. – The last paragraphs in non-fictional texts (e.g. scientific research, newspaper articles) often summarise the main ideas of the text.
Scanning	– Scanning is reading in order to find specific information. – Decide what specific information you are looking for. Ignore unrelated information. – Look out for relevant key words. Stop when you find one and read that part of the text carefully. Make notes if necessary. – How is the information given in the text? If you need a date, only look at the numbers in the text. – Headings can help you to identify sections which might contain the information. – The first sentence in a paragraph should indicate whether the information you need could be there, or not. Do not read the text in detail.
Close reading / reading for detail	– If it is necessary to understand a text in detail, make sure you understand every word. – Look up unknown words in a dictionary and use the information you find on word category, register, collocation and usage to identify the word that best fits the context.

KWL: This technique is useful if you are reading a text to learn more about a certain topic.

Pre-reading
- **K** What I KNOW (What do I already know about the topic and the author?)
- **W** What I WANT to know (Why am I reading the text? What exactly do I want to find out?)

While-reading
- **L** What I have LEARNED (What are my findings?)

SQ3R:
- **S** SURVEY what you are asked to read. (What additional information about the text can I find if I survey the title, subheadings, images, charts …?)
- **Q** Ask yourself QUESTIONS about the text. (What exactly am I looking for?)
- **3R** READ the text and look for answers.
  RECITE what you have found out in your own words.
  REVIEW the text and your notes. (What am I going to do with my findings?)

S 5 Writing skills

S 5.1 Dealing with writing tasks

In order to improve the quality of your writing, consider following this step-by-step approach.

6. Proofread your text. Pay special attention to tenses, prepositions, word order and spelling.
5. Write a first draft of your text.
4. Your text should develop in a logical way. Use structuring devices and connectives. Pay attention to style and register.
3. Organise your ideas. Put your notes in a logical order and finalise them.
2. Brainstorm ideas and make notes on how to include the given material.
1. Make sure you understand the assignment.

SKILLS FILES

S 5.2 Improve your writing

Use connectives to make your writing more logical. They are used to illustrate a connection between certain aspects or ideas.

💡	Adding ideas	*moreover, besides, furthermore, in addition to that*
→→→	Sequencing	*first of all, to begin with, next, then, finally*
👍	Emphasising	*above all, in particular, especially, significantly, indeed*
=	Similarity	*in the same way, similarly, likewise*
🍒🍒🍒	Cause and effect	*therefore, thus, however, although, unless*
✍	Illustrating	*for example, for instance, as revealed by, in the case of, nevertheless, despite, in spite of, on the contrary*
◣	Contrasting	*instead of, alternatively, otherwise, unlike, on the one hand …, on the other hand*
Σ	Conclusion	*In conclusion …, Therefore …, All in all …, To sum up …*

> **Proofreading**
> Before finalising your text, check it according to the following categories:
> – spelling mistakes   – sentence structure
> – use of tenses   – style and register

S 6 Writing specific text types

For each text type, you need to consider the typical structure, contents, purposes and writing style.

S 6.1 Mediation German – English

In the exam, your task is to write a coherent text in English of about 150 words. You will be given one or two German texts.
Your English text should be a summary comprising the required aspects of the German text.
You will be presented with a situation (*Für ein Referat zum Thema X bereiten Sie eine Übersicht vor …*) and a list of aspects your text must include (*Nennen Sie drei Gründe für …, Welche Bedenken nennt …*).

1 Before you write

- Read the instructions and the German text carefully.
- Find the relevant parts. It can help if you highlight or underline the different aspects with different colours. Remember that the instructions do not always present what is required in the same order as the text.
- Check how the different aspects are related. Are the points in a temporal sequence? Is one a condition or a consequence of another? Are some points examples for others?

2 While you write

- Focus on the essential parts and aspects and do not add any extra or irrelevant information.
- Mediate the contents and avoid translating. Mediation is not a word-by-word translation. In fact, often the German texts will use words or idiomatic expressions that are very difficult or even impossible to translate directly. You need to understand what the German text wants to say and then find a way of expressing this point in English. If you have problems finding the

right English words, try to paraphrase the required aspect in German. This might give you an idea how to paraphrase it in English.
- Use connectives and linking phrases (see the list of linking phrases in S 5.2) to make your text coherent. Make sure it follows the logic of the German original.
- Be precise and concise. Mediation is about efficient and focused communication.

3 After writing

- Check that you have included all necessary aspects
- Make sure your grammar and spelling are correct.

S 6.2 Material-based writing: Writing a composition

In a written exam, you will have to write a composition about a certain topic. You will usually have to deal with a controversial issue, including your own thoughts, your previous knowledge and information from up to three materials. At the end you draw a conclusion.

1 Preparation

- Define the topic clearly.
- Brainstorm ideas. Write down what you know about the topic in a mind map, table or list.
- If necessary, collect facts, arguments, statistics and other information from sources, e. g. your library or the Internet.
- Formulate your opinion on the topic.

2 Arranging your material

- Decide on the most important facts, arguments or pieces of information that you want to include in your composition (maximum 5 items).
- Look at the material and decide how it can help you with your arguments. Don't analyse or quote it, just consider the content.
- For each main argument try to think of two supporting arguments.
- Put your facts or arguments in a logical order. For example, you could:
  - start with general ideas and then go on to talk about details.
  - put things into chronological order.
  - start by giving all the arguments in favour and then give all the counter-arguments.
  - follow each argument in favour with a counter-argument.

3 Writing your composition

The introduction
- The introductory paragraph should introduce your topic and catch the reader's interest. You could:
  - give a relevant quotation.
  - make a provocative statement.
  - describe a relevant (humorous) personal experience.
- In your introductory paragraph you should also:
  - say clearly what your composition is going to be about in one or two sentences.
  - ask a question or questions which you will answer in your composition.
  - give a brief outline of the problem/topic at present and in the past.
- Don't forget the topic sentence at the end of the introduction.

The main part
- Start a new paragraph for each new idea and begin it with a main idea or argument. Follow it up with your supporting or counterarguments (examples, statistics, personal experience etc.).
- Arrange sentences in a logical order and join them using suitable connectives.
- Use adverbs to emphasise points and examples where possible.

The conclusion
- Do not introduce new ideas!
- Make a brief concluding statement summarising what you have written in your composition.
- You may: give an outlook on further consequences / future developments / possible solutions; state your own opinion / give a recommendation or appeal to the readers to reach their own conclusion.

SKILLS FILES

4 Checking your composition

- Check that all your sentences are complete and that they make sense.
- Check your composition for grammar, spelling and punctuation mistakes. (Tip: Leave it overnight before checking.)
- Write or print out the final version of your composition.

5 Writing a model composition

USEFUL PHRASES

Presenting aspects and examples
… consists of (two) aspects. | It is a … rather than a … problem/issue. | … should also be considered/mentioned. | … is relevant/completely irrelevant to … | There are various reasons why … | This also raises questions about … | Some researchers say … / Studies show … | Proponents/Opponents say/point out …

Referring to someone's statement/theory/opinion (in a text)
The author believes/states/suggests/claims that … | The author holds the view/is of the opinion that … | The author argues/demands that … | According to the text, the problem is that … | Recently, there has been a debate on how to …

Expressing your criticism (in general)
Whereas the author thinks that … I feel very different about … | Unlike the author, I find it hard to believe that … | Contrary to the speaker, I am doubtful whether … | To be quite honest, I do not think that / I cannot (fully) agree with … / I am not convinced by … / I would like to question the view that … / I reject the idea that … | In my opinion/view this argument is wrong/weak/unconvincing because … | … the author ignores a fact/forgets to mention sth / is not aware of sth / focuses too much on sth / does not realise that …

Expressing your support (in general)
The author is absolutely right in saying that … | I do not think anyone would disagree with the author's statement that … | The speaker has my full support when he argues that … | In fact/As a matter of fact, I believe it is fully justified to say that … | I agree entirely with the speaker saying that … | I am of exactly the same opinion as … | I share the view that … | To my mind, … | this argument is very strong/powerful/convincing/plausible | the author presents convincing arguments/discusses the topic in detail/ | the author's argumentation is thoroughly convincing/logical

Making concessions
To a certain extent, I can accept … | However, we shouldn't forget that … | Most of the arguments are hard to dismiss. | Yet there are experts who … | I agree in principle, but … |
Although …, we should accept/must admit that … |
In spite of all this, … | Admittedly, …, but …

Giving arguments/reasons
One reason for my criticism/scepticism is that … | Another / A second / A further / An additional argument I would like to present is that … | I would also argue that … | Another point I would like to make is that … | The main reason, however, is that … | The most convincing argument is that … | That brings me neatly to my final and most important point: …

Your conclusion/summary
To sum up, … | In short, … | Considering all these arguments, … | I would conclude that … | I have come to the conclusion that … | It is safe to say that … | I would support the view that … | My suggestion is that … | My appeal to … is: … | In conclusion … | Having weighed up all the arguments, I would like to conclude with a quote: "…"

S 6.3 Writing a comment

In a comment you also deal with a controversial issue, a quote or a statement and give your personal opinion about it.

Structure your comment as follows:

Introduction
- Define the problem or topic.
- Get the reader's attention.
- Clearly state your opinion.

Main part
- Give reasons for your opinion.
- Support arguments with examples.
- Use connectives.

Conclusion
- Summarise the best argument.
- Restate your opinion.
- Give an outlook.

- Before writing, read the quote or statement carefully and decide if you agree or disagree.
- Start with the weakest argument and end with the strongest.
- Write your comment in the simple present.
- When writing a comment on a computer, run the spelling and grammar checker.

USEFUL PHRASES

Giving examples
for example | for instance | in another case | take the case of | to illustrate | as shown/expressed by …

Referring to a point already made
As I have already said/noted | as suggested above …

Emphasising your statements
definitely | indeed | extremely | absolutely | positively …

Balancing pros and cons
On the one hand …, on the other hand … | although | however | We shouldn't forget that … | In contrast to … | On the contrary … | Weighing up the pros and cons …

Drawing a conclusion
That's why … | For this reason / these reasons | therefore | as a result | consequently | Taking everything into account … | The arguments seem to indicate that … | It is clear therefore that … | Thus it could be concluded that … | The evidence seems to be strong that …

S 6.4 Writing a blog post

A well-structured blog post will catch the readers' attention and make them want to read on.

BLOG

Choose an interesting, eye-catching headline

- Put the main point you are writing about in the first paragraph.
- All further details, explanations, examples etc. can go in the following paragraphs.
- It is always a good idea to end with a kind of conclusion, i.e. a final thought that summarises your main ideas.
- Try to write in a friendly and informal style.
- Always be polite and respectful of other cultures and opinions.
- Use the first person 'I' and try to include examples/anecdotes from your own experience.
- Think about your readers and what they might want to learn from what you are telling them.
- Use phrases and expressions that are suitable for expressing your opinion in a clear way.
- It might even be a good idea to directly invite your readers to join the discussion.
- In some blog posts it is common to add your username and the date of your post.

Never
include links to commercial sites or resources.
include links to inappropriate material.
give specific names, places, addresses or contact details.

SKILLS FILES

S 6.5 Writing an email

A great deal of today's communication is done via email. Formal emails are written in a polite and formal style. Therefore, use suitable forms of politeness and appropriate modal verbs.
Make sure that your salutation and complimentary close corresponds with your relationship with the person you are writing to. Depending on the topic you are writing about, you will need to use technical terms too.
Formal emails contain a salutation, a subject line, a complimentary close and the name of the person writing the email. The text itself should have clear structure and consist of short paragraphs only.

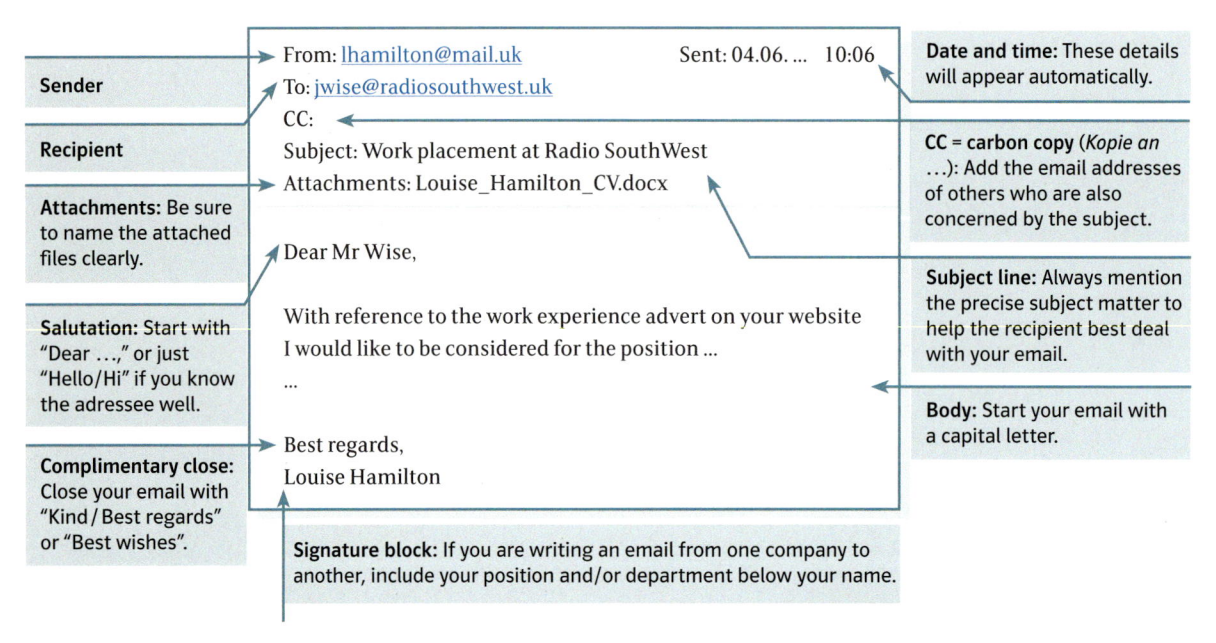

Sender

Recipient

Attachments: Be sure to name the attached files clearly.

Salutation: Start with "Dear …," or just "Hello/Hi" if you know the adressee well.

Complimentary close: Close your email with "Kind / Best regards" or "Best wishes".

From: lhamilton@mail.uk   Sent: 04.06. …   10:06
To: jwise@radiosouthwest.uk
CC:
Subject: Work placement at Radio SouthWest
Attachments: Louise_Hamilton_CV.docx

Dear Mr Wise,

With reference to the work experience advert on your website I would like to be considered for the position …
…

Best regards,
Louise Hamilton

Date and time: These details will appear automatically.

CC = carbon copy (*Kopie an* …): Add the email addresses of others who are also concerned by the subject.

Subject line: Always mention the precise subject matter to help the recipient best deal with your email.

Body: Start your email with a capital letter.

Signature block: If you are writing an email from one company to another, include your position and/or department below your name.

Email etiquette
– Limit your email to one subject only, be precise and clear.
– Make sure your email has a clear structure.
– Even though emails tend to be less formal than letters, remain polite.
– Do not use colloquial language or emoticons.
– Proofread your emails (grammar, spelling, punctuation, choice of words …).

SKILLS FILES

EMAIL

Structure
- Use an appropriate salutation and a complimentary close.
- In personal letters also include the date.
- Very often, personal emails or letters start with stating the reason for writing.
- In the main part, go into more detail and focus on the purpose of your correspondence.
- You might want to end your email or letter by asking the person you are writing to a question, a favour etc.

Language and style
- Use the first-person perspective (1st person singular/1st person plural) in your text.
- The language you use very much depends on the topic you are writing about and on the relationship between you and the person reading your email or letter.
- Specific topics might require technical terms even in personal correspondence.

> Before you send emails, always check for spelling and typing mistakes, and also for any sentences which could be misunderstood.

S 6.6 Creating an information sheet

In a brochure or flyer you inform an interested group of people about facts, issues, events or a problem.

Structure
- Give your text a very clear, concise heading so that the readers know at a glance what your brochure or flyer is about.
- Subheadings will provide a clear structure.

Language and style
- Depending on the situation or the topic you might consider addressing your readers directly.
- Use factual and objective language only; colloquial language is not suitable for a brochure or flyer.
- Listing points or facts one by one will make your text easier to understand.
- Depending on the topic you are writing about, you will also be expected to use technical terms.

SKILLS FILES

S 6.7 Writing a story

When writing a story, you can either rely completely on your own imagination or you may choose to write on a given theme or topic.

1. Planning

Before beginning to write, you'll need to make a few decisions regarding the following elements:

The narrator
- The first-person narrator tells the story from his or her perspective.
- The third-person narrator takes on the perspective of one person telling other people's stories.

The characters
- Choose your protagonist and other characters. You may take inspiration from people around you (someone you notice who is always giggling/someone who speaks very fast/slowly etc.).

The setting
- Choose the place where you wish to set your story.

The time
- Decide on when your story will be set: this could, for example, be yesterday, last year or in the century to come.

The plot
- The beginning: You can either start by introducing the protagonist, or open in the midst of the action.
- The main part: Consider what could drive your plot. This might be some unresolved conflict or a problem, a funny or surprising incident.
- The ending: At the end of your story, the situation may be resolved; or you may choose to leave it unresolved (i.e. offer an open ending).

2. Writing

- Think about what your characters might say in specific situations.
- Look up any new words or expressions you would like to use.
- In writing your story, use either the past or present tense forms.
- Include adjectives and adverbs (e.g. for sensory perception, i.e. in order to describe sounds, colours, smells etc.) and describe details (e.g. of people und places).

The following example will give you an idea of how your story could begin:

It was evening and there were no cars or people on the street. I ran until I came to a big, old building, which looked dark and dirty. The sign said, 'Magic bought and sold here.' I pushed the door open.
"Good evening, young lady," said the old man behind the desk. He spoke very slowly and looked at me closely. I knew he was thinking, 'What has she got for me?'
"Buying or selling?" he asked curiously.
"Er … selling … I think." My voice sounded less nervous than I was. My father would go crazy if he knew I was here, talking to a man who could take some of my magic skills, put them into a bottle and sell them to a stranger. But we needed money, and this was the only way to get some fast. I hated this place, hated this man, but he had what I needed, and I had what he wanted. "Show me what you've got for me then," he said. Although I was really scared, I took a deep breath and showed him my hands. His eyes suddenly looked round and shocked. "I can't believe it," he said. …

S 7 Analysing language

S 7.1 Stylistic devices

Whenever you are asked to analyse the language of a text, you have to mention the stylistic devices used by the author. It is equally important to explain their function. What might be the desired effect on the reader?

Stylistic device	Definition	Example
Alliteration	A series of words beginning with the same letter or sound.	bold, bright and beautiful
Anaphora	The first part of the sentence is repeated to create a certain effect.	I didn't like his hairstyle. I didn't want to tell him.
Ambiguity	When something can be understood in more than one possible way and therefore be unclear or confusing.	Kids Make Nutritious Snack (a headline meaning either "Kids make good food" or "Eating kids is good for you")
Contrast	An obvious difference between two or more words.	a fire-and-ice relationship
Enumeration	Aspects are repeated step by step so as to create a list.	old, grey, majestic
Euphemism	Expressions that replace words that stand for something negative.	"to pass away" instead of "to die"
Exaggeration/Hyperbole	Ideas or opinions are made more important for the sake of effect.	Her old mobile weighs a ton.
Irony	Words are used in such a way that the actual meaning differs from the intended meaning.	That was clever! Now it's broken.
Metaphor	A word or phrase comparing something to something else which shows that they are similar.	a heart of gold
Metonymy	Referring to something by the name of something else that is closely connected with it.	Number 10 (referring to the British Prime Minister or government)
Oxymoron	Two words with opposite meanings are joined together to create a strong effect.	a deafening silence
Paradox	A statement that appears to contradict itself.	"I'm nobody," he said to introduce himself.
Pun	A play on words that produces an often comical effect.	"All she ever wanted was a camouflaged blouse, but she couldn't find one."
Rhetorical question	Does not expect a real answer. It is just asked to emphasise a certain point.	You are enjoying the party, aren't you?
Sarcasm	Like irony, the literal meaning differs from the intended meaning. Often used to criticise or mock somebody.	"Wow, you're a genius!" (when someone made an obvious statement)

S 7.2 Style, tone and register

When analysing a text, you might be asked to have a close look at the language used. Part of this is the analysis of style, tone and register:

> **Style** is the typical way of writing or speaking used by a person; their choice of tone, grammar and narrative techniques.
> **Tone** is the general mood, feeling or attitude being expressed; it is the emotional content of a text rather than the devices used.
> **Register** is the choice of words, style and grammar used in a certain social context. It reflects status and situations often have rules for appropriate register.

SKILLS FILES

Situation	Features	Examples
Formal: in a formal speech or letter; adressing someone unknown or higher in a hierarchy	– respectful, neutral, detached style – complete and complex sentences – formal expressions – foreign/specialist words	*After analysing the evidence, the hypothesis was concluded to be correct.* *I would be grateful for your advice on this.*
Informal: used in spoken rather than written language, when speakers know each other well	– more personal and familiar style – simple sentences, can be incomplete or ungrammatical, dialect or slang – vivid, colloquial or vulgar expression	*Morning all! How's things? Fancy a cuppa? Gotta go get a donut. Ain't you got brains? C'mon, stupid.*
Literary: used mainly in written literary texts	– eloquent/elevated style – complex sentences – rich vocabulary – use of stylistic devices – can combine registers for various effects	*"So we went on in the quiet, and the twilight deepened into night. The clear blue of the distance faded, and one star after another came out."* (Wells, The Time Machine)

- Style, tone and register are difficult to separate and are thus mainly considered together.
- It is useful to note the way a character speaks.
- Don't forget: Form follows function. Comment on the way these devices are used to convey an impression.

S 8 Analysing fictional texts

S 8.1 Fictional text types

Fictional texts are made up, which means that they are based on imagination.

Fictional texts	Novel	– a long, written, fictional prose narrative – has multiple characters, a plot and a narrator – is written in the past tense in most cases
	Short story	– same as novel but shorter – focuses on one major character
	Graphic novel	– comic strip format published as a book – written for adults – texts can be fictional or non-fictional
	Play	– written to be performed on stage – consists of dialogues and monologues
	Poem	– artful arrangement of words to create rhythm – words are used to create images in the readers' mind

S 8.2 Analysing novels and short stories

A Characteristics of the novel

Function	– tells a fictional story, which transports the reader into a fictional world (which can be close to real life or fantastical) – to entertain and sometimes educate the reader
Focus	– able to give large amounts of detail because length is unlimited – can focus on any number of characters/protagonists and show developments over time – different narrative perspectives possible → S 8.4 – may cover several events or locations – can focus on a long period of time, sometimes over several generations – time settings could be historical, contemporary or futuristic
Structure	– long, informative introduction or direct start 'in the middle of things' (in medias res) – order of the plot can be chronological or written with narrative techniques such as frame story, flashbacks, back story or foreshadowing → S 8.5 – mainly separated into chapters – cliffhangers (exciting endings to chapters, making the reader want to read more) – ending can be closed, open, predictable or unexpected – effect created by the relationship between style and content
Language and style	– always in the genre of prose (following the flow of natural speech) – can be written in many different styles – contains descriptive sections, reported speech and direct speech

B Characteristics of the short story

Function	– gives a short glimpse of a life-changing event or revelation – captures an important moment or an important feeling
Focus	– single event, single setting, short time span – only one or two characters
Structure	– direct beginning, little or no introduction – central turning point or surprising 'twist in the tale' near the end
Language and style	– often elliptical (details or sentence parts left out) – one distinctive language or style choice

SKILLS FILES

S 8.3 Narrative perspectives

The effect of a story is strongly influenced by the point of view, or perspective, from which it is told. Narrative types can be mixed and the point of view can sometimes change over the course of the story.

Third-person omniscient narrator
This narrator does not play a part in the story. Although they are telling the story from the sidelines, they know everything about the characters' thoughts and feelings.
This style of narration is mainly neutral and more distanced than others.

Third-person limited narrator
This narrator describes feelings and thoughts from the perspective of one particular character. It is often one of the main characters.
This point of view enables us to feel quite close to this character.

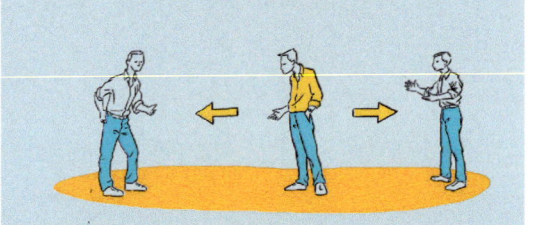

First-person narrator
This narrator is a character who tells the story from his/her own perspective ("I"). We understand and sympathise easily with this type of narrator. Keep in mind that the first-person narrator is not the author unless the text is autobiographical.

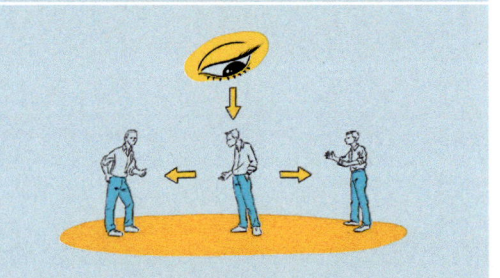

Objective narrator
The objective point of view does not reveal any of the characters' feelings or thoughts. It is as if the narrator was watching the action and describing it objectively. This perspective usually does not create a sense of proximity to the characters.

> **USEFUL PHRASES**
>
> **Writing about narrative perspective**
> The story is told by a … narrator. | The narrator's views are very personal and subjective which can be seen … | The fact that the narrator is involved in the story leads to the effect that … | The narrator remains outside the plot. | The effect on the reader is … | The narrator describes the action and characters objectively.

S 8.4 Narrative techniques

When you analyse a fictional text, you should not only think about the story itself, but also about the ways in which it is told. These 'narrative techniques' influence the way the reader sees the story.

A Structure

The plot, i.e. the main events and the theme of a story, is usually structured in the following way:

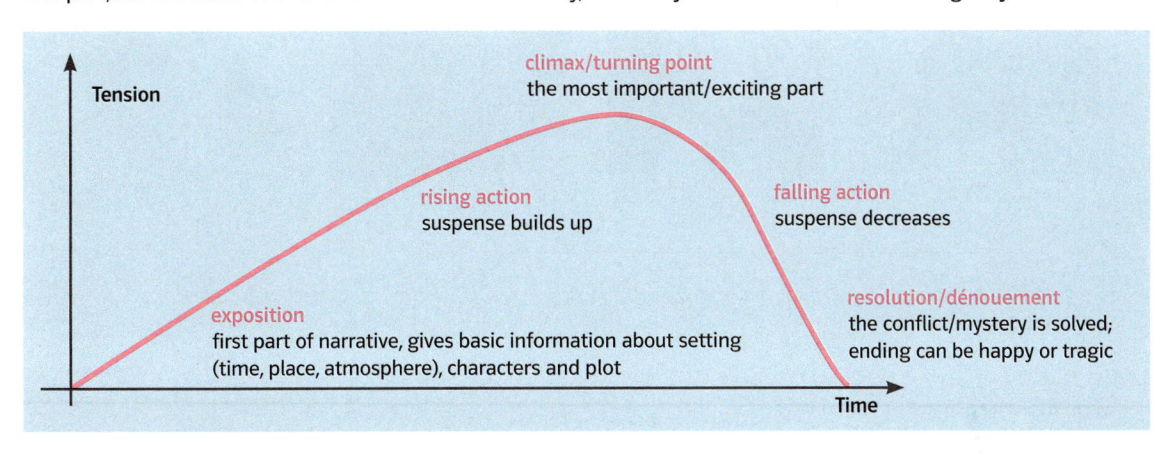

- **exposition**: first part of narrative, gives basic information about setting (time, place, atmosphere), characters and plot
- **rising action**: suspense builds up
- **climax/turning point**: the most important/exciting part
- **falling action**: suspense decreases
- **resolution/dénouement**: the conflict/mystery is solved; ending can be happy or tragic

(Diagram: Tension plotted against Time, showing a curve rising from exposition through rising action to the climax/turning point, then falling through falling action to resolution/dénouement.)

Tense as narrative technique
Tense influences the distance between readers and characters.
The use of **present tense** makes you feel closer to the action.
More distance is created when the narrator uses **indirect speech**.

B Chronology
Authors use different possibilities of relating the events in a story.

Back story	gives the history of characters, objects, places or events in the story
Flashback	the narrative is taken back in time
Flash-forward	future events are revealed
Foreshadowing	clues in the story that hint at a future development

C Narrative situation

Point of view	the narrator shows his/her attitude to the characters and can limit what the reader knows
Suspense	created by not giving away too much information; typical of crime or adventure stories
Tense	influences the distance between reader and characters (e.g. if the narrator uses present tense, you feel close to the action)
Irony	can be used as a distancing effect by the narrator
Narration	can vary between dialogues (direct speech), description and comments

SKILLS FILES

S 8.5 Characterisation

When dealing with a novel, film or play, you will often be asked to analyse a certain character and his/her behaviour. In general there is a main character (protagonist, hero/heroine) and an antagonist (another important character who is in conflict with the protagonist).

Types of characters

Static / Flat character	Round character	Dynamic character
– shows no development – has no depth	– complex – shows inner conflict – is presented in detail	– changes over time – shows development

How to analyse a character:

Preparing
– Collect any relevant information from the text about the character (personal details, appearance, behaviour, what he/she says and what others say about him/her).
– Collect these facts as quotations and include line references.

Writing
1. Briefly present the character (personal details). Say what his/her function in the story is and how he/she relates to the other characters.
2. Describe the character's personality and behaviour.
3. Sum up their most important traits.

Direct characterisation
The narrator or a character tells the reader explicitly what a character is like.

Indirect characterisation
It is the reader's job to interpret a character through what the character thinks, does or says.

USEFUL PHRASES

Personal details
The protagonist is young/middle-aged/single/married …

Outward appearance
He/She is described as being tall/small/good-looking …

Positive character traits
He/She is/seems to be friendly/cheerful/good-natured/attentive/observant, intelligent/honest/trustworthy/sensitive/brave/generous/optimistic/polite …

Negative character traits
He/She seems to be bad-tempered/rude/violent/unreliable/pessimistic/dishonest/untrustworthy/mean/selfish/foolish/careless/ignorant …

Drawing conclusions about a character
The plot reveals that … |
His/Her statement "…" (line …) shows/proves that … |
He/She appears to be portrayed as … |
His/Her behaviour clearly indicates that … |
The character is described/presented/portrayed as …

Talking about relationships
to build up / to continue / to break off a relationship

S 9 Analysing non-fictional texts

S 9.1 Non-fictional text types

Non-fictional texts are based on facts and provide information and opinions about real-world issues. They can be categorised according to their **intention**, i.e. what effect they want to have on the reader:

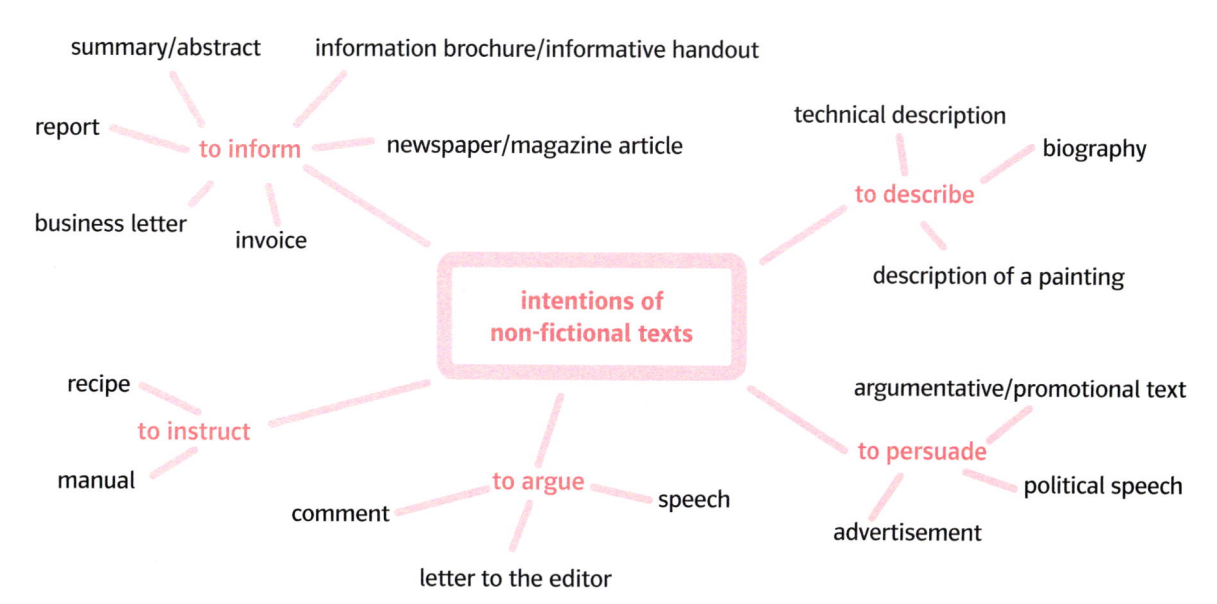

intentions of non-fictional texts

- **to inform**: summary/abstract, report, business letter, invoice, information brochure/informative handout, newspaper/magazine article
- **to describe**: technical description, biography, description of a painting
- **to instruct**: recipe, manual
- **to argue**: comment, letter to the editor, speech
- **to persuade**: argumentative/promotional text, political speech, advertisement

S 9.2 Structure of non-fictional texts

One of the key steps in dealing with non-fictional texts is to analyse the text structure. How is the information generally organised and presented?

Text structure	Explanation	Signal words and phrases
Chronological order / Sequence	Events are revealed in a sequence from beginning to end.	*first, then, next, finally*
Cause and effect	Cause and effect-relationships are described: – What causes a certain event? – What are the consequences?	*for, since, because, … is caused by … (cause), as a result, consequently, for this reason, therefore, … leads to … (effect)*
Problem and solution	A problem is described and possible solutions are presented.	*The problem is …, The question is …, A solution might be …, One answer is …*
Compare and contrast	Various comparisons are used to effectively describe and contrast ideas.	*Different from/to …, Same as …, Similar to …, As opposed to …, Instead of …, Compared with/to …, On the other hand …, although, however, but*
Description	Ideas or concepts are described and illustrated. Visual details such as illustrations and diagrams are often added.	*for instance, for example, such as, to illustrate, to show*

SKILLS FILES

S 9.3 Analysing argumentative texts

A Types of arguments

Argumentative texts offer a lot of claims and theses, each of which is or should be supported by logical arguments. In order to analyse an argumentative text, find out which types of arguments are used.

Practical argument	Refers to widely known facts and common experience in order to appear logical.	*Humans need oxygen to survive and plants produce oxygen – that's why it is important to protect the environment.*
Argument by illustration	Uses examples to support and illustrate a claim.	*The death penalty should be abolished because innocent people may be put to death. In 1990, for example, a man was executed in Florida for the murders of two police officers. Two years later he was found innocent.*
Argument by authority	Uses the opinion of experts and the results of statistics to prove a point.	*Recent studies show that very frequent use of social media affects mental health.*
Normative argument	Refers to accepted norms and values. Often based on common sense.	*To save our planet we will have to drastically reduce water and air pollution.*
Argument by analogy	The reader can easily draw parallels to other areas of life.	*In sports as well as in business, we can see globalisation, monopolies and illegal actions to "win at all costs" increasing.* *Sport is more and more heavily regulated to ensure that competition is fair and equal, thus business should be too.*

B Line of argumentation

Analysing the line of argumentation in a text includes describing and explaining how the argumentation is being developed throughout the text. How are the various parts of the text connected? What is the function of each individual paragraph?

S 9.4 Analysing newspaper articles

If you are asked to analyse a newspaper article, you need to identify the topic and the main points in the text. You will also have to identify and explain the type of article and its intention, as well as the article's structure.

A Types of articles

Reports / News articles	– discuss current or recent news of general interest or on a specific topic – are formal and objective – focus only on the facts – answer general questions like Who? What? When? Where? Why? How? – may contain photographs, personal accounts, statistics, graphs, polls etc. – are often written in the simple past tense
Feature articles	– deal in depth with a topic, person or event by providing a great deal of a background information – analyse a series of events or a development that is of human interest – have a storyline and are entertaining – may contain quotations, personal interviews and descriptions
Editorials	– are written by the editor of the paper or magazine – focus on current events – include the writer's opinion – are usually run all together on a specific page of the paper or magazine (editorial page)

SKILLS FILES

> **Quality of news reports**
> News reports are supposed to inform the public about interesting and important events in an unbiased way. However, their quality and neutrality differ depending on the newspaper or magazine.

B Structure of articles

Newspaper articles are often structured like an inverted pyramid with the most important aspect at the top. More facts and additional details follow, with the least important ones at the end, so readers can stop reading when they feel they have enough information. The typical parts of a newspaper article are explained in the following example:

British backpacker Sam Woodhead missing in Australian outback

A British backpacker has disappeared after he set out on a run in the Australian outback.

The last picture Sam Woodhead posted, two days before he went missing.

Sam Woodhead was reported missing from a cattle station after he failed to return from a jog two days ago.

Local authorities launched a hunt for him amid fears he may have lost his way in a hot, isolated region of central Queensland. His mother is understood to have urged police to widen the search on the grounds that her son, an experienced long-distance runner, could have travelled some way from his base, near the town of Longreach.

Sister uses social media to reach out

His sister, Rebecca, issued an anxious plea for news on her social media. "If anyone hears from my brother, please contact me ASAP" she posted. In another posting, she added: "Thanks so much for all your messages regarding Sam. Still no further news but we have the helicopter going out again in the morning, Aus time, and hundreds of people going on voluntary search party. Will keep you all posted."

The **headline** catches the reader's attention.

Pictures often have a **caption**.

Subheadings are used to split articles into sections.

The **lead paragraph** introduces the news story by telling the most important facts (who, what, when, where, why, how).

Newspaper articles are usually written in **columns**.

SKILLS FILES

S 10 Analysing and using visuals

Among the materials you get for writing a composition or for having a group discussion, there are often visuals like pictures, cartoons or diagrams. The content of the material should be used, but it should not be described or quoted.

S 10.1 Analysing and using pictures and paintings

Introduction	– Give information about the type of picture and the artist/photographer. – Say when the painting/photo was most likely painted/taken. – Give a general description of what is in the picture and what you can see.
Analysis	– Describe the message conveyed by the picture and how this message is communicated. – Consider aspects like colour, contrast, tone, composition, focus, light and perspective. – Is the picture intended to have a certain effect on the viewer? Describe how this is achieved.
Evaluation	– Based on the results of your analysis, state whether the picture is effective and which elements are responsible for it being successful or unsuccessful. – Give your personal opinion (if asked) or your thoughts on what topic the picture represents.

USEFUL PHRASES

Introduction
The photo/sketch/portrait/still life/oil painting was taken/drawn/painted by … and published in (year) … | The main focus is … | The picture illustrates …

Evaluation
The overall effect of the picture is … because … | In my opinion, the painting/photo only shows one aspect of/idealises/… | The picture reminds me of … because … | It is effective/moves me deeply because …

Analysis
The artist/photographer (probably) wants to express/show/criticise … | The artist presents … | The light/colours of … create an … atmosphere/give an impression of/contribute to … | The position of …

S 10.2 Analysing and using cartoons

A cartoon usually combines a drawing with a text and/or a caption. Cartoons often pick up on current events and criticise people, institutions or developments in society and politics. Some cartoons are just intended to be entertaining, e.g. making fun of a public figure. On the other hand, others can make a serious and important critical point, simply by using visual means. However, when analysing a cartoon, make sure you consider the emotional level of language it conveys.

Introduction	– Give information on the context (artist, date of publication and source). – Briefly say what the cartoon is about (a topic, an event, a person etc.).
Analysis	– Examine each important element (people, objects, text) and explain the message they convey. – Pay attention to the function of the characters (Do they represent well-known people or a particular group of people?) and typical techniques (see tip box).
Evaluation	– State whether you think the cartoon is effective and which elements are responsible for it being successful/unsuccessful. – Give your personal opinion (if asked) or your thoughts on the topic presented in the cartoon.

Typical techniques used by cartoonists
– caricature (exaggerating certain striking characteristics)
– irony (depicting the opposite of what is really meant)
– exposing inconsistencies (e.g. contrasting a statement with a picture showing the exact opposite)
– emphasising stereotypes
– using wordplay and symbolism

SKILLS FILES

USEFUL PHRASES

Introduction
The cartoon was drawn by … and was published / appeared in (source) on (date). | It was created in response to … | It shows / deals with / refers to / comments on … | The cartoonist makes fun of … / criticises … for (doing sth).

Analysis
The cartoon satirises / represents / is a caricature of … | This figure is a stereotype of … / is exaggerated / supposed to represent … / supports the message of … | The cartoonist is making fun of … | It is obvious that the artist wants to criticise / express / show …

Evaluation
The cartoon (only partly) achieves its aim of (doing sth). | I (do not) think the cartoon is funny / easy to understand because … | In my opinion, the cartoonist is (not) successful in presenting / criticising … because … | I (do not) like the cartoon because … | The cartoon appeals / does not appeal to me. | In my opinion, it is convincing / confusing / unfair / …

S 10.3 Analysing and using diagrams and statistics

Diagrams visualise statistics and make them much easier to understand. Data can be graphically presented in different ways:

Bar chart
Bar charts present data in coloured bars so as to make it easier to compare figures directly.

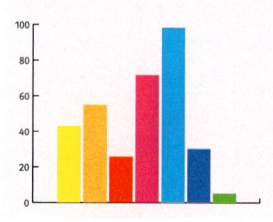

Pie chart
A pie chart is usually used to illustrate percentages or proportions.
The entire circle represents 100%. Each segment shows a percentage of the whole.

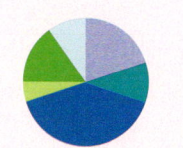

Line graph
A line graph shows a change / development over a certain period of time.

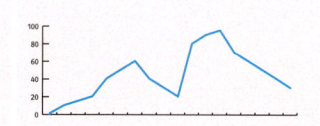

Flow chart
A flow chart shows the links between elements and their influence on each other.
It is best used to describe processes that contain decisions at certain points and where alternatives need to be shown.

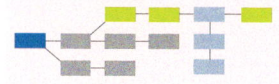

If you want to practise describing and analysing diagrams, you can search online for:
– Eurostat, the European Union statistical office
– ONS, the Office for National Statistics in the UK
– US data and statistics
– UNSD, the United Nations Statistics Division

USEFUL PHRASES

Bar chart
The vertical / horizontal axis shows / represents … | The chart indicates / makes clear that … | The number of … is far greater than / is significant in comparison to …

Line graph
The line graph of … shows the development of … from … to … | The vertical axis shows the number / percentage / amount of … | The horizontal axis shows the time from … to … | The number of … increased / rose / remained constant / decreased / fell (gradually / steadily / rapidly / steeply / significantly) until … | This change was possibly caused by …

Pie chart
The chart is divided into … segments. | The pie chart shows / represents … | The segments compare … | As you can see from the pie chart …

Flow chart
The process is divided into … stages / phases. | The first stage of the process is … | The process starts with / by … | In this phase … | First / Second / Third | Then | After that … | Before that … | Following … | This is followed by … | The next step is … | Alternatively … | There are then two possibilities … | Having completed … the … moves onto … | Finally … | The process concludes with …

SKILLS FILES

S 11 Vocabulary skills

S 11.1 Expanding your vocabulary

In order to fill in the gaps in exam tasks correctly, you will need to be able to recognise *parts of speech* and know how to form them (e.g. *noun* → *verb*). To this end, it is helpful to learn words in their *word families* and to be aware of the basic rules regarding *word order* in sentences.

1. Recognising parts of speech

Parts of speech are the 'building blocks' of a language which are required for forming sentences. The most important parts of speech are:

noun	Hauptwort/Nomen	book, Sam, girl, parents
verb	Tuwort/Verb	go, eat, feel, think
adjective	Wie-Wort/Adjektiv	small, intelligent, blue
adverb	Umstandswort/Adverb	slowly, yesterday, always
preposition	Verhältniswort/Präposition	next to, on, over , in, until
pronoun	Fürwort/Pronomen	he, them, yourselves, ones
article, determiner	Artikel, Begleiter	the, a, an, this, those
conjunction	Konjunktion	and, but, when, although
quantifier	Mengenbezeichnung	some, any, a couple of

2. Word order

When doing a 'fill in the gaps' task requiring various parts of speech, pay attention to the position of each gap in a sentence and to the words before and after it:
- Before a noun, there is most often an article or an adjective.
- An adjective always refers to a noun or pronoun.
- Every sentence has a verb in it.
- The basic word-order rule is **S-V-O**: *subject – verb – object*.
- In a sentence containing several adverbs, these parts of speech are often found in the following order: *manner – place – time*.

SKILLS FILES

3. Mind maps

Mind maps are a great tool to cluster and organise new vocabulary which makes it easier to learn new words. You can either make a mind map for each new word you want to learn or you can collect vocabulary that relates to a specific topic.

A Learning new words

- **increase**
  - word class: noun
  - sample sentence: There was an increase in the number of college students last year.
  - meaning: a rise in the size or number of something
  - word family: to increase, increasing
  - synonyms: rise, growth
  - antonyms: decrease, drop

> antonym = a word with the opposite meaning
> synonym = a word with a similar or the same meaning

B Collecting topic vocabulary

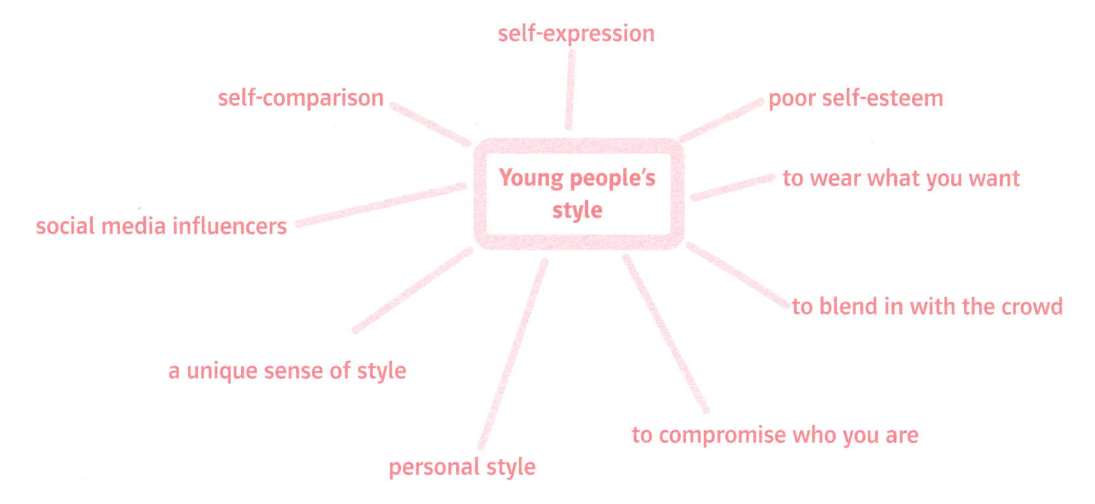

- **Young people's style**
  - self-expression
  - self-comparison
  - poor self-esteem
  - to wear what you want
  - social media influencers
  - to blend in with the crowd
  - a unique sense of style
  - to compromise who you are
  - personal style

SKILLS FILES

S 11.2 Guessing unknown words

There is no need to be afraid of texts containing new words. You already know many different ways of guessing their meanings. After applying your guessing technique, it is likely that there are still some words you don't know the meaning of, but you will probably understand the most important points in the text.

Guessable words	Examples
Words that are also used in a German context	*bestseller, boycott, clown, laptop, track …*
Words that are similar to German words → watch out for false friends!	*individuality, install, parallel, to wander, …*
Words that are similar to words you know from another foreign language (e.g. French, Latin, Spanish, Italian) → watch out for false friends!	*academic, announcement, artificial, descendant, dignity, individuality, junior, minor, pasta, phase, …*
Compounds of words you already know	*handwriting, heartfelt, mixed ability, single-sex, washing machine, whole-heartedly, …*
Words from a word family you already know	*adventurous, announcement, to mirror, nationalism, relevance, …*
Words with prefixes or suffixes whose root you already know	*to dislike, impatient, to rewrite, profitable, paperless, …*
Words you already know, but with a different meaning – the new meaning may be guessed from the context	*to admit, light, plain, pretty, to report sb, …*
Words whose meaning you can guess from the context	*(he) dozed off (in his chair); (it's old-fashioned) out of date*

> **prefix** = an element placed before a word that changes its meaning (*dis*like, *im*patient)
> **suffix** = an element placed after a word that changes its meaning or word class (profit*able*, paper*less*)

S 11.3 Working with a dictionary

When you cannot guess a word from its context in the text, you can look it up in a dictionary. Using a dictionary takes time however, so decide if you really need to know the meaning of the word in order to understand the sentence or text.

A English-German, German-English (bilingual)
This type of dictionary is best used for translating or finding the meaning of new words quickly. You can use a bilingual dictionary to do mediation exercises.

Check the following information in your dictionary:

- Which word class does the word belong to?
- Which words does it often go together with?
- What topic or word field does it belong to?
- How is it pronounced?
- Are there irregular forms?
- What translations are given?
- Which of the translations can only be used in a limited context (AE, formal, slang etc.)?
- Which of the translations fits the context?

Example

fo·cus[ˈfəʊkəs] <pl focuses, foci> [pl ˈfəʊkaɪ] s ❶ (MATH OPT) Brennpunkt m ❷ (fig) Brennpunkt, Herd m, Zentrum nt; ~ (un)scharf eingestellt; ~ scharf einstellen vt ❶ (OPT PHOT) einstellen (on auf) ❷ (fig) konzentrieren (on auf); focus group s (in marketing) [ausgewählte]

B English-English (monolingual)

This type of dictionary is best used for writing an English text when you are not quite sure which is the best word to choose in a given context.

An English-English dictionary provides you with the following information:

- What part of speech is the word?
- Which words does it often go together with?
- What topic or word field does it belong to?
- How is it pronounced?
- Are there irregular forms?
- What synonyms and/or definitions are given?
- Which of the given meanings fits the context?
- Examples show how the word is typically used.

- Before looking up a word, identify whether it is a verb, noun, adjective, adverb etc.
- When you have found the entry for the word, make sure you look at the meaning for the correct word class.
- Read any additional information which the dictionary gives you about the word.
- Take your time to read the entry carefully.
- Make sure you find the entry which matches the use of the word in the given context.

Example

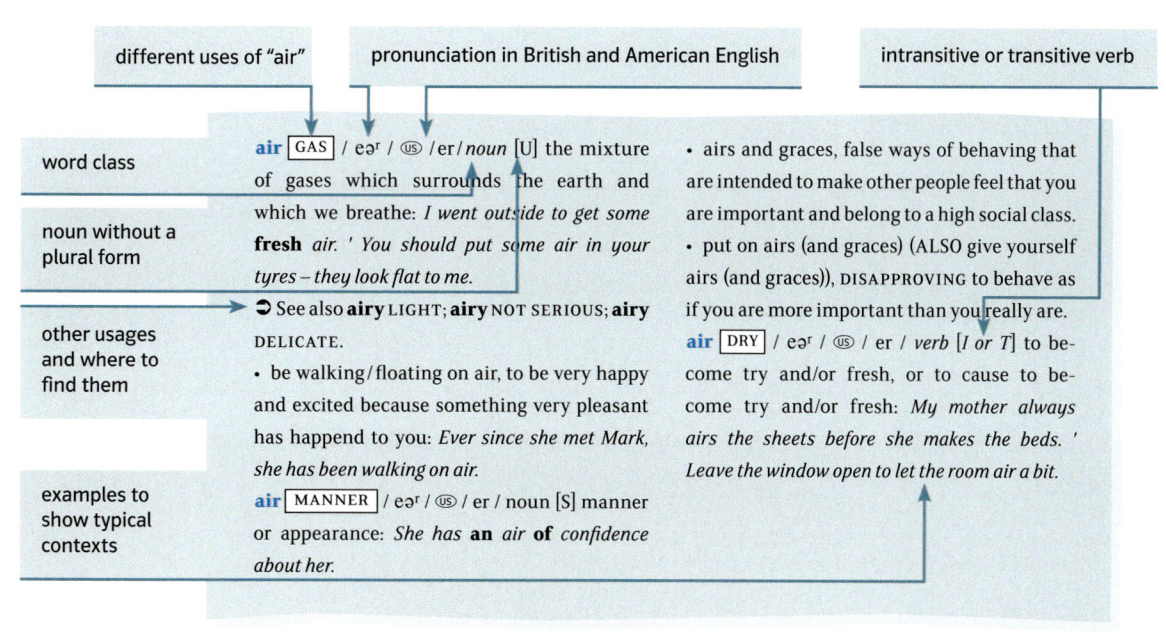

Labels (pointing to dictionary entry):
- different uses of "air"
- pronunciation in British and American English
- intransitive or transitive verb
- word class
- noun without a plural form
- other usages and where to find them
- examples to show typical contexts

air [GAS] /eəʳ/ US /er/ *noun* [U] the mixture of gases which surrounds the earth and which we breathe: *I went outside to get some fresh air.* ' *You should put some air in your tyres – they look flat to me.*

↪ See also **airy** LIGHT; **airy** NOT SERIOUS; **airy** DELICATE.

• be walking/floating on air, to be very happy and excited because something very pleasant has happend to you: *Ever since she met Mark, she has been walking on air.*

air [MANNER] /eəʳ/ US /er/ *noun* [S] manner or appearance: *She has **an** air **of** confidence about her.*

• airs and graces, false ways of behaving that are intended to make other people feel that you are important and belong to a high social class.
• put on airs (and graces) (ALSO give yourself airs (and graces)), DISAPPROVING to behave as if you are more important than you really are.

air [DRY] /eəʳ/ US /er/ *verb* [I or T] to become try and/or fresh, or to cause to become try and/or fresh: *My mother always airs the sheets before she makes the beds.* ' *Leave the window open to let the room air a bit.*

SKILLS FILES

S 12 Making a video

Preparing a video

Preparation
– find suitable actors, location(s) and setting
– decide on the use of light (bright, fading, …), colours (e.g. dark, warm, …), space (e.g. interior or exterior, wide or narrow) and cinematic devices → S 10.2
– produce a film script and a storyboard

Filming
– follow your storyboard
– repeat takes if necessary

Editing
– use suitable editing techniques (e.g. cut, fade in, fade out, slow motion, fast motion)
– add sound (e.g. music, dubbing, voiceover, effects)

Example of a script (adaptation of the first scene from *The White Tiger* by Aravind Adiga)

```
1 EXT. Beijing, Great Hall of the People -- DAY
    Fade-in to time lapse of PEOPLE of all kinds walking across Tiananmen Square past
    the façade, including businessmen and street vendors. Chinese music.

2 INT. Beijing, Premier Wen Jiabao's office -- SAME TIME
    Crosscut to Chinese PREMIER at desk, leaning back in chair, reading a printout
    letter (several pages). Secretary, nervous, stands waiting for reaction. Silence.
                PREMIER
    (annoyed, irritated; speaks in Chinese. Subtitle in English appears)
            It's in English.
                VOICEOVER BALRAM
    (Balram, speaking in English with an Indian accent)
            Mr Premier, Sir.
            Neither you nor I can speak English, but there are some things
            that can be said only in English.

3 INT. Bangalore, India, huge and shabby room, nearly empty, one large 70's chandelier;
  fan above, splitting up the light; radio -- NIGHT
    Fade-in to Balram cross-legged on floor with a silver laptop but talking, not
    typing. Dreamy look on his face.
                BALRAM
            … and at 11:32 p.m. today, which was about ten minutes ago, when
            the lady on All India Radio announced, "Premier Jiabao is coming
            to Bangalore next week", I said that thing at once.
```

Example of a storyboard (shot 3 from the film above)

Audio	Near silence, voice fades in	Radio background: Indian music	Fade out radio, Balram louder
Video			
Shot	Fade-in establishing shot: bird's eye view, chandelier to left, Balram small, centre	Move: slow crane zoom round back of Balram to front close-up at "announced"	Stop at: close-up frontal shot Balram, from "I said that thing at once."

S 13 Online research and checking sources

S 13.1 Checking sources

You will often have to research a topic before you can talk or write about it. There are many different ways of finding out information: by researching online, by going to a library and looking in books, newspapers or magazines or by talking to an expert. However, sources differ in quality and reliability, especially online. Therefore, it is absolutely vital that you check your sources before using them. Here is how you distinguish between reliable and unreliable sources:

Reliable	Unreliable
– written by respectable journalists, professors, experts or institutions	– without a named author – written by hobby "experts" – from the popular press
– up to date	– too old to be useful
– neutral and objective	– expressing a biased opinion
– covering both sides of a controversial topic	– offering one-sided information only
– with expert proof or personal experience	– just hearsay
– correct grammar and spelling	– many grammar and spelling mistakes

> Don't believe everything you read! Anyone can publish anything on the internet.
> Printed articles and books have normally been more carefully chosen and edited,
> but these can also be biased or too generalised and simple.

If you are unsure about certain news or facts, use a fact check website to validate your source.

S 13.2 Citing sources

You must document all the sources (texts, pictures, statistics, videos …) you have used in a presentation or written text. There are different citing styles, for example MLA, APA, Harvard or Chicago. The examples below are in MLA style since this is the most commonly used style.

A Citing in the text
Within your text, you can either cite your sources in a footnote or in brackets within the text. Add the footnote or brackets at the end of the sentence or paragraph in which you reference or use the source.

Bill Smith analyses migration problems in Britain. He writes that real life is about integration.[1]

[1] Smith, Bill. *Real Life in the UK*. London, Brown, 2014, p. 23.

Bill Smith analyses migration problems in Britain. He writes that real life is about integration (Smith 23).

SKILLS FILES

B Creating a list of references
For each of the sources that you have used and referenced in your text, include the following details in your list of references:

Author's name, Author's surname. *Title*. Place of publication, Publishing house, Year of publication.

References/Bibliography

Books:
Eggers, Dave. *The Circle*. New York, Knopf, 2013.
Smith, Bill. *Real Life in the UK*. London, Brown, 2014.

Articles:
Jones, Owen. "London riots – one year on." *The Independent*, 24 July 2012.

Online sources:
Darzi, Ara. "Great communication in healthcare can save lives." *The Guardian* online, 18 November 2015, theguardian.com/healthcare-network/2015/nov/18/nhs-great-communication-healthcare-save-lives-behavioural-insight-nudge. Accessed 5 June 2019.

Copyrighted material
It is important to check whether the material you are including is copyrighted, i.e. it can only be used with the permission of the author. You can include copyrighted material in your presentation in class if you cite it correctly, but you are not allowed to publish or upload it online. Check the material for a copyright notice: the symbol "©" or the word "copyright" followed by the date of publication and the author's name. Pictures may have a watermark to show that they are copyrighted.

S 13.3 Quoting

Always make a clear difference between text you wrote yourself and text or facts written by others.
You can cite a text in different ways:

Direct quotation: Copy the exact words of the source text and cite them with quotation marks. If you cite a whole sentence, add a colon (…: "…").

Indirect quotation: Paraphrase the source using your own words.

In her article "Great communication in healthcare can save lives", Ara Darzi states: "More than one in 15 hospital prescriptions contains some kind of error […]". She argues that "the most frequent cause of avoidable harm to patients in hospital" is that prescriptions are not written clearly and do not contain all the necessary information (Darzi, *The Guardian.com*).

Symbols and abbreviations
[…]   to add to or leave words out of a direct quote
l. / ll.   to indicate the line or lines you are quoting (e.g. in a poem or newspaper article)
p.   to indicate the page you are quoting from
ff.   to indicate the page on which the quote starts (ff. stands for "and the following pages")
'…'   to mark direct speech in a quote
/   to mark the beginning of a new line in a quoted poem

USEFUL PHRASES

Direct quotation (whole sentence)
In his/her book/article …, X states: "…" (p. 7ff.).

Direct quotation (built into your sentence)
X claims/argues/assumes/concludes that "…" (l. 6).
X presents … as "…", which … (p. 12).

Indirect quotation (paraphrasing)
X claims/reports/writes in … that… | According to X, … is/has/was/could … (ll. 7–9). | In X's article, he/she describes …, which is based on / gives reasons for / explains why … (l. 4). | While X argues that …, Y gives reasons for … (l. 23ff.; l. 76ff.).

S 14 Preparing for an exam

Dealing with exam tasks

Get hold of some mock (practice) exams and take the time to do them in a situation like the exam.

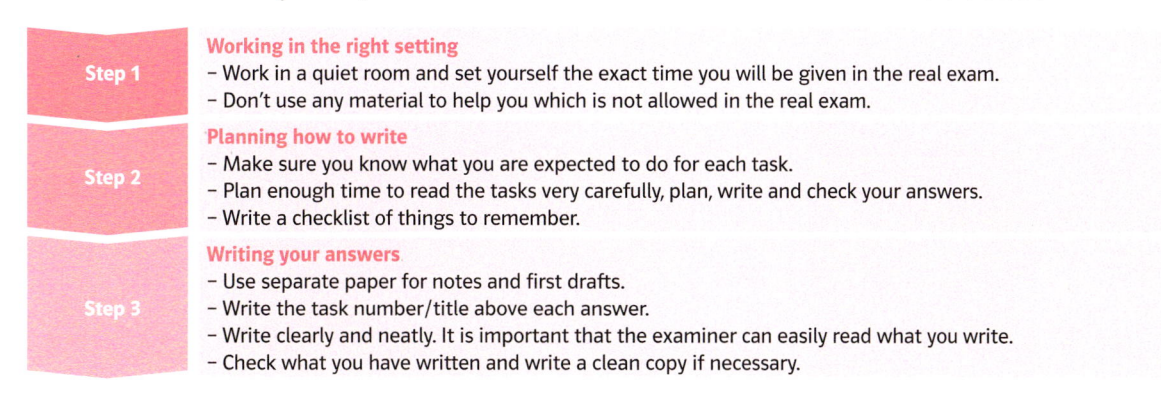

Step 1
Working in the right setting
– Work in a quiet room and set yourself the exact time you will be given in the real exam.
– Don't use any material to help you which is not allowed in the real exam.

Step 2
Planning how to write
– Make sure you know what you are expected to do for each task.
– Plan enough time to read the tasks very carefully, plan, write and check your answers.
– Write a checklist of things to remember.

Step 3
Writing your answers
– Use separate paper for notes and first drafts.
– Write the task number/title above each answer.
– Write clearly and neatly. It is important that the examiner can easily read what you write.
– Check what you have written and write a clean copy if necessary.

S 15 Methods

Milling around Marktplatz

1. Bearbeiten Sie die Aufgabe zunächst allein. Auf ein Signal der Lehrkraft stehen Sie auf und gehen durch den Raum. Nehmen Sie die Aufgabe und einen Stift mit.

2. Wenn erneut ein Signal ertönt, bleiben Sie stehen. Besprechen Sie die Aufgabe mit der Person, die Ihnen am nächsten steht.

3. Beim nächsten Signal trennen Sie sich und gehen weiter durch den Raum. Wiederholen Sie Schritt 2.

Think-pair-share Nachdenken-austauschen-teilen

Think: Schreiben Sie Ihre Ideen, Gedanken oder Lösungen zur Aufgabe alleine auf.

Pair: Tauschen Sie Ihre Notizen mit einem Partner / einer Partnerin aus und besprechen Sie diese.

Share: Präsentieren Sie Ihre Ergebnisse anderen Paaren oder der gesamten Klasse.

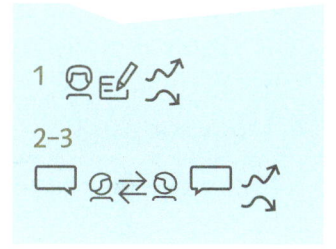

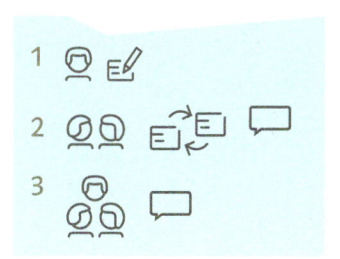

SKILLS FILES

1-minute presentation Kurzpräsentation

Nehmen Sie sich ein DIN A4-Blatt. Falten Sie es so, dass das untere Drittel nach hinten wegknickt.

Schreiben Sie den Text Ihrer Präsentation auf die oberen zwei Drittel.

Notieren Sie nun die wichtigsten Stichpunkte noch einmal auf dem unteren Drittel. Dies ist Ihr Spickzettel.

In Ihrer Präsentation verwenden Sie nur den Spickzettel. Wenn Sie nicht mehr weiter wissen, dürfen Sie kurz auf den Text oben schauen.

Placemat Platzdeckchen

1. Bilden Sie Vierergruppen.
2. Teilen Sie ein großes Blatt Papier in fünf Bereiche ein.
3. Setzen Sie sich so hin, dass jeder in eine Ecke des Blattes schreiben kann.
4. Jedes Gruppenmitglied denkt allein über das Thema nach und schreibt Ideen auf seinen / ihren Teil des Blattes.
5. Tauschen Sie sich über die Ideen aus. Einigen Sie sich auf die besten Ideen und schreiben Sie diese in die Mitte des Blattes.

Round robin Blitzlicht

Überlegen Sie sich einen Satz zu der Aufgabe / der Frage / dem Thema.

Wenn alle bereit sind, tauschen Sie sich in der Klasse / in Gruppen aus, indem Sie nacheinander Ihren Satz sagen.

Alle anderen hören aufmerksam zu, kommentieren aber nicht.

Opinion line Meinungslinie

Überlegen Sie, welche Meinung Sie zum genannten Thema haben. Sind Sie dafür oder dagegen? Warum?

Stellen Sie sich auf einer gedachten Linie im Klassenzimmer auf. Auf der linken Seite stehen die Schüler/-innen, die DAFÜR sind. Auf der rechten Seite stehen die Schüler/-innen, die DAGEGEN sind.

Tauschen Sie sich zunächst innerhalb Ihrer Gruppe (a) und danach mit der anderen Gruppe (b) aus. Nennen Sie Ihre Argumente und Gründe.

Am Schluss positionieren Sie sich erneut. Haben Sie Ihre Meinung geändert?

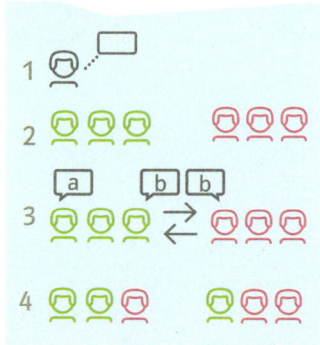

SKILLS FILES

Peer correction Partnerkontrolle

1. Bearbeiten Sie die Aufgabe zunächst selbstständig.
2. Tauschen Sie Ihre Lösungen mit einem Partner / einer Partnerin oder in Kleingruppen untereinander. Kontrollieren Sie die Lösungen.
3. Tauschen Sie sich danach zu der Aufgabe aus und korrigieren Sie den Text.

Tip-top Feedback

Sagen Sie zunächst, was Ihnen gut gefallen hat – also „top" war.

Sagen Sie nun, was noch nicht so gut war. Geben Sie einen Tipp, was man verbessern könnte.

Gallery walk Galerierundgang

Hängen Sie nach Ihrer Gruppenarbeit Ihr Produkt gut sichtbar im Klassenzimmer auf.

Eine/r von Ihnen, der „Experte"/die „Expertin", bleibt bei Ihrem Projekt stehen und erklärt es den anderen. Die anderen gehen herum. Nach jedem Durchgang wechselt der „Experte"/die „Expertin".

Sehen Sie sich die Produkte der anderen an und geben Sie Feedback.

Werten Sie im Anschluss Ihre Ergebnisse in der Klasse aus.

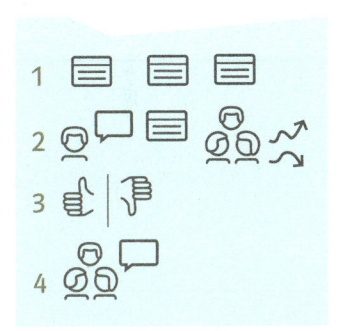

GRAMMAR FILES

G1	**Tenses**	169
	G1.1 Simple present	169
	G1.2 Present progressive	169
	G1.3 Simple past	170
	G1.4 Past progressive	170
	G1.5 Present perfect simple	171
	G1.6 Present perfect progressive	171
	G1.7 Past perfect simple	172
	G1.8 Past perfect progressive	172
	G1.9 Going to-future	173
	G1.10 Future simple (will-future)	173
	G1.11 Future progressive	174
	G1.12 Future perfect simple	174
	G1.13 Future perfect progressive	175
	G1.14 Conditional I	175
	G1.15 Conditional II	176
G2	**If-clauses**	176
	G2.1 Type 1	176
	G2.2 Type 2	177
	G2.3 Type 3	177
G3	**The passive**	178
G4	**Relative clauses**	179
	G4.1 Defining relative clauses	179
	G4.2 Non-defining relative clauses	179
G5	**Adjectives**	179
G6	**Adverbs**	180
G7	**Question tags**	181
G8	**Modal auxiliaries**	181
G9	**-ing forms**	182
	G9.1 The present participle	182
	G9.2 The gerund	182
G10	**Reported speech**	183
G11	**Word order**	184
	G11.1 Statements	184
	G11.2 Questions	184
	G11.3 Negated statements	184
Übersicht Erklärvideos und interaktive Übungen		185

G1 Tenses

G1.1 Simple present

Positive sentences	Negative sentences	Questions
I use social media. You use social media. He/she/it uses social media. We use social media. You use social media. They use social media.	I don't use social media. You don't use social media. He/she/it doesn't use social media. We don't use social media. You don't use social media. They don't use social media.	Do I use social media? Do you use social media? Does he/she/it use social media? Do we use social media? Do you use social media? Do they use social media? Questions with a question word: Why do I use social media? Why do you use social media? Why does he/she/it use social media? Why do we use social media? Why do you use social media? Why do they use social media?

> **!** Be careful with these verbs: be, have.

Talking about the present
V 1 ▶   I 13 👆

Examples of typical use:
- Facts and general statements: The cartoon shows a family.
- Everyday activities or habits: Justin listens to podcasts on the bus.
  Tense markers: always, often, sometimes, never, usually, every day/week/month/year, on Mondays/Tuesdays…, at 7 o'clock/11 o'clock…
- A set sequence of events or actions: Young people spend too much time on their phones, get very little sleep and are tired the next day at school.
- For scheduled future events with an adverbial phrase of time: The programme finishes at ten o'clock.

G1.2 Present progressive

Positive sentences	Negative sentences	Questions
I am studying. You are studying. He/she/it is studying. We are studying. You are studying. They are studying.	I'm not studying. You aren't studying. He/she/it isn't studying. We aren't studying. You aren't studying. They aren't studying.	Am I studying? Are you studying? Is he/she/it studying? Are we studying? Are you studying? Are they studying? Questions with a question word: What am I studying? What are you studying? What is he/she/it studying? What are we studying? What are you studying? What are they studying?

Talking about the present
V 1 ▶   I 13 👆

> **!** Some verbs are never used in the progressive form, especially those which express feelings or a belief: believe, love, hate, seem, have (in the sense of own), can, mean, want to, feel, notice, realise.

GRAMMAR FILES

Examples of typical use:
- An activity that is going on right now and will continue for a limited period of time: Reese is giving an interview (now).
  Tense markers: now, just now, at the moment
- Planned future events with an adverbial phrase of time: Reese is flying to London next week.

G1.3 Simple past

Talking about the past
V 2 ▶ I 14

Positive sentences	Negative sentences	Questions
I played a video game. You played a video game. He/she/it played a video game. We played a video game. You played a video game. They played a video game.	I didn't play a video game. You didn't play a video game. He/she/it didn't play a video game. We didn't play a video game. You didn't play a video game. They didn't play a video game.	Did I play a video game? Did you play a video game? Did he/she/it play a video game? Did we play a video game? Did you play a video game? Did they play a video game? Questions with a question word: Why did I play a video game? Why did you play a video game? Why did he/she/it play a video game? Why did we play a video game? Why did you play a video game? Why did they play a video game?

❗ Be careful with irregular verbs.

Examples of typical use:
- For activities that began and ended at a specific time in the past: The technical team tested the device last week.
  Tense markers: yesterday, ago, last week/month/year, in 2017/…, on Tuesday/…
- For a series of events in the past, as in a story, often called the 'narrative past':
  As Kate didn't have a job, she went to Australia. Her aunt found her a job there and one thing led to another. After six months, Kate had a permanent job.

G1.4 Past progressive

Talking about the past
V 2 ▶ I 14

Positive sentences	Negative sentences	Questions
I was thinking. You were thinking. He/she/it was thinking. We were thinking. You were thinking. They were thinking.	I wasn't thinking. You weren't thinking. He/she/it wasn't thinking. We weren't thinking. You weren't thinking. They weren't thinking.	Was I thinking? Were you thinking? Was he/she/it thinking? Were we thinking? Were you thinking? Were they thinking? Questions with a question word: What was I thinking? What were you thinking? What was he/she/it thinking? What were we thinking? What were you thinking? What were they thinking?

GRAMMAR FILES

Examples of typical use:
- An activity in the past that was already in progress when something else happened:
  Kate was working in a bar when she heard about the job in a bank.
- Several activities or events that were happening at the same time in the past:
  While Kate was living in England, she only had temporary jobs.

G1.5 Present perfect simple

Positive sentences	Negative sentences	Questions
I have finished. You have finished. He/she/it has finished. We have finished. You have finished. They have finished.	I haven't finished. You haven't finished. He/she/it hasn't finished. We haven't finished. You haven't finished. They haven't finished.	Have I finished? Have you finished? Has he/she/it finished? Have we finished? Have you finished? Have they finished?
		Questions with a question word: What have I finished? What have you finished? What has he/she/it finished? What have we finished? What have you finished? What have they finished?

> **Talking about the present perfect**
> V 3 ▶ I 15

❗ Be careful with irregular verbs.

❗ With the present perfect simple the result of the action is usually more important than the action itself. Never use the present perfect with adverbs of past time, e.g. yesterday, last week, three years ago, in 2017…

Examples of typical use:
- Activities that happened recently and whose effects are still being felt in the present: Kate has moved to Australia and she is still getting used to the different accent there.
- With certain adverbs: just, so far, ever, never, recently, lately, today, this week, already, (not) yet
  He has listed all his work experience so far. – Has he ever worked abroad?
- With for and since, for activities that started in the past and are continuing:
  Lisa hasn't checked her emails for two days. – She has received 20 emails since Tuesday.

G1.6 Present perfect progressive

Positive sentences	Negative sentences	Questions
I have been waiting. You have been waiting. He/she/it has been waiting. We have been waiting. You have been waiting. They have been waiting.	I haven't been waiting. You haven't been waiting. He/she/it hasn't been waiting. We haven't been waiting. You haven't been waiting. They haven't been waiting.	Have I been waiting? Have you been waiting? Has he/she/it been waiting? Have we been waiting? Have you been waiting? Have they been waiting? Questions with a question word: Why have I been waiting? Why have you been waiting? Why has he/she/it been waiting? Why have we been waiting? Why have you been waiting? Why have they been waiting?

> **Talking about the present perfect**
> V 3 ▶ I 15

GRAMMAR FILES

Examples of typical use:
- Activities that have been going on either continuously or at intervals up to the present, often with adverbials of time such as all day, for a week, etc.: We have been looking at job adverts all evening.
- There is no mention of time but the activity has taken place very recently and the result is still visible: It has been raining.

G1.7 Past perfect simple

Positive sentences	Negative sentences	Questions
I had finished. You had finished. He/she/it had finished. We had finished. You had finished. They had finished.	I hadn't finished. You hadn't finished. He/she/it hadn't finished. We hadn't finished. You hadn't finished. They hadn't finished.	Had I finished? Had you finished? Had he/she/it finished? Had we finished? Had you finished? Had they finished? Questions with a question word: What had I finished? What had you finished? What had he/she/it finished? What had we finished? What had you finished? What had they finished?

! Be careful with irregular verbs.

Examples of typical use:
- An activity that happened before another activity in the past, showing the connection between the two activities:
  When I arrived at college, the lesson had already started.
  After I had finished my homework, I decided to go out.
- In reported speech, when the original statement is in the past or present perfect:
  Jane said that she had forgotten to do her homework.

G1.8 Past perfect progressive

Positive sentences	Negative sentences	Questions
I had been waiting. You had been waiting. He/she/it had been waiting. We had been waiting. You had been waiting. They had been waiting.	I hadn't been waiting. You hadn't been waiting. He/she/it hadn't been waiting. We hadn't been waiting. You hadn't been waiting. They hadn't been waiting.	Had I been waiting? Had you been waiting? Had he/she/it been waiting? Had we been waiting? Had you been waiting? Had they been waiting? Questions with a question word: Why had I been waiting? Why had you been waiting? Why had he/she/it been waiting? Why had we been waiting? Why had you been waiting? Why had they been waiting?

GRAMMAR FILES

Examples of typical use:
- An activity that occurred over a period of time, and before another activity, in the past. The two activities are directly related: He was tired because he had been working so hard.
- In reported speech, when the original statement is in the present perfect progressive:
He said that he had been working hard.

G1.9 Going to-future

Positive sentences	Negative sentences	Questions
I am going to leave early. You are going to leave early. He/she/it is going to leave early. We are going to leave early You are going to leave early. They are going to leave early.	I'm not going to leave early. You're not going to leave early. He/she/it's not going to leave early. We're not going to leave early. You're not going to leave early. They're not going to leave early.	Am I going to leave early? Are you going to leave early? Is he/she/it going to leave early? Are we going to leave early? Are you going to leave early? Are they going to leave early?

Talking about the future
V 4 ▷ I 16 👋

Examples of typical use:
- For an action in the future that has already been planned or prepared:
They're going to buy new tablets for the whole school.
- For a prediction about the future, when you can see that something is about to happen:
Look at those clouds. It's going to rain soon.

G1.10 Future simple (will-future)

Positive sentences	Negative sentences	Questions
I will finish college. You will finish college. He/she/it will finish college. We will finish college. You will finish college. They will finish college.	I won't finish college. You won't finish college. He/she/it won't finish college. We won't finish college. You won't finish college. They won't finish college.	Will I finish college? Will you finish college? Will he/she/it finish college? Will we finish college? Will you finish college? Will they finish college? Questions with a question word: When will I finish college? When will you finish college? When will he/she/it finish college? When will we finish college? When will you finish college? When will they finish college?

Talking about the future
V 4 ▷ I 16 👋

❗ English will = German werden
English want = German wollen

Examples of typical use:
- Things that are likely to happen at a defined or undefined time in the future:
You'll be a great business person one day.
- For forecasts, such as the weather forecast: On Saturday, it will rain for most of the day.
- In if-clauses Type 1 – future situations that are probable/possible:
If the weather is nice, I'll revise for my test in the park.

173

GRAMMAR FILES

G1.11 Future progressive

Positive sentences	Negative sentences	Questions
I will be learning. You will be learning. He/she/it will be learning. We will be learning. You will be learning. They will be learning.	I won't be learning. You won't be learning. He/she/it won't be learning. We won't be learning. You won't be learning. They won't be learning.	Will I be learning? Will you be learning? Will he/she/it be learning? Will we be learning? Will you be learning? Will they be learning? Questions with a question word: What will I be learning? What will you be learning? What will he/she/it be learning? What will we be learning? What will you be learning? What will they be learning?

Example of typical use:
- Events – which are often planned – that will be going on at a certain time in the future when another event occurs: You will be sleeping by the time I get home.

G1.12 Future perfect simple

Positive sentences	Negative sentences	Questions
I will have finished. You will have finished. He/she/it will have finished. We will have finished. You will have finished. They will have finished.	I won't have finished. You won't have finished. He/she/it won't have finished. We won't have finished. You won't have finished. They won't have finished.	Will I have finished? Will you have finished? Will he/she/it have finished? Will we have finished? Will you have finished? Will they have finished? Questions with a question word: When will I have finished? When will you have finished? When will he/she/it have finished? When will we have finished? When will you have finished? When will they have finished?

❗ Be careful with irregular verbs.

Example of typical use:
- For an activity in the future that takes place before a second activity, to show the relation between them. The second activity is in the present tense:
Joanna will have finished the college course by the time she is 20.

GRAMMAR FILES

G1.13 Future perfect progressive

Positive sentences	Negative sentences	Questions
I will have been waiting. You will have been waiting. He/she/it will have been waiting. We will have been waiting. You will have been waiting. They will have been waiting.	I won't have been waiting. You won't have been waiting. He/she/it won't have been waiting. We won't have been waiting. You won't have been waiting. They won't have been waiting.	Will I have been waiting? Will you have been waiting? Will he/she/it have been waiting? Will we have been waiting? Will you have been waiting? Will they have been waiting?

Example of typical use:
- Used in the same way as the future perfect simple, but it places more emphasis on the length of time the activity is expected to take:
  They will have been studying English for eight years by the time they take the exam.

G1.14 Conditional I

Positive sentences	Negative sentences	Questions
I would take a gap year. You would take a gap year. He/she/it would take a gap year. We would take a gap year. You would take a gap year. They would take a gap year.	I wouldn't take a gap year. You wouldn't take a gap year. He/she/it wouldn't take a gap year. We wouldn't take a gap year. You wouldn't take a gap year. They wouldn't take a gap year.	Would I take a gap year? Would you take a gap year? Would he/she/it take a gap year? Would we take a gap year? Would you take a gap year? Would they take a gap year? Questions with a question word: Why would I take a gap year? Why would you take a gap year? Why would he/she/it take a gap year? Why would we take a gap year? Why would you take a gap year? Why would they take a gap year?

Talking about conditions
V 5 I 17

Examples of typical use:
- For suggestions, polite questions and requests:
  Which country would you visit? – Well, I would visit Australia.
  Would you like a drink?
  Would you help me, please?

- In if-clauses Type 2 – future situations that are improbable/unlikely:
  If I had enough money, I would start my own company.

GRAMMAR FILES

Talking about conditions
V 5 ▶ I 17

G1.15 Conditional II

Positive sentences	Negative sentences	Questions
I would have applied for the job. You would have applied for the job. He/she/it would have applied for the job. We would have applied for the job. You would have applied for the job. They would have applied for the job.	I wouldn't have applied for the job. You wouldn't have applied for the job. He/she/it wouldn't have applied for the job. We wouldn't have applied for the job. You wouldn't have applied for the job. They wouldn't have applied for the job.	Would I have applied for the job? Would you have applied for the job? Would he/she/it have applied for the job? Would we have applied for the job? Would you have applied for the job? Would they have applied for the job? Questions with a question word: Why would I have applied for the job? Why would you have applied for the job? Why would he/she/it have applied for the job? Why would we have applied for the job? Why would you have applied for the job? Why would they have applied for the job?

❗ Be careful with irregular verbs.

Example of typical use:
- In if-clauses Type 3 – past situations that are unreal/impossible/hypothetical:
  If you had prepared before the interview, they would have given you the job.

Talking about conditions
V 5 ▶ I 17

G2 If-clauses

There are three main types of if-clauses (or conditional sentences) in English. They are basically used in the same way as conditional sentences in German. You can put the if-clause at the beginning or at the end of the sentence.

G2.1 Type 1 – Future situations (probable/possible)

a) if-clause: simple present – main clause: will-future
   If you study hard, you will pass the exam.
   Wenn du fleißig lernst, wirst du die Prüfung bestehen.

b) if-clause: present perfect – main clause: will-future
   If you have studied hard, you will pass the exam.
   Wenn du fleißig gelernt hast, wirst du die Prüfung bestehen.

c) if-clause: simple present – main clause: can + infinitive
   If you study hard, you can pass the exam.
   Wenn du fleißig lernst, kannst du die Prüfung bestehen.

d) if-clause: simple present – main clause: might + infinitive
   If you study hard, you might pass the exam.
   Wenn du fleißig lernst, wirst du eventuell die Prüfung bestehen.

G2.2 Type 2 – Future situations (improbable/unlikely)

a) if-clause: simple past – main clause: conditional I (would + infinitive)
   If you studied hard, you would pass the exam.
   Wenn du fleißig lernen würdest, würdest du die Prüfung bestehen.

b) if-clause: simple past – main clause: could + infinitive
   If you studied hard, you could pass the exam.
   Wenn du fleißig lernen würdest, könntest du die Prüfung bestehen.

G2.3 Type 3 – Past situations (unreal/impossible/hypothetical)

a) if-clause: past perfect – main clause: conditional II (would + have + past participle)
   If you had studied hard, you would have passed the exam.
   Wenn du fleißig gelernt hättest, hättest du die Prüfung bestanden.

b) if-clause: past perfect – main clause: could + have + past participle
   If you had studied hard, you could have passed the exam.
   Wenn du fleißig gelernt hättest, hättest du die Prüfung bestehen können.

c) if-clause: past perfect – main clause: might + have + past participle
   If you had studied hard, you might have passed the exam.
   Wenn du fleißig gelernt hättest, hättest du eventuell die Prüfung bestanden.

! Exceptions to the rules:

- The present tense is used in both clauses in general statements and for repeated activities or habits:
  If plants don't get enough water, they die. – If she has time, she goes to the gym.

- For recommendations and advice use 'were' in the if-clause and conditional I in the main clause: If I were you, I would study a bit harder.

- 'If' can be left out when the order of the verb and subject are reversed:
  Had I studied harder, I would have passed the exam.

! Be careful!

- If you start a sentence with an if-clause, use a comma. Don't use a comma if you start with the main clause:
  If you study hard, you will pass the exam.
  You will pass the exam if you study hard.

- Don't use 'will' in the if-clause, except to express willingness:
  They can come to Britain if they'll work.

- Don't use 'would' in the if-clause except when you are making a polite request:
  I would be grateful if you would hand in your homework on time in future.

GRAMMAR FILES

Talking about processes

V 6 ▶   I 18

G3 The passive

The passive is often used when the action is more important than who or what performed it. The passive is frequently used in scientific and technical writing. The passive can be formed with or without an 'agent'. The 'agent' is the person or thing that causes an action to occur.

Form the passive using a form of 'to be' + past participle (+ by + agent)

The Youth Agency carries out research projects.

Research projects are carried out by the Youth Agency.

Simple present	Present progressive
I am invited for an interview. You are invited for an interview. He/she/it is invited for an interview. We are invited for an interview. You are invited for an interview. They are invited for an interview.	I am being interviewed for a survey. You are being interviewed for a survey. He/she/it is being interviewed for a survey. We are being interviewed for a survey. You are being interviewed for a survey. They are being interviewed for a survey.
Simple past	Past progressive
I was invited for an interview. You were invited for an interview. He/she/it was invited for an interview. We were invited for an interview. You were invited for an interview. They were invited for an interview.	I was being interviewed for a survey. You were being interviewed for a survey. He/she/it was being interviewed for a survey. We were being interviewed for a survey. You were being interviewed for a survey. They were being interviewed for a survey.
Present perfect	Modal verbs
I have been invited for an interview. You have been invited for an interview. He/she/it has been invited for an interview. We have been invited for an interview. You have been invited for an interview. They have been invited for an interview.	I can be contacted online. You must be contacted online. He/she/it mustn't be contacted online. We needn't be contacted online. You ought to be contacted online. They should be contacted online.
Future	Future perfect
I will be invited for an interview. You will be invited for an interview. He/she/it will be invited for an interview. We will be invited for an interview. You will be invited for an interview. They will be invited for an interview.	I will have been invited for an interview. You will have been invited for an interview. He/she/it will have been invited for an interview. We will have been invited for an interview. You will have been invited for an interview. They will have been invited for an interview.

! Be careful with irregular verbs.

GRAMMAR FILES

G4 Relative clauses

Relative clauses are used to describe people or things. A relative clause usually begins with a relative pronoun.

Relative pronoun	refers to
who	people (subject or object)
whom	people (object), formal English
which	things
that	people or things (subject or object)
whose	possessions

> **Talking about describing people or things in more detail**
> V 7 ▶ I 19 ✋

G4.1 Defining relative clauses

- A defining relative clause is important for the meaning of the sentence. Without the relative clause the sentence would not make any sense. Defining relative clauses are not separated from the rest of the sentence by commas:
  The text message that/which you sent me didn't arrive.
  This is the woman who(m) I emailed yesterday.
  This is the boy whose smartphone was stolen.

- The pronouns 'that', 'which' and 'who(m)' can be left out if the pronoun is the object of the relative clause. This type of relative clause is known as a 'contact' clause:
  The apps we use are all free.
  This is the woman I emailed yesterday.

G4.2 Non-defining relative clauses

- The information in non-defining relative clauses is additional and descriptive. Even without the relative clause the sentence is clear. Non-defining relative clauses are separated from the rest of the sentence by commas:
  Aiden, who is still a teenager, runs a successful online business.

G5 Adjectives

Adjectives describe people and things: the tall man – bright lights

> **Talking about qualities**
> V 8 ▶ I 20 ✋

- The present participle (-ing form) and past participle of verbs can often be used as adjectives:
  an interesting book – the finished report

- Verbs are usually followed by adverbs, however some verbs are followed by adjectives:

to be	The laptop is heavy.
to become	Anne became nervous before the interview.
to feel	Thomas felt excited about his new job.
to get	Her smartphone got broken.
to look	The office block looks modern.
to seem	My new colleagues seem nice.

- Adjectives can be used as collective nouns. In such cases, the + adjective refers to a particular group of people as a whole:
  It is important to help the unemployed to find work.
  The very young and the very old are particularly at risk.

GRAMMAR FILES

- The comparison of adjectives:

Positive form	Comparative form	Superlative form
cold	colder	the coldest
hot	hotter	the hottest
funny	funnier	the funniest
modern	more modern	the most modern

! Remember the irregular forms:	good – better – the best much – more – the most bad – worse – the worst far – further – the furthest

Use more/-er than, as … as and not as … as to make comparisons:
An email is more modern than a letter.
My smartphone is newer than yours.
Tablets are just as popular as laptops.
The internet at school is not as fast as the internet at home.

G6 Adverbs

Talking about qualities
V 8 I 20

Adverbs are formed by adding -ly/-ily to an adjective:

Adjective	Adverb
safe	safely
happy	happily
real	really
reasonable	reasonably

! Remember the irregular forms:	good – well fast – fast hard – hard

- Adverbs describe actions (verbs): He walked quickly. She spoke slowly.
- Adverbs before other adjectives: This is an extremely good essay.
- Adverbs before other adverbs: He was driving incredibly fast.
- Adverbs before past participles: Credit cards are frequently accepted.
- Some useful adverbs: always, usually, often, frequently, sometimes, seldom, rarely, never, recently, soon, lately, in the past, in the future, largely, for the most part, partly, probably, possibly, hardly, definitely, obviously, clearly, basically, consequently, as a result
- The comparison of adverbs:

Positive form	Comparative form	Superlative form
fluently	more fluently	the most fluently

! Remember the irregular forms:	well – better – the best badly – worse – the worst fast – faster – the fastest

G7 Question tags

A question tag is added to the end of a sentence to turn it into a question. In German you use expressions like '…, *nicht wahr?*' and '…, *oder?*' in a similar way.

- If the statement is positive, the question tag is negative:
  He uses social media, doesn't he?

- If the statement is negative, the question tag is positive:
  He doesn't use social media, does he?

- The subject of the sentence is also the subject of the question tag:
  Lisa never turns off her smartphone, does she?

- If the statement is in the simple present, the question tag is formed with 'is/are' or 'isn't/aren't', 'do/does' or 'don't/doesn't':
  He likes video games, doesn't he?

- For statements in the simple past, the question tag is formed with 'was/were' or 'wasn't/weren't' or 'did/didn't':
  He took a gap year, didn't he?

- If the statement uses an auxiliary verb (to be, to have, will, etc.) or a modal (can, must, etc.), use the modal or auxiliary in the same tense in the tag:
  Tom is here, isn't he?
  Roger has bought a new laptop, hasn't he?
  Jill will be at the interview, won't she?
  You can contact me by email, can't you?

G8 Modal auxiliaries

> **Talking about ability, permission and necessity**
> V 9 I 21

- Will/would/can/could/may:

  Asking someone to do something:
  Will/Would/Can/Could you do me a favour?

  Asking for permission/giving permission:
  May I use your phone? – Yes, of course, you may.

  Talking about abilities:
  She can speak English.

- Must/mustn't/needn't:

  Instructing someone to do something or not to do something:
  You must prepare before an interview.
  You mustn't tell lies at an interview.

  Talking about a necessity or duty:
  I must send in my job application by Friday.
  You needn't be nervous before the interview.

- May/might/could/must/will:

  Expressing a possibility or probability:
  It may/might/could/will rain.
  You must be Mr Jones.

  Making a suggestion:
  We could look for typical interview questions online.

GRAMMAR FILES

- Should/ought to/shouldn't/ought not to:

  Giving advice:
  You should/ought to use a dictionary.
  You shouldn't/ought not to arrive late for the interview.

- Modal auxiliaries only have a present and/or past tense form. Substitutes are used for other tenses:

Modal auxiliary	Substitutes	Examples
can/could	be able to	He won't be able to to work under pressure.
may/mustn't	be allowed to not be allowed to	We were allowed to use our smartphones in class. We weren't allowed to play music.
must/needn't	have to not have to	She will have to work this weekend. We didn't have to work late.

> **Talking about likes and dislikes**
> V 10 ▶ I 22

G9 -ing forms

An -ing form can be either a present participle or a gerund.

G9.1 The present participle

- The present participle is used in the progressive tenses (present progressive, past progressive, etc.):
  Mary is checking her emails. – The class was discussing the topic 'Take a gap year or find a job?'.

- The present participle can be used as an adjective: the winning party – a growing child

- The present participle can be used to shorten clauses, often after a conjunction, e.g: after, while, before, when
  I was riding my bike to work when I saw her. → While riding my bike to work, I saw her.
  The class listened to the entrepreneur who was talking about start-ups. → The class listened to the entrepreneur talking about start-ups.
  After we had collected ideas in a word web, we discussed them. → After collecting ideas in a word web we discussed them.
  Read the text before you answer the questions. → Read the text before answering the questions.

G9.2 The gerund

- The gerund is used after prepositions: You're very good at speaking English.

- The gerund is often used after certain verbs: like, hate, enjoy, love, mind, prefer
  I don't mind watching TV but I prefer reading and I also enjoy playing computer games.

- The gerund can be used as a noun: Laughing is good for you. – Studying is very important.

- Some verbs have the construction verb + preposition + gerund:
  to be afraid of, to look forward to, to feel like, to talk about, to insist on, to decide against, to think about/of, to succeed in, to apologise for
  I'm afraid of flying.

- When the following expressions are followed by a verb, use the gerund:
  There's no point in waiting any longer.
  It's not worth going to see the new James Bond film.
  A waste of money/time: It's a waste of time talking to you.
  To spend/to waste time/money: He spends all of his time sitting in front of a computer.

G10 Reported speech

Talking about passing on information
V 11 ▶ I 23 👆

Reported speech (or indirect speech) is used to report what someone has said without quoting them.

- Start the reported speech with a reporting verb:
  a) Statements: say (that), tell sb. (that), answer, mention, explain, reply, etc.
     "I'm tired." → She says (that) she's tired.
  b) Questions: ask, want to know
     "Are you hungry?" → She asks me if I'm hungry.
     "Where do you go to school?" → She wants to know where I go to school.
  c) Commands: tell sb. to + infinitive
     "Leave me alone!" → She told me to leave her alone.

- If the reporting verb is in the present, present perfect or future tense, the tense stays the same:
  "Spending hours on social media is bad for you".
  → Mr Jones says spending hours on social media is bad for you.
  → Mr Jones has said spending hours on social media is bad for you.
  → Mr Jones will say spending hours on social media is bad for you.

- If the reporting verb is in the past tense, the tense of the reported speech changes:

simple present "I text my best friend every day."	→ simple past She said she texted her best friend every day.
present progressive "I am texting my best friend."	→ past progressive She said she was texting her best friend..
simple past "I texted my best friend last night."	→ past perfect She said she had texted her best friend the night before.
past progressive "I was texting my best friend."	→ past perfect progressive She said she had been texting her best friend.
present perfect "I have texted my best friend."	→ past perfect She said she had texted her best friend.
present perfect progressive "I have been texting my best friend."	→ past perfect progressive She said she had been texting her best friend.
past perfect "I had texted my best friend."	→ past perfect She said she had texted her best friend.
past perfect progressive "I had been texting my best friend."	→ past perfect progressive She said she had been texting her best friend.
will-future I will text my best friend every day."	→ conditional I She said she would text her best friend every day.

- Questions follow the same tense changes as statements:
  "How many jobs have you applied for?" → My friend asked me how many jobs I had applied for.
- Some adverbs of time also change in reported speech, for example:

now	→	then
yesterday	→	the day before/the previous day
here	→	there
last year	→	the year before/the previous year
today	→	that day
tomorrow	→	the next day

- Statements involving truths and facts do not have to change in reported speech:
  "The novel is by Zadie Smith." → The teacher said that the novel is by Zadie Smith.

GRAMMAR FILES

Talking about qualities
V 8 ▶ I 20

G11 Word order

Generally, the word order in English sentences is subject – verb – object.
This is the case in main clauses and subordinate clauses:
We live in a world that is heavily influenced by the media.
I like Las Vegas because it has something for everyone.

G11.1 Statements

- Normally, place comes before time:
  I went to school yesterday.
  I've wanted to visit the UK for years.

- The adverbs in a sentence generally follow the sequence: adverb of manner – adverb of place – adverb of time:
  I was waiting patiently for tickets outside the stadium all morning.
  I will be working hard in London this summer.

- In English, adverbs of frequency (never, sometimes, often, always, etc.) are directly in front of the verb:
  I usually check my phone as soon as I wake up.
  I never leave home without my phone.

  > **!** But be careful – there is an exception when you use the verb to be:
  > I'm always in the gym on Fridays.

G11.2 Questions

- Questions never begin with a main verb:
  Do you like British food?
  Did you get my message last night?

  > **!** But be careful – there is an exception when you use the verb to be:
  > Are you thinking of taking a gap year?
  > Am I the first person to arrive?

- Negative questions do not end with a main verb like they do in German:
  Aren't you going to miss German food?

G11.3 Negated statements

- The negation of don't/doesn't comes before the main verb, unlike in German:
  I don't have school on Friday afternoons.
  I don't use my mobile phone during lessons.

GRAMMAR FILES

Erklärvideos ▷ und interaktive Übungen

Mit Hilfe von Erklärvideos und interaktiven Übungen können grammatische Phänomene wiederholt und gefestigt werden.
Die Videos sowie die Übungen finden Sie in den Medien zum Schülerbuch und im eBook.

Talking about the present	– simple present, present progressive
	– questions and negative sentences
Talking about the past	– simple past, past progressive
Talking about the present perfect	– present perfect simple, present perfect progressive
	– present perfect, simple past
Talking about the future	– will-future, going to-future, present with future meaning
Talking about quantities	– some, any, every, no and their compounds
Talking about qualities	– adjectives, adverbs
	– comparison of adjectives and adverbs, exceptions
Talking about ability, permission and necessity	– modal auxiliaries and their substitutes
Talking about describing people or things in more detail	– relative clauses: who, which, that, whose
Talking about conditions	– if-clauses
Talking about likes and dislikes	– the gerund
Talking about processes	– the passive: present, past, future
Talking about passing on information	– reported speech

IRREGULAR VERBS

be	was/were, been	sein
beat	beat, beaten	schlagen
become	became, become	werden
begin	began, begun	anfangen
bite	bit, bitten	beißen
break	broke, broken	(zer)brechen
breed	bred, bred	züchten, erzeugen
bring	brought, brought	(mit)bringen
build	built, built	bauen
buy	bought, bought	kaufen
catch	caught, caught	fangen
choose	chose, chosen	wählen
come	came, come	kommen
cost	cost, cost	kosten
cut	cut, cut	schneiden
do	did, done	tun, machen
draw	drew, drawn	zeichnen
drink	drank, drunk	trinken
drive	drove, driven	fahren
eat	ate, eaten	essen
fall	fell, fallen	fallen
feel	felt, felt	(sich) fühlen
fight	fought, fought	(be)kämpfen
find	found, found	finden
flee	fled, fled	fliehen, flüchten
fly	flew, flown	fliegen
forbid	forbade, forbidden	verbieten
forget	forgot, forgotten	vergessen
freeze	froze, frozen	frieren
get	got, got	bekommen
give	gave, given	geben
go	went, gone	gehen, fahren
grow	grew, grown	wachsen
hang	hung, hung	hängen
have	had, had	haben
hear	heard, heard	hören
hide	hid, hidden	(sich) verstecken
hit	hit, hit	schlagen
hold	held, held	(fest)halten
hurt	hurt, hurt	(sich) wehtun
keep	kept, kept	aufbewahren
know	knew, known	wissen; kennen
lead	led, led	führen
leave	left, left	(ver)lassen
lend	lent, lent	(ver)leihen

IRREGULAR VERBS

let	let, let	lassen
lie	lay, lain	liegen
lose	lost, lost	verlieren
make	made, made	machen
mean	meant, meant	meinen, bedeuten
meet	met, met	treffen
pay	paid, paid	bezahlen
read	read, read	lesen
ride	rode, ridden	reiten, fahren
ring	rang, rung	klingeln
rise	rose, risen	steigen
run	ran, run	laufen
say	said, said	sagen
see	saw, seen	sehen
seek	sought, sought	suchen
sell	sold, sold	verkaufen
send	sent, sent	senden
shoot	shot, shot	(er)schießen
show	showed, shown	zeigen
shrink	shrank, shrunk	schrumpfen
shut	shut, shut	schließen
sing	sang, sung	singen
sink	sank, sunk	sinken
sit	sat, sat	sitzen
sleep	slept, slept	schlafen
speak	spoke, spoken	sprechen
spend	spent, spent	ausgeben; verbringen
spread	spread, spread	ausbreiten
stand	stood, stood	stehen
steal	stole, stolen	stehlen
stick	stuck, stuck	kleben, feststecken
strike	struck, struck	schlagen; betreffen
strive	strove, striven	anstreben, sich bemühen
swim	swam, swum	schwimmen
take	took, taken	nehmen
teach	taught, taught	unterrichten
tear	tore, torn	zerreißen
tell	told, told	sagen; erzählen
think	thought, thought	denken
throw	threw, thrown	werfen
understand	understood, understood	verstehen
wake	woke, woken	aufwachen
wear	wore, worn	tragen
win	won, won	gewinnen
write	wrote, written	schreiben

CLASSROOM PHRASES

Asking about words and meanings

What does (the word) … mean?	Was bedeutet (das Wort) …?
I don't understand the word …/the expression …/this sentence.	Ich verstehe das Wort … nicht/den Ausdruck … nicht/diesen Satz nicht.
How do you say … in English?	Wie sagt man … auf Englisch?
Could you repeat that/say that again?	Würden Sie das wiederholen/nochmal sagen?
Can you explain the meaning of …?	Können Sie die Bedeutung von … erklären?
Could you provide an example sentence with …?	Könnten Sie einen Beispielsatz mit … geben?

Giving your opinion

I think (that) …	Ich denke/meine, dass …
In my opinion …	Meiner Meinung nach …
I find … (really) good/interesting/boring.	Ich finde … (echt) gut/interessant/langweilig.
It seems to me that …	Es scheint mir, dass …
I have a positive/negative impression of …	Ich habe einen positiven/negativen Eindruck von …

Agreeing and disagreeing

I agree (with Martina).	Ich stimme (Martina) zu.
I share (Anna's) opinion.	Ich teile (Annas) Meinung.
I disagree/don't agree (with Bernd).	Ich stimme (Bernd) nicht zu.
Yes, I think the same/I think that, too.	Ja, ich denke das Gleiche/das meine ich auch.
I think you are wrong.	Ich finde, dass du Unrecht hast.
I have a different perspective.	Ich habe eine andere Perspektive.
I see it differently.	Ich sehe das anders.

CLASSROOM PHRASES

Talking about texts

In the text the reader learns that …	Im Text erfährt der Leser/die Leserin, dass …
Throughout the article, we discover that …	Im Laufe des Artikels erfahren wir …
The headline indicates that …	Die Überschrift deutet darauf hin, dass …
The first paragraph tells us that …	Der erste Absatz sagt uns, dass …
In the second paragraph we read/learn that …	Im zweiten Absatz liest/erfährt man, dass …
The last paragraph is about …	Im letzten Absatz geht es um …
The main idea presented in the text is …	Die Hauptidee, die im Text präsentiert wird, ist …
In the text it (also) says that …	Im Text steht (auch), dass …
The author highlights that …	Der Autor/die Autorin betont, dass …
The author uses … to illustrate their point.	Der Autor/die Autorin verwendet …, um seinen/ihren Standpunkt klar zu machen.
One can infer from the text that …	Man kann aus dem Text schließen, dass …
Finally, we learn/read that …	Zuletzt erfährt/liest man, dass …
The main message of the text is …	Die Hauptaussage des Textes ist …

Working in class

Would you write that on the board, please?	Würden Sie das bitte an die Tafel schreiben?
Could you play the CD again, please?	Würden Sie die CD bitte nochmal vorspielen?
I didn't understand the instruction.	Ich habe die Anweisung nicht verstanden.
I'm not sure what we have to do.	Ich bin nicht sicher, was wir tun müssen.
I haven't got a partner.	Ich habe keinen Partner/keine Partnerin.
We need another person in our group.	Unserer Gruppe fehlt eine Person.
Our group's finished.	Unsere Gruppe ist fertig.
We need a bit more time.	Wir brauchen noch ein bisschen Zeit.
Could you give us feedback on these ideas?	Könnten Sie uns Feedback zu diesen Ideen geben?
Could I borrow a/your dictionary?	Darf ich ein/Ihr Wörterbuch leihen?

Bildquellennachweis

8 plainpicture GmbH & Co. KG, Hamburg (Cavan Images/Cavan Social); **10.1** ShutterStock.com RF, New York (Silvia Truessel); **10.2** Alamy stock photo, Abingdon (Ken Gillespie Photography); **10.3** Alamy stock photo, Abingdon (keith morris); **10.4** Alamy stock photo, Abingdon (Stuart Forster); **10.5** graphitecture book & edition, Bernau am Chiemsee ; Three-Circle Model of World Englishes. Braj Kachru, 1985; **18.1** ShutterStock.com RF. New York (Net Vector); **18.2** Sara Barnard (unbekannt); **22.1** ShutterStock.com RF, New York (Farknot Architect); **22** graphitecture book & edition, Bernau am Chiemsee ; April 2021, World Health Organization; (Deafness and hearing loss); Elizabeth Dougherty, March 2017, The Brink, Boston University; (Auszug aus Infographic: Sign Language Rights for All!); **23.1** Getty Images Plus, München (iStock / martin-dm); **25** ShutterStock.com RF, New York (DFree); **26.1** ShutterStock.com RF, New York (Lulu877); **26.2** ShutterStock.com RF, New York (MaryValery); **26.3** ShutterStock.com RF, New York (FlyIntoSpace); **26.4** ShutterStock.com RF, New York (infostocker); **28** ShutterStock.com RF, New York (Far_Away); **29.1** www.CartoonStock.com, Bath (Zeitler, Martina); **30.1** ShutterStock.com RF, New York (Visual Generation); **31** ShutterStock.com RF, New York (LightField Studios); **32.1** ShutterStock.com RF, New York (pathdoc); **32.2** Getty Images Plus, München (iStock / PeopleImages); **32.3** Getty Images Plus, München (E+ / FluxFactory); **32.4** ShutterStock.com RF, New York (Olena Yakobchuk); **33** stock.adobe.com, Dublin (Lubo Ivanko); **35** stock.adobe.com, Dublin (Bubble beanie); **36.1** ShutterStock.com RF, New York (baranq); **38** Getty Images Plus, München (NicolasMcComber E+); **39.1** Getty Images Plus, München (iStock / sturti); **39.2** graphitecture book & edition, Bernau am Chiemsee ; Source: National Student Accommodation Survey 2022; ("Where university students live"); **40.1** ShutterStock.com RF, New York (BRO.vector); **40.2** Getty Images, München (Getty Images North America / Donna Ward); **44.1** ShutterStock.com RF, New York (AlexLMX); **47.1** ShutterStock.com RF, New York (Vector pro); **47.2** laif, Köln (Davide Lanzilao/Contrasto); **51.2** ShutterStock.com RF, New York (PeopleImages.com - Yuri A); **53** ShutterStock.com RF, New York (Elizaveta Galitckaia); **54.1** ShutterStock.com RF, New York (Gorodenkoff); **54.2** Getty Images Plus, München (iStock / kynny); **54.4** ShutterStock.com RF, New York (vchal); **54.4** ShutterStock.com RF, New York (ducu59us); **54.5** ShutterStock.com RF, New York (ImageFlow); **59** ShutterStock.com RF, New York (franz12); **60.1** laif, Köln (Murat Tueremis); **60.2** Alamy stock photo, Abingdon (JEP Celebrity Photos); **62** ShutterStock.com RF, New York (Alexander Limbach); **63.1** ShutterStock.com RF, New York (CECIL BO DZWOWA); **63.2** Alamy stock photo, Abingdon (RZAF_Images); **63.3** Picture-Alliance, Frankfurt/M. (REUTERS/Noor Khamis); **67.1** ShutterStock.com RF, New York (AlexLMX); **67.2** Nach: wearesocial.com 2018.; **68.1** ShutterStock.com RF, New York (Visual Generation); **70** graphitecture book & edition, Bernau am Chiemsee ; Data from: Survey conducted April23-May 6, 2018. Pew Research Center; (Larger shares of Americans belive negative effects of widespread use of gene editing are very likely); **71.1** Getty Images Plus, München (iStock / EvgeniyShkolenko); **71.3** graphitecture book & edition, Bernau am Chiemsee ; Data from: Bitkom Research 2020; (KI-Anwendungen sind im Alltag angekommen); **73** ShutterStock.com RF, New York (Net Vector); **74.1** Mauritius Images, Mittenwald (Graham, David / Alamy / Alamy Stock Photos); **74.2** ShutterStock.com RF, New York (Everett Collection); **74.3** ShutterStock.com RF, New York (Vyntage Visuals); **74.4** ShutterStock.com RF, New York (Monkey Business Images); **74.5** Getty Images Plus, München (E+ / franckreporter); **74.6** ShutterStock.com RF, New York (PRESSLAB); **76.1** Alamy stock photo, Abingdon (MediaPunch Inc); **76.2** Alamy stock photo, Abingdon (JOHN KELLERMAN); **79** ShutterStock.com RF, New York (Macrovector); **80.1** Getty Images Plus/Microstock, München (iStock / solar22); **83** Getty Images Plus, München (iStock / Ivan Martynov); **84.1** www.CartoonStock.com, Bath (John Morris); **86** graphitecture book & edition, Bernau am Chiemsee ; Source: World Economic Forum, Global Gender Gap Report 2022; (Gender Gap Global, Top 10); **87.1** stock.adobe.com, Dublin (Daniel Coulmann); **90** www.evanscartoons.com/Malcolm Evans, Auckland; **91.2** graphitecture book & edition, Bernau am Chiemsee ; Source: AP-NORC, 2021. APNORC.org; (Grafik To fight terrorism, do you think it is..); **94.1** Getty Images Plus, München (DigitalVision / Jacobs Stock Photography Ltd); **94.2** Getty Images, München (Getty Images AsiaPac / Don Arnold); **94.3** Getty Images, München (Monument / bugto); **94.4** Alamy stock photo, Abingdon (TEK IMAGE / SCIENCE PHOTO LIBRARY); **96.1** ShutterStock.com RF, New York (desdemona72); **97** Kate Raworth and Christian Guthier. CC-BY-SA 4.0 https://creativecommons.org/licenses/by-sa/4.0/deed.de, Mountain View ; CC-BY-SA-4.0 Lizenzbestimmungen: https://creativecommons.org/licenses/by-sa/4.0/legalcode, siehe *3; **99** graphitecture book & edition, Bernau am Chiemsee. Nach: Joseph Poore & Thomas Nemecek, Science (2018) und MarketWatch reporting, 2019; **100.1** Alamy stock photo, Abingdon (Ron Adar); **103.1** Picture-Alliance, Frankfurt/M. (Albert Llop / NurPhoto); **105** Getty Images, München (AFP / BRENDAN SMIALOWSKI); **106.1** ShutterStock.com RF, New York (Nicole Glass Photography); **109.1** CartoonStock Ltd, Bath (Karsten Schley); **109.3** graphitecture book & edition, Bernau am Chiemsee ; Source: Eurostat, 2021; (Armutsgefährdungsquote von Erwerbstätigen 2021); **111** ShutterStock.com RF, New York (Octus_Photography); **112.1** Getty Images, München (AFP / DANIEL BELOUMOU OLOMO); **112.2** stock.adobe.com, Dublin (Andrey Popov); **112.3** Getty Images, München (LightRocket / Subhendu Sarkar); **112.4** Getty Images, München (NurPhoto); **113** Alamy Ltd., Abingdon; **114.1** Ernst Klett Verlag GmbH, Stuttgart; **114.2** laif, Köln (Hannah Assouline /opale.photo); **116** stock.adobe.com, Dublin (LIGHTFIELD STUDIOS); **117.1** Getty Images Plus, München (iStock / SHansche); **119** www.CartoonStock.com, Bath (Carré); **120.1** ShutterStock.com RF, New York (Photographer RM); **123.1** graphitecture book & edition, Bernau am Chiemsee ; Source: United Nations 2022; (Percentage of working people living on less than $1.90 a day); **123.2** ShutterStock.com RF, New York (RURI BYAKU); **124.1** Bláha, Marek, Offenbach am Main; **126** Getty Images, München (AFP / JOSEPH EID); **127.1** CartoonStock Ltd, Bath

(Karsten Schley); **127.2** graphitecture book & edition, Bernau am Chiemsee ; Nach: YouGov plc. 2016; (Statistic Most Patriotic Countries 2022); **129** ShutterStock.com RF, New York (Boris15); **133** iStockphoto, Calgary, Alberta (clu); **134** Alamy stock photo, Abingdon; **136.1** stock.adobe.com, Dublin (Igor Mojzes); **136.2** Thinkstock, München (iStock / gpointstudio); **139** iStockphoto, Calgary, Alberta (R-J-Seymour); **140** ShutterStock.com RF, New York (Jacob Lund); **144** ShutterStock.com RF, New York (Rawpixel.com); **145** ShutterStock.com RF, New York (Diego Cervo); **148** stock.adobe.com, Dublin (kaipong); **150.1** Romo, Virginia, Stuttgart; **150.2** Romo, Virginia, Stuttgart; **150.3** Romo, Virginia, Stuttgart; **152.1** ShutterStock.com RF, New York (Yulai Studio); **152.2** MEV Verlag GmbH, Augsburg; **152.3** Thinkstock, München (iStockphoto); **152.4** Avenue Images GmbH, Hamburg (Stockbyte RF, George Doyle); **155** Getty Images Plus, München (swissmediavision/E+); **157.1** Ernst Klett Verlag GmbH, Stuttgart; **157.2** Ernst Klett Verlag GmbH, Stuttgart; **157.3** Ernst Klett Verlag GmbH, Stuttgart; **159** www.panthermedia.net, München (keerati); **160** plainpicture GmbH & Co. KG, Hamburg (plainpicture); **162** Romo, Virginia, Stuttgart; **Umschlag** Getty Images RF, München (Hero Images)

*3 Lizenzbestimmungen zu CC-BY-SA-4.0 siehe: http://creativecommons.org/licenses/by-sa/4.0/legalcode

Textquellennachweis

12 Sandra Richter, Deutsche Welle, 02.10.2018. https://www.dw.com; **14.1** From: Heart Force One: Need No Gun to Defend Society ©2021 Abhijit Naskar; **14.2** Gloria Steinem, quoted in Gender Issues in Society: Myths, Reality and Responsibility, Jantu Das, 2021; **14.3** From: Language: The Basics ©1999 Robert Lawrence Trask; **14.4** From: 7 Things You Should Never Ask a Transgender Person, Hari Nef, Teen Vouge, 2016; **14.5** Reed Blaylock, 08.01.2020, https://theconversation.com; **18.3** From: A quiet kind of thunder ©2017 Sara Barnard; **22.3** April 2021, World Health Organization; Zur besseren altersgemäßen Verständlichkeit wurde der Originaltext verändert, ohne den Inhalt und/oder Sinn zu verändern.; **22.4** Elizabeth Dougherty, March 2017, The Brink, Boston University; Zur besseren altersgemäßen Verständlichkeit wurde der Originaltext verändert, ohne den Inhalt und/oder Sinn zu verändern.; **23.2** Ludovic Hunter-Tilney, 2019, The world no longer wants to learn to sing in English, The Financial Times, Used under licence from the Financial Times. All Rights Reserved.; **26.5** Philip Seargeant, 21.03.2022, https://theconversation.com; **29.2** Hermione Foster, https://www.languageservicesdirect.co.uk/social-media-changing-english-language/; **29.3** Attributed to Helmut Schmidt; **30.2** Christoph David Piorkowski, 20.09.2021, https://www.tagesspiegel.de; **32.5** From: Mortals and Others: American Essays 1931-35, Betrand Russell, 1975; **32.6** Shane Claiborne, Plotting Goodness Together: An Interview with Shane Claiborne, https://www.jonathanmerritt.com, 22.05.2013; **32.7** Attributed to Gelett Burgess; **32.8** From: God's Men ©1975 Pearl S Buck; **35** From: A quiet kind of thunder ©2017 Sara Barnard; **36.2** Donald Hirsch, https://theconversation.com, 18.01.2019; **40.3** From: One for the Money ©1996 Janet Evanovich; **44.2** Jessica Klein, bbc.com, 01.04.2022; **47.3** From: The Monk of Mokha ©2019 Dave Eggers; **51.1** https://www.wuestenrot.de/de/ihr_wohnwunsch/altersgerecht_wohnen/mehrgenerationenhaus.html; **51.3** From: Nada ©1945 Carmen Laforet, translated into English by Edith Grossman; **52** 20.07.2021, www.haufe.de; **56.1** Chris Milk, Chris Milk Talks Empathy in VR, the Commerce of Art and Waiting for The Holodeck, indiewire.com, 02.02.2016; **56.2** Martin Rees, 2011; **56.3** Attributed to Hilary Clinton; **56.4** Sarah Baxter, ©2020, Guardian News&Media Ltd.; **60.3** From: Machines like me ©2020 Ian McEwan; **63.4** Revolutionary technologies will drive African prosperity – this is why, Cathy Smith, World Economic Forum, 2019; **68.2** Sahotra Sarkar, https://theconversation.com, 22.04.2021; **71.2** From: Brief Answers to Big Questions ©2018 Stephen Hawking; **72** Gero Rueter, Deutsche Welle, 31.05.2022; **74.7** Attributed to Carl Honoré; **76.3** © 2021, Amanda Gorman; **80.2** Robert Skidelsky and Edward Skidelsky, How much is enough? Other Press, 2013, pp. ix-xii.; **84.2** Jannine Poletti-Hughes, The Conversation, 2022; **87.2** Noreen Nasir, Russell Contreras, 2020, APNews.com; **91.1** From: Beyond Equality: A Manual for Human Rights Defenders, Mahnaz Afkhamim, Ann Eisenberg, 2015; **91.3** 2004, Jutta Limbach in Terror - Eine Bewährungsprobe für die Demokratie für tagesschau.de; **92.1** Regina Bluhme, Süddeutsche Zeitung, 16.05.2022; **92.2** Regina Bluhme, Süddeutsche Zeitung, 21.07.2022; **93** 27.01.2017 https://acerforeducation.acer.com; **94.5** from: Doughnut Economics: Seven Ways to Think Like a 21st-Century Economist , ©2018 Kate Raworth; **94.6** Attributed to Sashi Tharoor; **94.7** Attributed to Ban Ki-Moon; **96.2** Robert Raymond, 26.01.2021, www.shareable.net; **100.2** Joe Biden, 4th February 2021, www.whitehouse.gov; **103.2** From: Empire of Pain: The Secret History of the Sackler Dynasty ©2021 Patrick Radden Keefe; **106.2** Diederik Baazil and Laura Millan Lombrana, 04.06.2021, www.bloomberg.com; **109.2** Larry Elder; **110** "Ecstasy vom Erzfeind", Christian Buß, DER SPIEGEL 40/2020; **112.5** ©1995 Judy Small; **114.3** From: The Overstory ©2019 Richard Powers; **117.2** © Lela London / Telegraph Media Group Limited 2019; **120.2** http://www.vossfoundation.org/; **124.2** Gillian Brock, Debating Brain Drain, Part 1, Oxford University Press, 2015, p. 11-13; **127.3** Aus Identität und Kultur in einer globalisierten Welt, 27.06.2012, Bundeszentrale für politische Bildung, www.bpb.de; **128** Christine Haas, WELT online, 2019